AF531709

Mass Media & Journalism

Mass Media And Journalism

Ajay Das

OMEGA PUBLICATIONS
NEW DELHI-110 002 (INDIA)

OMEGA PUBLICATIONS
4378/4B, G-4 JMD House
Murari Lal Street, Ansari Road
Daryaganj, New Delhi - 110 002
Phone : 011-23278062,9811787417
e-mail : omega_publications@yahoo.com

Edition : 2023

ISBN : 978-81-8455-126-6

Price : 1195/-

PRINTED IN INDIA

Published by Mahender Garg for Omega Publications, New Delhi- 110002
Printed at Tarun Offest Press Delhi-110053

Mass Media and Journalism

by Ajay Das

Preface

Mass media is a term used to denote a section of the media specifically designed to reach a very large audience such as the population of a nation state. It was coined in the 1920s with the advent of nationwide radio networks, mass-circulation newspapers and magazines, although mass media (like books and manuscripts) were present centuries before the term became common. The concept of mass media includes Internet media (like blogs, message boards, podcasts, and video sharing) because individuals now have a means to exposure that is comparable in scale to that previously restricted to a select group of mass media producers.

Journalism in the 21st century will be fundamentally different from the Big Media oligarchy that prevails today. Mass media and Journalism casts light on the future of journalism, and invites us all to be part of it. An independent press is essential to sound and equitable economic development. The media helps to give a voice to the poor and the disenfranchised. An independent press also provides a solid foundation for a free and transparent society. This book explores the role of the media as a watchdog of government and the corporate sector, and the policies that prevent the media from exercising that role. The Right to Tell assesses the media's function as transmitters of new ideas and information. This book also evaluates the damaging effects that an unethical or irresponsible press can cause to a society.

Combining textual analysis and extensive in-depth interviews with political journalists, editors, presenters and documentary makers, the author offers a more optimistic evaluation of the contemporary public sphere. He argues that the quantity of political information in mass circulation has expanded hugely in the late twentieth century, and that it has become steadily more rigorous and effective in its criticism of elites, more accessible to the public, and more thorough in its coverage of the political process. This book will serve as a theoretical base for all media friendly community.

Ajay Das

Contents

1

INTRODUCTION

Mass media is a term used to denote a section of the media specifically designed to reach a very large audience such as the population of a nation state. It was coined in the 1920s with the advent of nationwide radio networks, mass-circulation newspapers and magazines, although mass media like books and manuscripts were present centuries before the term became common. The term public media has a similar meaning: it is the sum of the public mass distributors of news and entertainment across media such as newspapers, television, radio, broadcasting, which may require union membership in some large markets such as Newspaper Guild, AFTRA, & text publishers.

The concept of mass media includes Internet media, like blogs, message boards, podcasts, and video sharing because individuals now have a means to exposure that is comparable in scale to that previously restricted to a select group of mass media producers. The communications audience has been viewed by some commentators as forming a mass society with special characteristics, notably atomization or lack of social connections, which render it especially susceptible to the influence of modern mass-media techniques such as advertising and propaganda. The term "MSM" or "mainstream media" has been widely used in the blogosphere in discussion of the mass media and media bias.Types of drama in numerous cultures were probably the first mass-media, going back into the Ancient World.

The first dated printed book known is the "Diamond Sutra", printed in China in 868 AD, although it is clear that books were printed earlier. Movable clay type was invented in 1041 in China. However, due to the slow spread of literacy to the masses in China, and the relatively high cost of paper there, the earliest printed mass-medium was probably European popular prints from about 1400. Although these were produced in huge numbers, very few early examples survive, and even most known to be printed before about 1600 have not survived. Johannes Gutenberg printed the first book on a printing press with movable type in 1453. This invention transformed the way the world received printed materials, although books remained too expensive really to be called a mass-medium for at least a century after that.

Newspapers developed around from 1612, with the first example in English in 1620; but they took until the nineteenth century to reach a mass-audience directly. During the 20th century, the growth of mass media was driven by technology that allowed the massive duplication of material. Physical duplication technologies such as printing, record pressing and film duplication allowed the duplication of books, newspapers and movies at low prices to huge audiences. Radio and television allowed the electronic duplication of information for the first time.

Mass media had the economics of linear replication: a single work could make money An example of Riel and Neil's theory proportional to the number of copies sold, and as volumes went up, units costs went down, increasing profit margins further. Vast fortunes were to be made in mass media. In a democratic society, independent media serve /electorate about issues regarding government and corporate entities. Some consider the concentration of media ownership to be a grave threat to democracy.

Purposes

Mass media can be used for various purposes:

- Advocacy, both for business and social concerns. This can include advertising, marketing, propaganda, public relations, and political communication.
- Entertainment, traditionally through performances of acting, music, and sports, along with light reading; since the late 20th century also through video and computer games.
- Public service announcements.

Negative Characteristics of Mass Media

Another description of Mass Media is central media which implies:

- An inability to transmit tacit knowledge (or perhaps it can only transfer bad tacit).
- The manipulation of large groups of people through media outlets, for the benefit of a particular political party and/or group of people.
- Marshall McLuhan, one of the biggest critics in media's history, brought up the idea that "the medium is the message.
- Bias, political or otherwise, towards favoring a certain individual, outcome or resolution of an event.
- "The corporate media is not a watchdog protecting us from the powerful, it is a lapdog begging for scraps."

This view of central media can be contrasted with lateral media, such as email networks, where messages are all slightly different and spread by a process of lateral diffusion.

Journalism

Journalism is the discipline of collecting, analyzing, verifying and presenting information regarding current events, trends, issues and people. Those who practice journalism are known as journalists. News-oriented journalism is sometimes described as the "first rough draft of history" (attributed to Phil Graham), because journalists often record important events, producing news articles on short deadlines. While under pressure to be first with their stories, news media organizations usually edit and proofread their reports prior to publication, adhering to each organization's standards of accuracy, quality and style. Many news organizations claim proud traditions of holding government officials and institutions accountable to the public, while media critics have raised questions about holding the press itself accountable.

Public Relations

Public relations is the art and science of managing communication between an organization and its key publics to build, manage and sustain its positive image. Examples include:

- Corporations use marketing public relations (MPR) to convey information about the products they manufacture or services they provide to potential customers to support their direct sales efforts. Typically, they support sales in the short and long term, establishing and burnishing the corporation's branding for a strong, ongoing market.
- Corporations also use public-relations as a vehicle to reach legislators and other politicians, seeking favorable tax, regulatory, and other treatment, and they may use public relations to portray themselves as enlightened employers, in support of human-resources recruiting programs.
- Non-profit organizations, including schools and universities, hospitals, and human and social service agencies, use public relations in support of awareness programs, fund-raising programs, staff recruiting, and to increase patronage of their services.
- Politicians use public relations to attract votes and raise money, and, when successful at the ballot box, to promote and defend their service in office, with an eye to the next election or, at career's end, to their legacy.

Forms

Electronic media and print media include:

- Broadcasting, in the narrow sense, for radio and television.
- Various types of discs or tapes. In the 20th century, these were mainly used for music. Video and computer uses followed.
- Film, most often used for entertainment, but also for documentaries.
- Internet, which has many uses and presents both opportunities and challenges. Blogs and podcasts (such as news, music, pre-recorded speech, and video)
- Mobile phones, often called the 7th Mass Media, used for rapid breaking news, short clips of entertainment like jokes, horoscopes, alerts, games, music, and advertising
- Publishing, including electronic publishing
- Video games, which have developed into a mass form of media since cutting-edge devices such as the PlayStation 3, XBox 360, and Wii broadened their use.

Audio Recording and Reproduction

Sound recording and reproduction is the electrical or mechanical re-creation and/or amplification of sound, often as music. This involves the use of audio equipment such as microphones, recording devices and loudspeakers. From early beginnings with the invention of the phonograph using purely mechanical techniques, the field has advanced with the invention of electrical recording, the mass production of the 78 record, the magnetic wire recorder followed by the tape recorder, the vinyl LP record. The invention of the compact cassette in the 1960s, followed by Sony's Walkman, gave a major boost to the mass distribution of music recordings, and the invention of digital recording and the compact disc in 1983 brought massive improvements in ruggedness and quality. The most recent developments have been in digital audio players.

An album is a collection of related audio recordings, released together to the public, usually commercially. The term record album originated from the fact that 78 RPM Phonograph disc records were kept together in a book resembling a photo album. The first collection of records to be called an "album" was Tchaikovsky's *Nutcracker Suite*, release in April 1909 as a four-disc set by Odeon records. It retailed for 16 shillings — about £15 in modern currency.

A music video (also promo) is a short film or video that accompanies a complete piece of music, most commonly a song. Modern music videos were primarily made and used as a marketing device intended to promote the sale of music recordings. Although the origins of music videos go back much further, they came into their own in the 1980s, when Music Television's format was based around them. In the 1980s, the term "rock video" was often used to describe this form of entertainment, although the term has fallen into disuse.

Music videos can accommodate all styles of filmmaking, including animation, live action films, documentaries, and non-narrative, abstract film. The sequencing of content in a broadcast is called a schedule. With all technological endeavours a number of technical terms and slang are developed please see the list of broadcasting terms for a glossary of terms used.

Television and radio programs are distributed through radio broadcasting over frequency bands that are highly regulated. Such regulation includes determination of the width of the bands, range, licencing, types of receivers and transmitters used, and acceptable content. Cable programs are often broadcast simultaneously with radio and television programs, but have a more limited audience. By coding signals and having decoding equipment in homes, cable also enables subscription-based channels and pay-per-view services.

A broadcasting organisation may broadcast several programs at the same time, through several channels (frequencies), for example BBC One and Two. On the other hand, two or more organisations may share a channel and each use it during a fixed part of the day. Digital radio and digital television may also transmit multiplexed programming, with several channels compressed into one ensemble.

When broadcasting is done via the Internet the term webcasting is often used. In 2004 a new phenomenon occurred when a number of technologies combined to produce podcasting. Podcasting is an asynchronous broadcast/ narrowcast medium, with one of the main proponents being Adam Curry and his associates the Podshow.

FILM

Film is a term that encompasses motion pictures as individual projects, as well as the field in general. The origin of the name comes from the fact that photographic film (also called filmstock) has historically been the primary medium for recording and displaying motion pictures. Many other terms exist — *motion pictures* (or just *pictures* and "picture"), *the silver screen, photoplays, the cinema, picture shows, flicks* — and commonly *movies*.

Films are produced by recording people and objects with cameras, or by creating them using animation techniques and/ or special effects. They comprise a series of individual frames, but when these images are shown rapidly in succession, the illusion of motion is given to the viewer. Flickering between frames is not seen due to an effect known as persistence of vision — whereby the eye retains a visual image for a fraction of a second after the source has been removed. Also of relevance is what causes the perception of motion; a psychological effect identified as beta movement.

Film is considered by many to be an important art form; films entertain, educate, enlighten and inspire audiences. Any film can become a worldwide attraction, especially with the addition of dubbing or subtitles that translate the film message. Films are also artifacts created by specific cultures, which reflect those cultures, and, in turn, affect them.

INTERNET

The Internet (also known simply as "the Net" or "the Web") is a more interactive medium of mass media, and can be briefly described as "a network of networks". Specifically, it is the worldwide, publicly accessible network of interconnected computer networks that transmit data by packet switching using the standard Internet Protocol (IP). It consists of millions of smaller domestic, academic, business, and governmental networks, which together carry various information and services, such as electronic mail, online chat, file transfer, and the interlinked Web pages and other documents of the World Wide Web.

Contrary to some common usage, the Internet and the World Wide Web are not synonymous: the Internet is the system of interconnected *computer networks*, linked by copper wires, fiber-optic cables, wireless connections etc.; the Web is the contents, or the interconnected *documents*, linked by hyperlinks and URLs. The World Wide Web is accessible through the Internet, along with many other services including e-mail, file sharing and others described below.

Toward the end of the 20th century, the advent of the World Wide Web marked the first era in which any individual could have a means of exposure on a scale comparable to that of mass media. For the first time, anyone with a web site can address a global audience, although serving to high levels of web traffic is still relatively expensive. It is possible that the rise of peer-to-peer technologies may have begun the process of making the cost of bandwidth manageable. Although a vast amount of information, imagery, and commentary (i.e. "content") has been made available, it is often difficult to determine the authenticity and reliability of information contained in web pages (in many cases, self-published). The invention of the Internet has also allowed breaking news stories to reach around the globe within minutes. This rapid growth of instantaneous, decentralized communication is often deemed likely to change mass media and its relationship to society.

"Cross-media" means the idea of distributing the same message through different media channels. A similar idea is expressed in the news industry as "convergence". Many authors understand cross-media publishing to be the ability to publish in both print and on the web without manual conversion effort. An increasing number of wireless devices with mutually incompatible data and screen formats make it even more difficult to achieve the objective "create once, publish many".

The internet is quickly becoming the center of mass media. Everything is becoming accessible via the internet. Instead of picking up a newspaper, or watching the 10 o'clock news, people will log onto the internet to get the news they want, when they want it. Many workers listen to the radio through the internet while sitting at their desk. Games are played through the internet. The Internet and Education: Findings of the Pew Internet & American Life Project. Even the education system relies on the internet. Teachers can contact the entire class by sending one e-mail. They have web pages where students can get another copy of the class outline or assignments. Some classes even have class blogs where students must post weekly, and are graded on their contributions. The internet thus far has become an extremely dominant form of media.

Blogs (Web Logs)

Blogging has become a huge form of media, popular through the internet. A blog is a website, usually maintained by an individual, with regular entries of commentary, descriptions of events, or other material such as graphics or video. Entries are commonly displayed in reverse chronological order. Many blogs provide commentary or news on a particular subject; others function as more personal online diaries. A typical blog combines text, images, and links to other blogs, web pages, and other media related to its topic. The ability for readers to leave comments in an interactive format is an important part of many blogs. Most blogs are primarily textual, although some focus on art (artlog), photographs (photoblog), sketchblog, videos (vlog), music (MP3 blog), audio (podcasting) are part of a wider network of social media. Micro-blogging is another type of blogging which consists of blogs with very short posts.

RSS Feeds

RSS is a format for syndicating news and the content of news-like sites, including major news sites like Wired, news-oriented community sites like Slashdot, and personal blogs. It is a family of Web feed formats used to publish frequently updated content such as blog entries, news headlines, and podcasts. An RSS document (which is called a "feed" or "web feed" or "channel") contains either a summary of content from an associated web site or the full text. RSS makes it possible for people to keep up with web sites in an automated manner that can be piped into special programs or filtered displays.

Podcast

A podcast is a series of digital-media files which are distributed over the Internet using syndication feeds for playback on portable media players and computers. The term podcast, like broadcast, can refer either to the series of content itself or to the method by which it is syndicated; the latter is also called podcasting. The host or author of a podcast is often called a podcaster.

Mobile

Mobile phones were introduced in Japan in 1979 but became a mass media only in 1998 when the first downloadable ringing tones were introduced in Finland. Soon most forms of media content were introduced on mobile phones, and today the total value of media consumed on mobile towers over that of internet content, and was worth over 31 billion dollars in 2007. The mobile media content includes over 8 billion dollars worth of mobile music (ringing tones, ringback tones, truetones, MP3 files, karaoke, music videos, music streaming services etc); over 5 billion dollars worth of mobile gaming; and various news, entertainment and advertising services. In Japan mobile phone books are so popular that five of the ten best-selling printed books were originally released as mobile phone books.

Similar to the internet, mobile is also an interactive media, but has far wider reach, with 3.3 billion mobile phone users at the end of 2007 to 1.3 billion internet users (source ITU). Like email on the internet, the top application on mobile is also a personal messaging service, but SMS text messaging is used by over 2.4 billion people. Practically all internet services and applications exist or have similar cousins on mobile, from search to multiplayer games to virtual worlds to blogs. Mobile has several unique benefits which many mobile media pundits claim make mobile a more powerful media than either TV or the internet, starting with mobile being permanently carried and always connected. Mobile has the best audience accuracy and is the only mass media with a built-in payment channel available to every user without any credit cards or paypal accounts or even an age limit. Mobile is often called the 7th Mass Medium and either the fourth screen (if counting cinema, TV and PC screens) or the third screen (counting only TV and PC).

Newspaper

A newspaper is a publication containing news and information and advertising, usually printed on low-cost paper called newsprint. It may be general or special interest, most often published daily or weekly. The first printed newspaper was published in 1605, and the form has thrived even in the face of competition from technologies such as radio and television. Recent developments on the Internet are posing major threats to its business model, however. Paid circulation is declining in most countries, and advertising revenue, which makes up the bulk of a newspaper's income, is shifting from print to online; some commentators, nevertheless, point out that historically new media such as radio and television did not entirely supplant existing.

Software Publishing

A software publisher is a publishing company in the software industry between the developer and the distributor. In some companies, two or all three of these roles may be combined (and indeed, may reside in a single person, especially in the case of shareware). Software publishers often license software from developers with specific limitations, such as a time limit or geographical region. The terms of licensing vary enormously, and are typically secret. Developers may use publishers to reach larger or foreign markets, or to avoid focussing on marketing. Or publishers may use developers to create software to meet a market need that the publisher has identified.

Mass Wire Media

Mass wire media is a new frontier of news reporting in the high-tech age. A few decades ago news reporting was through newspapers and radio and television. The radio broadcasts that were made famous by Franklin D. Roosevelt during World War II changed the way radio was looked at. These fireside chats made the radio news and news radio. Things are different now as we are witnessing a revolution of people-oriented reporting in real time and other times. This element of intimate knowledge of the event or story being reported has dramatically changed the way we all view news stories.

This is called by some the Social Media Revolution. This revolution has intrinsically altered the way news is reported almost the way it happens. The trend of people-oriented reporting is only on the rise as reporting news becomes more personal and more accurate - although also more subjective.

2

Evolution of Indian Media Power

Compared with many other developing countries, the Indian press has flourished since independence and exercises a large degree of independence. British colonialism allowed for the development of a tradition of freedom of the press, and many of India's great English-language newspapers and some of its Indian-language press were begun during the nineteenth century. As India became independent, ownership of India's leading English-language newspapers was transferred from British to Indian business groups, and the fact that most English-language newspapers have the backing of large business houses has contributed to their independence from the government. The press has experienced impressive growth since independence. In 1950 there were 214 daily newspapers, with forty-four in English and the rest in Indian languages. By 1990 the number of daily newspapers had grown to 2,856, with 209 in English and 2,647 in indigenous languages.

The expansion of literacy and the spread of consumerism during the 1980s fueled the rapid growth of news weeklies and other periodicals. By 1993 India had 35,595 newspapers—of which 3,805 were dailies—and other periodicals. Although the majority of publications are in indigenous languages, the

English-language press, which has widespread appeal to the expanding middle class, has a wide multicity circulation throughout India.

There are four major publishing groups in India, each of which controls national and regional English-language and vernacular publications. They are the Times of India Group, the Indian Express Group, the Hindustan Times Group, and the Anandabazar Patrika Group. The *Times of India* is India's largest English-language daily, with a circulation of 656,000 published in six cities. The *Indian Express* , with a daily circulation of 519,000, is published in seventeen cities. There also are seven other daily newspapers with circulations of between 134,000 and 477,000, all in English and all competitive with one another. Indian-language newspapers also enjoy large circulations but usually on a statewide or citywide basis. For example, the Malayalam-language daily *Malayala Manorama* circulates 673,000 copies in Kerala; the Hindi-language *Dainik Jagran* circulates widely in Uttar Pradesh and New Delhi, with 580,000 copies per day; *Punjab Kesari*, also published in Hindi and available throughout Punjab and New Delhi, has a daily circulation of 562,000; and the *Anandabazar Patrika* , published in Calcutta in Bengali, has a daily circulation of 435,000. There are also numerous smaller publications throughout the nation. The combined circulation of India's newspapers and periodicals is in the order of 60 million, published daily in more than ninety languages.

India has more than forty domestic news agencies. The Express News Service, the Press Trust of India, and the United News of India are among the major news agencies. They are headquartered in Delhi, Bombay, and New Delhi, respectively, and employ foreign correspondents.

Although freedom of the press in India is the legal norm—it is constitutionally guaranteed—the scope of this freedom has often been contested by the government. Rigid press censorship was imposed during the Emergency starting in 1975 but quickly retracted in 1977. The government has continued, however, to exercise more indirect controls. Government advertising accounts for as much as 50 percent of all advertisements in Indian newspapers, providing a monetary incentive to limit harsh criticism of the administration. Until 1992, when government regulation of access to newsprint was liberalized, controls on the distribution of newsprint could also be used to reward favored publications and threaten those that fell into disfavor. In 1988, at a time when the Indian press was publishing investigative reports about corruption and abuse of power in government, Parliament passed a tough defamation bill that mandated prison sentences for offending journalists.

Vociferous protests from journalists and opposition party leaders ultimately forced the government to withdraw the bill. Since the late 1980s, the independence of India's press has been bolstered by the liberalization of government economic policy and the increase of private-sector advertising provided by the growth of India's private sector and the spread of consumerism.

Broadcast Media

The national television (Doordarshan) and radio (All India Radio, or Akashwani) networks are state-owned and managed by the Ministry of Information and Broadcasting. Their news reporting customarily presents the government's point of view. For example, coverage of the 1989 election campaign blatantly favored the government of Rajiv Gandhi, and autonomy of the electronic media became a political issue. V.P. Singh's National Front government sponsored the Prasar Bharati (Indian Broadcasting) Act, which Parliament considered in 1990, to provide greater autonomy to Doordarshan and All India Radio.

The changes that resulted were limited. The bill provided for the establishment of an autonomous corporation to run Doordarshan and All India Radio. The corporation was to operate under a board of governors to be in charge of appointments and policy and a broadcasting council to respond to complaints. However, the legislation required that the corporation prepare and submit its budget within the framework of the central budget and stipulated that the personnel of the new broadcasting corporation be career civil servants to facilitate continued government control. In the early 1990s, increasing competition from television broadcasts transmitted via satellite appeared the most effective manner of limiting the progovernment bias of the government-controlled electronic media.

Since the 1980s, India has experienced a rapid proliferation of television broadcasting that has helped shape popular culture and the course of politics. Although the first television program was broadcast in 1959, the expansion of television did not begin in earnest until the extremely popular telecast of the Ninth Asian Games, which were held in New Delhi in 1982. Realizing the popular appeal and consequent influence of television broadcasting, the government undertook an expansion that by 1990 was planned to provide television access to 90 percent of the population. In 1993, about 169 million people were estimated to have watched Indian television each week, and, by 1994, it was reported that there were some 47 million households with televisions. There also is a growing selection of satellite transmission and cable services available.

Television programming was initially kept tightly under the control of the government, which embarked on a self-conscious effort to construct and propagate a cultural idea of the Indian nation. This goal is especially clear in the broadcasts of such megaseries as the Hindu epics *Ramayana* and *Mahabharata* . In addition to the effort at nation-building, the politicians of India's ruling party have not hesitated to use television to build political support. In fact, the political abuse of Indian television led to demands to increase the autonomy of Doordarshan; these demands ultimately resulted in support for the Prasar Bharati Act.

The 1990s have brought a radical transformation of television in India. Transnational satellite broadcasting made its debut in January 1991, when owners of satellite dishes—initially mostly at major hotels—began receiving Cable News Network (CNN) coverage of the Persian Gulf War. Three months later, Star TV began broadcasting via satellite. Its fare initially included serials such as "The Bold and the Beautiful" and MTV programs. Satellite broadcasting spread rapidly through India's cities as local entrepreneurs erected dishes to receive signals and transmitted them through local cable systems. After its October 1992 launch, Zee TV offered stiff competition to Star TV. However, the future of Star TV was bolstered by billionaire Rupert Murdock, who acquired the network for US$525 million in July 1993. CNN International, part of the Turner Broadcasting System, was slated to start broadcasting entertainment programs, including top Hollywood films, in 1995.

Competition from the satellite stations brought radical change to Doordarshan by cutting its audience and threatening its advertising revenues at a time when the government was pressuring it to pay for expenditures from internal revenues. In response, Doordarshan decided in 1993 to start five new channels in addition to its original National Channel. Programming was radically transformed, and controversial news shows, soap operas, and coverage of high-fashion events proliferated. Of the new Doordarshan channels, however, only the Metro Channel, which carries MTV music videos and other popular shows, has survived in the face of the new trend for talk programs that engage in a potpourri of racy topics.

Media in India—initiated since the late 1700s with print media started in 1780, radio broadcasting initiated in 1927, and the screening of Auguste and Louis Lumière moving pictures in Bombay initiated during the July of 1895—is among the oldest and largest media of the world. Indian media—private media in particular—has been free and independent throughout most of its history. The period of emergency (1975–1977), declared by Prime Minister Indira Gandhi, was the brief period when India's media was faced with potential government retribution.

The country consumed 99 million newspaper copies as of 2007—making it the second largest market in the world for newspapers. By 2008, India had a total of 60,000,000 Internet users—comprising 6.0% of the country's population, and 4,010,000 people in India also had access to broadband Internet as of 2008— making it the 18th largest country in the world in terms of broadband Internet users. India also ranks 8th in the list of countries by number of television broadcast stations by 1997 statistics.

Print Media

Main articles: Print media in India and: Category: Newspapers published in IndiaFurther information: Press Trust of India, United News of India, and Category:Indian magazines. The first major newspaper in India—The Bengal Gazette—was started in 1780 under the British Raj. Other newspapers such as The India Gazette, The Calcutta Gazette, The Madras Courier (1785), The Bombay Herald (1789) etc. soon followed. These newspapers carried news of the areas under the British rule. The Times of India was founded in 1838 as The Bombay Times and Journal of Commerce by Bennett, Coleman and Company, a colonial enterprise now owned by an Indian conglomerate. The Times Group publishes The Economic Times (launched in 1961), Navbharat Times (Hindi language), and the Maharashtra Times (Marathi language).

During the 1950s 214 daily newspapers were published in the country. Out of these, 44 were English language dailies while the rest were published in various regional languages. This number rose to 2,856 dailies in 1990 with 209 English dailies. The total number of newspapers published in the country reached 35,595 newspapers by 1993 (3,805 dailies).

The main regional newspapers of India include the Malayalam language *Malayala Manorama* (published from: Kerala, daily circulation: 673,000), the Hindi-language *Dainik Jagran* (published from: Uttar Pradesh, daily circulation in 2006: 580,000), and the *Anandabazar Patrika* (published from: Kolkata, daily circulation in 2006: 435,000). The Times of India Group, the Indian Express Group, the Hindustan Times Group, and the Anandabazar Patrika Group are the main print media houses of the country.

Newspaper sale in the country increased by 11.22% in 2007. By 2007, 62 of the world's best selling newspaper dailies were published in China, Japan, and India. India consumed 99 million newspaper copies as of 2007—making it the second largest market in the world for newspapers.

Audio-Visual Media

Radio broadcasting was initiated in 1927 but became state responsibility only in 1930. In 1937 it was given the name *All India Radio* and since 1957 it has been called *Akashvani*. Limited duration of television programming began in 1959, and complete broadcasting followed in 1965. The Ministry of Information and Broadcasting owned and maintained the audio-visual apparatus—including the television channel *Doordarshan*—in the country prior to the economic reforms of 1991.The Government of India played a significant role in using the audio-visual media for increasing mass education in India's rural swathes. Projected television screens provided engaging education in India's villages by the 1990s.

Following the economic reforms satellite television channels from around the world—including BBC, CNN, CNBC, PTV, and other foreign television channels gained a foothold in the country. 47 million household with television sets emerged in 1993, which was also the year when Rupert Murdoch entered the Indian market. Satellite and cable television soon gained a foothold. *Doordarshan*, in turn, initiated reforms an modernization. With 562 television stations as of 1997, the country ranks 8th in the list of countries by number of television broadcast stations.

Communications

The Indian Government acquired the EVS EM computers from the Soviet Union, which were used in large companies and research laboratories. Tata Consultancy Services — established in 1968 by the Tata Group — were the country's largest software producers during the 1960s. The 'microchip revolution' of the 1980s had convinced both Indira Gandhi and her successor Rajiv Gandhi that electronics and telecommunications were vital to India's growth and development. MTNL underwent technological improvements. Between 1986-1987, the Indian government embarked upon the creation of three wide-area computer networking schemes: INDONET (intended to serve the IBM mainframes in India), NICNET (network for the National Informatics Centre), and the academic research oriented Education and Research Network (ERNET).

The Indian economy underwent economic reforms in 1991, leading to a new era of globalization and international economic integration. Economic growth of over 6% annually was seen between 1993-2002. The economic reforms were driven in part by significant the internet usage in India. The new administration under Atal Bihari Vajpayee—which placed the development of Information Technology among its top five priorities— formed the Indian National Task Force on Information Technology and Software Development. Internet gained a foothold in India by 1996. India had a total of 60,000,000 Internet users—comprising 6.0% of the country's population—by 2008. By 2008, 4,010,000 people in India also had access to broadband Internet— making it the 18th largest country in the world in terms of broadband Internet users.

India had a total of 49,750,000 telephone lines in use by 2008. In the fixed line arena, BSNL and MTNL are the incumbents in their respective areas of operation and continue to enjoy the dominant service provider status in the domain of fixed line services. BSNL controls 79% of fixed line share in the country.

In the mobile telephony sector, Bharti Airtel controls 21.4% subscriber base followed by Reliance Communications with 20.3%, BSNL with 18.6%, Vodafone with 14.7% subscriber base as of June 2005. India had a total of 233,620,000 mobile phone connections by 2008. Total fixed-line and wireless subscribers reached 325.78 million as of June, 2008.

Cinema

The history of film in India begins with the screening of Auguste and Louis Lumière moving pictures in Bombay during the July of 1895. *Raja Harishchandra*—a full length feature film—was initiated in 1912 and completed later. *Alam Ara* (released 14 March 1931)—directed by Ardeshir Irani—was the first Indian movie with dialogs.

Indian films were soon being followed throughout Southeast Asia and the Middle East—where modest dressing and subdued sexuality of these films was found to be acceptable to the sensibilities of the audience belonging to the various Islamic countries of the region. As cinema as a medium gained popularity in the country as many as 1, 000 films in various languages of India were produced annually. Hollywood also gained a foothold in India with special effects films such as *Jurassic Park* (1993) and *Speed* (1994) being specially appreciated by the local audiences. Expatriates throughout the United Kingdom and in the United States continued to give rise to an international audiences to Indian movies, which—according to the The *Encyclopædia Britannica* (2008) entry on *Bollywood*—'continued to be formulaic story lines, expertly choreographed fight scenes, spectacular song-and-dance routines, emotion-charged melodrama, and larger-than-life heroes.'

CENSORSHIP IN INDIA

Censorship in India mainly targets religious issues. It is justified by the government as necessary to maintain communal harmony, peace and tranquillity, given the history of communal tension in India. The Constitution of India guarantees freedom of speech but places "reasonable restrictions" "in the interests of the sovereignty and integrity of India or public order or morality." The report Freedom in the World 2006 by Freedom House gave India a political rights rating of 2, and a civil liberties rating of 3, earning it the designation of *free*.

Obscenity Law

Pornography is illegal and attracts several penal provisions. Some media dealing with sex are frequently banned. Films, television shows and music videos are especially prone, however if any literature is banned, it is not usually for pornographic reasons. Pornographic magazines are technically illegal, but many softcore Indian publications are available through many news vendors, who often stock them at the bottom of a stack of non-pornographic magazines, and make them available on request. In practice, the police usually ignores this as long as the display itself does not contain nudity. Most non-Indian publications (including Playboy) are usually harder to find, whether softcore or hardcore. Mailing pornographic magazines to India from a country where they are legal is also illegal in India. In practice, the magazines are almost always confiscated by Customs and entered as evidence of law-breaking, which then undergoes detailed scrutiny. But the enforcement is very lax and pornographic films are easily available in the smallest of towns and villages.

National Security

The Official Secrets Act 1923 is used for the protection of official information, mainly related to national security.

Press

In 1975 Indira Gandhi government imposed censorship of press in the The Emergency. It was removed at the end of the Emergency rule.

Film

The Central Board of Film Certification, the regulatory film body of India, regularly orders directors to remove anything it deems offensive, including sex, nudity, violence or subjects considered politically subversive. In 2002, the film *War and Peace*, depicting scenes of nuclear testing and the 11 September atrocities, created by Anand Patwardhan, was asked to make 21 cuts before it was allowed to have the certificate for release. Patwardhan objected, saying "The cuts that they asked for are so ridiculous that they won't hold up in court" and "But if these cuts do make it, it will be the end of freedom of expression in the Indian media." The court decreed the cuts unconstitutional and the film was shown uncut.

In 2002, the Indian filmmaker and former chief of the country's film censor board, Vijay Anand, kicked up a controversy with a proposal to legalise the exhibition of X-rated films in selected cinemas across the country, saying "Porn is shown everywhere in India clandestinely... and the best way to fight this onslaught of blue movies is to show them openly in theatres with legally authorised licences".

He resigned within a year after taking charge of the censor board after facing widespread criticism of his moves. In 2003, the Indian Censor Board banned the film 'Gulabi Aaina (The Pink Mirror)', a film on Indian transsexuals produced and directed by Sridhar Rangayan. The censor board cited that the film was 'vulgar and offensive'. The filmmaker appealed twice again unsuccessfully. The film still remains banned in India, but has screened at numerous festivals all over the world and won awards. The critics have appluaded it for its 'sensitive and touching portrayal of marginalized community'.

In 2004, the documentary *Final Solution*, which looks at religious rioting between Hindus and Muslims, was banned. The film follows 2002 clashes in the western state of Gujarat, which left more than 1,000 people dead. The censor board justified the ban, saying it was "highly provocative and may trigger off unrest and communal violence". The ban was lifted in Oct.'04 after a sustained campaign.

In 2006, seven states (Nagaland, Punjab, Goa, Tamil Nadu, Andhra Pradesh) have banned the release or exhibition of the Hollywood movie *The Da Vinci Code* (and also the book), although India's Central Board of Film Certification cleared the film for adult viewing throughout India. However, the respective high courts lifted the ban and the movie was shown in the two states.

Dramas

In 1999 Maharashtra government banned the Marathi play 'Me Nathuram Godse Boltoy" or 'I am Nathuram Godse Speaking"

Books

In 1989, Salman Rushdie's *The Satanic Verses* was banned in India, as it was in many countries, for its purported attacks on Islam. India was the second country in the world (after Singapore) to ban the book. The book *Understanding Islam through Hadis* by Ram Swarup was also banned. In 1990 the Hindi translation of the book was banned, and in March 1991 the English original became banned as well.

A book on the Maharashtrian prince, Shivaji, by Queens University Professor Jayant Lele was also banned. This book asked the question of who was the father of Shivaji. Shortly thereafter, the Central government of the time, which contained the Shiv Sena, banned *Shivaji: Hindu King in Islamic India*, penned by American scholar James Laine, and another book *The Epic of Shivaji*, which contained the objectionable phrase "Oedipal rebel", following an attack by Sambhaji Brigade activists on the Bhandarkar Oriental Research Institute in Pune. The subsequent UPA government has not revoked the ban.

In Punjab the Bhavsagar Granth was banned by the state government, following clashes between mainstream Sikhs and the apostate Sikh sect that produced it. "It was said that the granth had copied a number of portions from the Guru Granth Sahib. In one of the photographs it showed Baba Bhaniara, wearing a shining coat and headdress in a style similar to that made familiar through the popular posters of Guru Gobind Singh, the tenth guru of the Sikhs. In another Baba Bhaniara is shown riding a horse in the manner of Guru Gobind Singh." The Polyester Prince, a biography of the Indian businessman Dhirubhai Ambani was banned nationally.

Internet

In 2004, a Yahoo! Groups discussion group was blocked because of fears the group, the Kynhun forum, had links with banned separatists. The ban resulted in the entire Yahoo! Groups being banned due to the internet service providers' inability to implement a sub-group ban, and hence a huge range of harmless material were made inaccessible. The government used new information technology laws to force Indian internet service providers to block the forum after Yahoo! refused to comply. The ban sparked outrage and led to many people calling for the ban to be lifted. Concerns have been voiced that despite the inherent power of ruling bodies, the actions of the Indian government are actually illegal: "But the route they have taken is completely illegal and will be struck down if challenged in court", says Indian cyberlaw expert, Pawan Duggal.

In 2001, the Bombay High Court appointed a Committee to oversee issues relating to cyber pornography and Cybercrime. The Court invited the petitioners Jayesh Thakkar and Sunil Thacker as special invitees to provide their inputs and recommendations on cyber laws. The Committee upon identifying key issues made recommendations such as licensing of Cyber cafe, introducing identity cards for Cyber cafe visitors, ensure that Cyber Cafe that have cubicles or partitions be required to ensure that minors are not allowed to use machines in cubicles or behind partitions, mandatory maintaining of IP logs by cyber cafe, and so on. The Committee made several other recommendations such as connectivity and authentication at Internet service provider level which provided that Internet service providers were responsible for time clock coordination and record keeping. The report addressed the issue of protecting minor children from accessing adult sites and made a recommendation that Internet Service Providers must protective parental software with every Internet connection. The committee placed a special emphasis on lack of technical knowledge in the police and recommended special training of cyber cops. The report of the committee was well accepted by the Courts and is being put in to practice by the Police and Cyber cafes jointly.

India has blocked Internet access to several blogs and web sites in July 2006 because of the 11 July 2006 Mumbai train bombings. As with the Yahoo! Groups case, the government had wished for a few blogs to be banned for spreading "hateful or inflammatory" material, but the internet service providers were either unable to ban a few blogs selectively or found it easier to block all the blogs directly. After outrage, blog service was restored within a few days.

3

The Press Comes of Age

The Press not only reports the history of the world, day by day, but helps to make it. Almost all that any person knows about public affairs is gleaned from newspapers. As it is not possible for him to have personal knowledge of activities outside a limited circle, he is obliged to depend upon others to keep him informed. In practice, it is the press which does this. It is equally certain that what any person knows, or thinks he knows, determines how he behaves. His opinion and his behavior, multiplied by the opinions and behavior of all those of his fellow-men, who are similarly influenced, determines the history of the world.

Local affairs or the policy of a nation, economic practices or social justice, the issues of war or peace, may be governed, in the final analysis, by the character of the information habitually provided by the press. The happiness of millions of persons, including those yet unborn, rests in the balance. It is this circumstance which gives importance to the news, as provided by the press. The news is the stuff of civilization, the substance of to-day, the echo of yesterday, the shadow of tomorrow.

Intelligent journalists cannot fail to be aware of the general responsibility of the press in the matter of relationships between peoples. Diplomats likewise know that news can be dynamite. Nor can thoughtful citizens ignore the press as a force in society, or remain indifferent to its influence and to the factors which shape that influence. Oddly enough, truth is unpalatable to many persons. This circumstance puts both journalists and their employers in a delicate position, since a penalty may be attached to telling the truth; yet if they play carelessly with such explosive material, and make truth secondary to popular prejudices, or deliberately create items which tend to provoke bad feelings or mislead readers, then they axe betraying humanity.

The world to-day is acting on the basis of information more plentiful than ever before, but still much distorted by prejudice, censorship and propaganda. Few countries have newspapers that are free of government control. There is a certain amount of poison in the news stream, and sometimes a sleeping potion is added. It behooves every individual who considers himself intelligent to keep awake to the persuasions of the press, as exercised through its news columns even more than through its editorials, or leaders. He must learn to make discounts in reading the news, estimating its sources and the influences that have touched it. He must demand more and better information-services, and cast his own weight on the side of good journalism, as a measure of self-protection, if for no more altruistic reason.

It examines its growth in enterprise and technical competence in pursuit of the news. It examines the organization for gathering and distributing the news of the present-day world. It examines two obstacles to the free flow of the news, that is, censorship and propaganda. And, finally, it considers obstacles existing in the minds of journalists, publisher-owners, and readers, with implications as to how all may contribute toward safeguarding human rights, where they yet survive.

1. News Fundamentals

Events are news; so are trends and tendencies, forecasts and reviews, summaries and interpretations. The journalist makes it possible for persons in all parts of the world to know about and understand what occurs at home and abroad. He is trained to know "news values," is experienced in the means of gathering the news-facts and in writing them concisely and interestingly.

He is one of the more essential, although least appreciated, cogs in the modern world machine. It is the reporter-journalist who comes into contact with the men and women who *make* the news by their thoughts, words and deeds. Upon him, for the most part, the editors in the office must depend. It is the editor-journalist at home, however, who prepares the written matter for actual publication, selects and rejects, and comments on it editorially. From his desk it goes to the mechanical department, which translates it into metal and sends it whirling from the presses as a part of the finished newspapers. News falls into certain general categories: Personalities, politics, government administration, including news of crime and the courts; economic, commercial, or financial; sports, Labor-class news, social problems, the arts.

Whether at home or abroad, most of this news flows in certain channels, which the journalist knows and has charted. Looking to the channels simplifies news gathering and, although it tends to standardize the newspapers somewhat, it has proved a generally satisfactory method. It is elastic enough so that any fresh type of news may promptly be included in the system. The result is that most news is anticipated and journalists are ready to "cover" a "story" when it "breaks," to use the technical jargon. Once having obtained any desired information, the journalist writes it into a report and then gets the report to the home office for publication. Good present-day news writing, in the American press at least, usually results in the presentation of a story in some one of perhaps five fairly distinct ways:

(*a*) **A "straight" account of the news.** This means that the first paragraph or so, called the "lead" of the story, gives a summary of the essential points involved; the who, what, when, where, why and how of it, and the details follow, usually in the order of diminishing importance or of interest. The writing is kept as simple, factual, and yet as effective as possible. This is journalism of information, primarily.

(*b*) **An "interpretative" account of the news.** This is much like the first in structure, but with the addition to plain facts of impartial explanations of the event or trend under consideration, in its present, future, and possibly in its historical significance. This may be called a "situation" story, or "think stuff." It may be journalism of ideas, to a greater or less extent.

(*c*) **A "feature" story.** This is a short or moderate length account intended primarily to entertain, and usually dealing with a matter of no great intrinsic importance. It is likely to be a "sidelight" on a news event, to be about persons or places of news interest, or merely intended to arouse a smile or a tear.

(d) **A "news feature" story.** This is a fairly long account of a matter of some importance, but written with the intent to entertain and at the same time to inform, with the emphasis on the entertainment side.

(*e*) **A "special article."** This is a relatively long consideration, analysis, or review of an important trend, tendency, or situation, rather than of an isolated event. Usually serious and partaking of the nature of an article in a magazine, it is not commonly so dependent for its reader-appeal upon trigger-like timeliness, although it probably is topical, at least.

News writing fashions have changed during the four centuries since the central European banking-houses began to receive letters of information from correspondents in other places. Doubtless they will change again.

The earliest printed sheets retained many of the characteristics of those first news-letters, offering a collection of paragraphs, usually brief, grouped according to the sources of the information. It was not until early in the eighteenth century that Addison and Steele, in England, introduced something new in their "essay papers," which were word-sketches of contemporary events, persons, and places. This style won the tribute of imitation in England and in the American colonies.

The so-called "human interest" formula brought a more important change. It consisted in selecting the news or aspects of the news that could be so written as to move the reader to feel some emotion—amusement, excitement, sorrow, even grief. The method seems to have been originated by John Wight in his "*Mornings at Bow Street,*" a series of brief little word-pictures, dramatized and fiction-like versions of cases in London's Bow Street police court. They appeared in the *Morning Herald* of London, beginning about 1820, and sent its circulation climbing.

It was a method to be widely used and extended, with application to the reports of many aspects of life in addition to policecourt incidents. It was given a constant new zest by the use of larger type, colored paper, colored inks, and pictures. It proved so appealing that papers which were clever in the use of the human interest formula attained great circulations and great wealth. It explains the material success of all the mass-circulation papers of England and America. It is the key to the power exercised by the James Gordon Bennetts, Joseph Pulitzer, E. W. Scripps, William Randolph Hearst, Lord Northcliffe, Lord Beaverbrook, Lord Rothermere, Colonel Robert McCormick, Joseph Patterson and others.

Despite the frequent misapplication of the human interest formula, it remains innocent and even praiseworthy in itself. Correctly used, it provides a means for giving wider interest to what might otherwise be dull matters by portraying them in their warm, personalized aspects, both from the standpoint of those involved and of those reading about them. It reclaims many a story from stodginess and wins for it an attention that it perhaps deserves. A combination of human interest journalism and the more serious style has resulted in some of the "best" newspapers.

A variant of the human interest story is the "interview," first used, so some reports say, by the New York *Herald* in

1859 at the time of the John Brown Raid at Harper's Ferry. Others credit its invention to J. B. McCullagh of the St. Louis Globe-Democrat. In any event, it was in wide use soon after the Civil War. Its adoption in other countries followed slowly; it was approximately 1890 before it was used in Great Britain, and then especially by W. T. Stead. It had been held in derision for many years as lacking in dignity. The style has always given great latitude in subject matter and in writing, and it does not necessarily depend for its effectiveness upon a "news peg," that is, upon the excuse of a conspicuous current incident or trend.

Fashions in news writing have been shaped, to some extent, by economic necessity. During the Civil War the electric telegraph came into general use as a means to speed the news to an eager public. But the telegraph was expensive to use. News writing prior to that date had tended to be somewhat florid and wordy. But it cost too much to be florid and wordy by telegraph. Correspondents were induced, therefore, to confine their dispatches to unadorned facts. These facts were necessarily the answers to the questions, What has happened? When? Where? Who was involved? How did it come to happen just so? Why did it happen so? In other words, the summary lead was born, due to a need for economy.

Much the same thing happened during the Great War. Cable costs were high, there was more factual material to be sent, and correspondents were permitted to sacrifice some details. So the what-when-where-why-how convention was further trimmed. Instead, correspondents would present in the leading paragraph only the absolute double-distilled essence of the story. In one brief sentence they told what had happened; that sentence was packed with as much drama, suspense, color and significance as it would hold in a line or two. It assumed that the reader was somewhat acquainted in advance with what was going on, and omitted what might have been unnecessary points from the lead, although they may have been included in the "body" of the story. While this new form of "lead" has not supplanted the summary lead in

American journalistic practice, it has taken its place in accounts of some "big" events.

In the British press, unlike the American, it is common to find stories written to present the facts of the news in chronological order, without any attempt to startle readers in the first sentence, but rather to interest them and then to build up to a climax, instead of beginning with one. These two opposing schools of news writing have their proponents in both countries, and either method might be used in writing individual stories in either country, but, generally speaking, the one is more common in Great Britain and the other in the United States. Newspapers in most other countries accept one or the other of these patterns for their own use.

What the future may bring in the way of changed methods of news writing can be mere speculation. It is reasonable to suppose, however, that these will continue to change, as they have in the past, always striving toward a more effective means of portraying the world for the benefit of the reading public. The trend toward an interpretative style of writing seems likely to wax stronger, and brevity may be more sought after.

Interpretation in news writing may, and does, take two forms. In one form it is an *editorial interpretation*. Some newspaper editors object to so-called "interpretative" news writing because they believe it must be this type, involving editorializing. Readers and editors alike are quite right in objecting to any critical appraisal by the reporter of the original facts. It would mean having the opinion of some individual foisted upon one instead of receiving facts, as accurate, impartial, and clearly defined as it is possible to make them. The good reporter wants facts, facts, and more facts, and then seeks to make those facts utterly clear. Readers then may have them as a basis for forming proper judgments and opinions.

The other form is *factual interpretation*. This is not merely legitimate, but useful. No opinions are expressed by the writer, directly or indirectly, but the event is put in its proper perspective, historically and otherwise, and the background, together with its possible meaning, is sketched in with clinical objectivity. There is no serving the reader with a ready-made opinion, but only an attempt to help him "place" and evaluate the news, relating it to what has gone before and linking it with its essential phases of human affairs.

In American newspaper offices there was for some years an almost fanatical insistence upon facts served so entirely without background as to be practically unintelligible to any save experts. This method of writing discouraged most readers from taking an interest in events occurring very far beyond their own personal ken. Almost nobody read foreign news, even national affairs left most persons apathetic, while economics and science were too difficult for consideration. In Great Britain the cult of pure factualism never was so widespread, and a certain amount of the second type of interpretation has characterized writing in the best papers for many years.

Perhaps it was the increasing complexity of all public affairs following the Great War that demanded a change of policy even in the United States. Efforts began to be made to explain the developments of science, then the workings of economics, later the operations of both national and foreign affairs so that more persons could understand them. At first the trend was confined to a few newspapers, directed by enlightened editors and publishers, and to a few feature syndicates. Its more general acceptance may be ascribed to efforts by the United Press and the Associated Press to "humanize" the news, that is, to give it increased interest and meaning, without distortion. The result was publication of far more news of a sort that might be described as "significant" rather than merely "interesting." Although some critics spoke of over-simplification, readers began to be much better informed through the press. Editors took notice of the generally favorable public response to this new policy, so that factual interpretation of the news has, in theory at least, been generally accepted as desirable.

2. In Pursuit of the News

Expansion of trade and political affairs bred an early demand for information. Proprietors of coffee houses, such as Lloyds in London and less prominent ones not only in

London, but in Paris, Amsterdam, and other great cities, found correspondents who would provide them with budgets of news. The printers of the corantos and news-books made similar arrangements on a limited scale.

The young newspapers in England and in the United States depended for non-local news almost entirely upon items reprinted from other newspapers published abroad or at home. This always meant a delay in news presentation, sometimes as much as several months, but the readers, unaccustomed to anything better, seemed not to mind. Only a very few of the richer newspapers had their own letters from correspondents, but even they were definitely not "staff" or "special" men sent by the newspapers in question to the cities from which they wrote. Rather, they were regularly employed at some task in that community, journalistic or otherwise, and their correspondence with the newspaper was more or less incidental.

The change that has occurred since then has been gradual and is to be attributed to a combination of circumstances. Before 1800, as well as since, mere curiosity supported much of an individual's interest, if any, in events removed from his own immediate orbit. Only a few persons had any special interest in far events, and they usually were business men, traders, some scholars, and especially money-lenders and speculators.

But better communications, better transportation, more general education, and the improved service of news established by the world press, especially by the Anglo-Saxon press, made information and ideas available to all, and this helped to create a further appetite for more and more information—News.

The history of the hunt for news is as exciting as the history of the world itself, and entirely inextricable from that history. It was about 1800 when the press began to develop enough independence of government restraint, economic strength, tradition and leadership to pursue the ends it considered right and desirable. This new freedom, it must be made clear, was almost exclusive to the press of Great Britain and the press of the United States, for in other countries the newspapers were held under so sharp a government supervision, or were so economically restricted, as to prevent any important display of enterprise, it is for this reason that the more dramatic portion of the history of press development during the nineteenth century and the first part of the twentieth century is concerned almost entirely with Anglo-American journalistic ventures.

Early in the nineteenth century, and even before, enterprising newspapers were laying the groundwork for the present-day system of news gathering. It was relatively simple to arrange to have letters of news written for publication and sent from Vienna, Paris, and other important capitals. It was far less simple and much more costly to send special correspondents to report specific events or to gather news in given places, or to make special arrangements for spreading the news, once obtained. It never had been done; there was no precedent.

When newspapers depended for their reports of foreign affairs upon other newspapers, published in foreign cities, rewriting or summarizing the reports given therein, translation of the news items often was necessary. An ability to translate such items brought some important figures into journalism. M. Charles Havas was one of them.

Early examples of journalistic enterprise concerned means by which certain newspapers were able to obtain copies of foreign newspapers more quickly than their competitors. This continued to be a factor of importance in newspaper publishing, particularly in the New World, up to the successful operation of the Atlantic cable in 1866. When events were moving rapidly in Europe at the end of the eighteenth century, British readers were especially anxious for news. Hence, after England declared war on France in 1793, and the importation of French newspapers was halted as contraband of war, the British newspapers and readers were left without a good supply of news from the Continent. John Walter, of *The Times*, which had been established in 1785, had a light cruiser crossing the Channel almost constantly.

It would bring communications from *Times* correspondents, who had been engaged in Brussels and Paris in 1792, and all the French and Belgian papers that could be obtained. These would be sent to the office of *The Times* by special messenger. Although the government sometimes interfered with the delivery of the foreign mail, this system enabled *The Times* to publish some most important news, including an eye-witness account of the execution of King Louis XVI, the surrender of Flushing in 1809, and the reports of Napoleon's rise and fall in the years up to 1815.

The first war correspondent actually to be sent out by a newspaper appears to have been an unidentified representative of the *Swedish Intelligencer*, among the earliest European newspapers. He went into the field in 1807 with the forces of King Gustavus Adolphus. *The Times*, continuing in its enterprising way, would seem to have been the first British newspaper, not merely to engage resident correspondents in European cities, as it had done in 1792 and 1794, but also to send out its own special correspondent to represent it specifically in a foreign place.

It was partly as a means to overcome interference with its news service by the Government, which resented the paper's political independence, that *The Times* sent Henry Crabb Robinson to Altona, Germany, in 1807. Altona and Hamburg were at that time important clearing centers for news of Northern and Central Europe, although they were not news sources in themselves. From Altona, Robinson went to Sweden. Then he returned to London, but in 1808 and 1809 he was in Spain for six months and observed matters leading up to and including the Battle of Corunna.

Both in Germany and in Spain Robinson was reporting wars, and his assignment seems to represent both the first major special correspondence and the first war correspondence. On the first assignment he devoted himself chiefly to preparing a summary of news from the newspapers published in the country of his residence, be it Germany or Sweden. In the later period he was somewhat more active in the pursuit of news facts.

Actually, Crabb Robinson, as he is generally known, took a most important part in improving foreign news service. While at Altona he urged upon John Walter an organization to gather news from abroad in time of peace as well as of war. He outlined his ideas of how such an organization should be formed and how the foreign news should be written. Mr. Walter appears to have liked the idea and to have liked Robinson, for he recalled him to London and made him the first Foreign Editor, and for a brief time virtual editor-in-chief of *The Times*. Under Robinson's direction and supervision, a system for obtaining foreign news was developed between 1807 and 1809, during part of which time he was at Corunna, Spain, for the campaign there.

Charles Lewis Gruneisen, representing the *Morning Post of London*, went to cover the Carlist wars in Spain in 1837. It was his work there, as much as anything, that soured the Duke of Wellington on war correspondents, and made difficulties for William Howard Russell some years later in the Crimean War, in which the British Army was directed by officers who had served with Wellington in Spain and had been taught to share his views, at least on this subject.

Despite the precedents set by Robinson and Gruneisen, no English papers covered the Afghan campaigns of 1838-1842, or the first and second Punjab wars, and it was not until the Crimean War of 1854 that the practice was resumed. By about 1840 the cost of obtaining foreign news had increased so much that Mr. Walter permitted the *Morning Chronicle* and the *Morning Post* to share *The Times'* news—and the expenses involved in getting it. The *Morning Herald*, which was excluded from this arrangement, set about building its own foreign service and succeeded so well that it won a wide reputation in Europe for quick and accurate accounts of foreign affairs.

Governments continued to interfere with the news dispatches, however. Guizot, in France, detained *The Times* courier in Paris in 1845 to delay delivery to the paper of messages from the Far East. This was to repay *The Times* for its unfavorable remarks about the government of Louis Philippe. *The Times*, however, re-routed its dispatches on an alternative course through Germany and so not only found itself able to avoid further French interference, but also to outstrip rival newspapers, notably the *Morning Herald*. This incident may be said to have *marked the beginning of competition* in rapid news delivery.

About 1850 the *Morning Post* was represented in Paris by Mr. Algernon Borthwick, son of the owner. He was one of the first special correspondents and eventually became editor of the paper, subsequently assuming the title of Lord Glenesk. In later years, under his direction, the paper developed a rather good foreign service.

The Times also had Henry Reeve as Paris correspondent in 1848. When suffering from gout, and unable to be about, he engaged John Palgrave Simpson to substitute for him. The letters that Simpson wrote to *The Times* concerning the revolutionary outbreaks in Europe, especially as they were reflected in Paris, now form a standard historical work on the events of that stormy period.

Although it is common to say that there was no extensive newspaper correspondence of importance, and, above all, no war correspondence, until William Howard Russell went to the Crimean War for *The Times* in 1854, this is not accurate. Quite apart from the expeditions of Robinson and Gruneisen, which are perhaps more important than usually is implied, marked honors must go to the press of the United States for progress between 1808 and 1854.

James Gordon Bennett, who started the *New York Herald* in 1835, was responsible for the chief developments in American news enterprise during these years. At that time, when most foreign news was reprinted from London papers, American newspapers sent representatives in fast boats to board incoming ships and get the papers. Bennett's impatience with existing means of meeting incoming ships to obtain news led him to set the pace with faster news boats. He organized the first American system, and the first extensive world system, of foreign correspondence, so setting a standard for other newspapers to follow for many years to come.

Mr. Bennett went to London to witness the coronation of Queen Victoria, which event he reported for the *Herald*. He organized in Europe, during 1838, a service of foreign news for the paper, Six regular correspondents were engaged, including Mr. Dionysius Lardner, who achieved a certain fame as head of the Paris office. Later he augmented this service with correspondents in Texas, then a foreign state; Mexico, Canada, and the larger cities of the United States.

In 1845 regular transatlantic passenger ship service began and ships called first at Halifax, N. S. Here some of the newspapers attempted to get the dispatches and foreign periodicals and rush them to New York ahead of the ship, but the *Herald* usually won the race, although not without competition, and finally was driven, partly as a measure of economy, perhaps, to subscribe to the service that Daniel H. Craig had arrange.

The *New York Sun* was the particular rival of the *Herald* in news enterprise at that time, and in 1843 it established a correspondent in London. He ran a special horse express to carry his dispatches from London to Bristol to get the very latest foreign news on to ships there just before departure for New York. Other American newspapers did not enjoy being "beaten" by the *Herald* any more than did the *Sun*, and in 1846 sixteen papers in several cities conspired to get in the fastest possible time the first news of the arbitration decision in the Oregon boundary dispute with England, which had given rise in America to the slogan, "54-40 or Fight!" These newspapers combined to charter a swift pilot boat, which was dispatched with the greatest secrecy across the Atlantic to get the news and speed it back to American shores. The cost of this enterprise to the group, which the *Herald* ironically called "The Holy Alliance," was about $10,000, and all to no purpose, for the *Herald* had the news first despite the opposing plans.

In England also the more enterprising newspapers went out to meet incoming ships. The ships from America were commonly met off Plymouth. Cape mail steamers also were watched for and boarded off that port.

During the Mexican War of 1846 to 1848 Mr. Bennett's correspondence system functioned very well, especially with the telegraph, which had become practicable only in 1844, speeding news from Washington to New York. But A. S. Abell of the *Baltimore Sun* established his own overland express between New Orleans and Baltimore, with sixty blooded horses housed at relay stations along the way. During the War dispatches received by water at New Orleans were carried by this pony express to Baltimore. All other transport was far outdistanced, and even the Government dispatches sometimes arrived more than thirty hours later.

From 1840 to 1850, a decade during which steam railroads and telegraph wires were being extended, the newspapers used both of them increasingly. As the transition was being made the old and the new methods were combined. The news boats meeting incoming ships off Sandy Hook would carry their messages to a nearby telegraph station and from there the messages would be wired the rest of the way into New York City, so saving considerable time. Similarly Daniel H. Craig, with a news service built upon speedy delivery of news from Halifax or from ships between Boston and Halifax, was able to hasten the news to New York by wire from Boston, where the telegraph line then reached.

Despite all of these methods, however, the normal time required for European news to see print in New York was from ten days to two weeks, until 1866, when the Atlantic cable went into successful operation. The first cable, laid in 1858, had broken almost at once, and the coming of the Civil War in America prevented the completion of another or the mending of the first until after the termination of hostilities.

After the Mexican War the *New York Tribune*, which had been established by Horace Greeley in 1841, joined the *Herald* and the *Sun* in the maintenance of several foreign correspondents. By 1850 it had four permanent European correspondents, two correspondents in Canada, and one each in Mexico, Cuba, and Central America.

Few foreign correspondents, however, whether for American or British newspapers, were natives of the country for whose newspapers they wrote, nor did they view impartially the events of which they wrote. It was considered preferable at that time, however, to engage as a correspondent some person long a resident and acquainted not only with the language, but with the intimate details of political and other affairs in the country in question. This usually resulted in the appointment of a native, preferably one able to write and speak English. Usually it was only at times of crisis, such as during wars, that staff members were sent from the home office to report events from a definitely national viewpoint.

Under such circumstances, therefore, occurred the next great stride in the history of bold news reporting. That came in 1854, when William Howard Russell, long a staff member of *The Times* of London, and previously its correspondent in Ireland, was sent to the Crimea to cover the war in which British and French forces met Russian forces.

Although he was coldly received and shunned by British staff officers, trained under Wellington in the Peninsular Campaign to regard war correspondents in the field as a distinct liability, he wrote a series of letters so vivid, so outspoken, and so powerful that they had far-reaching results. They won him fame, if no popularity, among military men at the time, but they also resulted in a much-needed reorganization of the British Army and its administration.

As another result, Miss Florence Nightingale went to the Crimea and laid the foundation for the great Red Cross organization and for numerous important advances in public sanitation. Mr. Russell's experiences in the Crimea are said to have started war correspondence. Mr. Atkins biography describes him on the fly-leaf as "The First Special Correspondent," and a memorial bust to Russell in the crypt of St. Paul's Cathedral, London, calls him *"The first and greatest of war correspondents."* Without wishing to detract in any way from Russell's accomplishments, which won him his knighthood, neither of these descriptions is accurate. Henry Crabb Robinson and Charles Lewis Gruneisen were war correspondents before him by many years, and Gruneisen, at least, had seen some real fighting. So had George Wilkins

Kendall of the New Orleans *Picayune*, who reported the Mexican War in 1846 to 1848, along with other American correspondents.

The distinction has been made between Gruneisen as the first definitely "commissioned" war correspondent, and Russell as the first "professional" war correspondent, but Kendall and some of his colleagues deserve recognition as setting the pace for the so called "modern" war correspondence. Russell, however, was the first "professional" correspondent in that he was to continue as a journalist specializing on wars, and he was one of the first actually to go into the field, instead of writing from somewhere well behind the lines. Russell subsequently reported the British campaigns in India in 1857, the American Civil War during 1861, the FrancoPrussian War of 1870, and other engagements.

The *Daily News* of London had Jesse White Mario in Italy from 1857 to 1860, or thereabouts, reporting the liberation of Italy. The *Daily News* continued to be prominent during the 'sixties and 'seventies for its excellent coverage of news, both relating to war activities and peace activities.

Henry J. Raymond, first editor of the *New York Times*, and one of its founders, was himself a witness of the battle of Solferino in 1859, with his Paris correspondent, Dr. W. E. Johnston, and contrived to get a good account of it to New York for publication in the *Times* ten days before any other paper had any news of it whatever. William Howard Russell also was a witness of this battle.

The American Civil War brought the war correspondent into active service. George W. Smalley, representing the *New York Tribune*, was one of the more famous. That war called Russell to the United States for a short and not especially happy time. Reuters, then a youthful British news agency, scored some of its most striking journalistic triumphs during the period and so helped to establish itself firmly. But Reuters' dispatches were interpreted in the North of the United States as biased in favor of the Southern cause, which was sympathetically viewed in England until the last year of the war. In fact, the only London newspaper that was favorable to the North in its dispatches was the *Daily News*, for which Edwin L. Godkin was correspondent in America.

Naturally, American newspapers covered the war in detail. The increasing use of the electric telegraph, as it was called, helped speed dispatches and fed the fires of public interest in the struggle, and sent American newspaper circulations mounting rapidly. This introduced a period of new prosperity and development for the American press. The *New York Herald*, always enterprising, had a particularly fine service, spending $500,000 on coverage during the period of the wax, a tremendous sum in those times.

After the Civil War, Mr. Smalley was sent to Europe to head a newly established London bureau to serve the *New York Tribune* and to apply to the coverage of European news some of the American practices of news gathering. He arrived in 1866 at the beginning of the brief war between Prussia and Austria, and he sent to the *Tribune* one of the first news cable dispatches, reporting a break in peace negotiations and the threat of renewed hostilities. His hundred-word dispatch cost $500. Altogether, the paper spent $125,506.97 on cable tolls during the short conflict, which was more than it had spent on telegraph tolls during the entire Civil War.

Mr. Smalley brought about a change in the technique of covering foreign news for American newspapers, and played an important part in the coverage of the War of 1870 between France and Prussia. Although he remained in his London office, it was his enterprise that brought some of the greatest news coverage of the war and revitalized British news practices into the bargain.

Late in 1866, after his first arrival in Europe, Mr. Smalley returned to New York. But in 1867 he was sent to London again by the *Tribune* under an agreement to remain until 1870. His previous experience had convinced him that the introduction of the cable into the news equation called for a revision of the system for covering international affairs. Just as Crabb Robinson in 1807 had suggested fundamental changes in news-gathering methods and so paved the way for the extension of *The Times* service, which set standards for other papers to follow, so. Smalley just sixty years later brought about another change in foreign news-handling methods.

Mr. Smalley believed London should be the distributing center of European news destined for publication in the United States. He maintained that the London correspondent, as the responsible agent in charge, ought to have increased authority, permitting him to organize the news service, appoint and dismiss correspondents, and exercise complete supervision over the European staff and the gathering of European news. Previously all direction had centered in the New York office but Mr. Smalley felt that the London correspondent was in a more advantageous position to sense a situation and to act quickly and wisely. When he returned to England, he was empowered to act on this theory. Other New York newspapers looked upon such an arrangement as tantamount to setting up a rival office, and considered it a mistaken policy. James Gordon Bennett was one who ridiculed the plan, but he was to adopt it later for the *Herald*.

The emergencies arising in connection with the coverage of the Franco-Prussian War in 1870 brought a test of the plan's value. In that year Mr. Smalley formed the first international alliance of newspapers when he arranged with the *Daily News* of London to exchange with the *Tribune* the news of the war. Both papers had men in the field. Mr. Smalley also found it advantageous to know what Reuters was distributing and what the Associated Press was sending to New York, so that unwarranted duplication would not occur in his own dispatches, involving waste of money on cable tolls.

The alliance turned out to be fortunate for both papers. Remarkable news dispatches by Holt White, Gustave Muller, M. Mejanel, a Mr. Hands, and Moncure D. Conway, a Unitarian pastor of, Washington, D. C., who witnessed the Battle of Gravelotte, all *Tribune* representative, when published by the *Daily News*, through its exchange arrangement with the *Tribune*, gave the *Daily News* a favorable reputation throughout Europe. The *Tribune* later benefited similarly by its right to the dispatches of Mr. Archibald Forbes, sent into the field for the

Daily News, and by the communications of Mr. Henry Labouchere, trapped in Paris when the French capital was surrounded by the Prussians, but whose dispatches were smuggled out by balloon post. These dispatches remain as remarkable historical documents.

The *Tribune* spent a great deal of money on its service, and the expenditure of the *Daily News* for war telegrams, exclusive of the salaries and expenses of correspondents, amounted to £1,200 a month. The entire tempo of the war correspondence was greatly speeded up, due to the general use of the telegraph, and the risk to the individual correspondent in the field was far greater than ever before because of the long-range rifles that had come into use.

William Howard Russell again went into the field for *The Times* during that conflict. As the "dean" of the correspondents, he took a prominent position and was made much of, so much, in fact, that he drew the fire of Matthew Arnold, in a satirical essay that lampooned the entire British press. The excellent handling of the news of the Franco-Prussian War marked the beginning of a lavish policy of sending almost all news by the fastest means, regardless of expense, and reduced the dependence upon the mails.

Although not a war exploit, the accomplishment of Henry Morton Stanley, who, on a commission for James Gordon Bennett Jr., of the *New York Herald*, went into the heart of Africa in 1869 seeking some trace of Dr. David Livingstone, stirred wide interest. Dr. Livingstone, a missionary and an explorer, had gone into the Equatorial regions of what was then a "Dark Continent" in March, 1868, and had not been heard of since. The *Daily Telegraph* of London shared with the *New York Herald* both the expense and the glory of the expedition. Stanley was gone from 1869 to 1872 on what has been called by some the greatest assignment in journalistic history, but which at first was considered a joke, if not a hoax, by certain London and New York papers. In November, 1871, he found Dr. Livingstone, but it was 1872 before he himself returned to civilization. When he did so his reports occasioned a new sensation.

Previous to this African adventure, Stanley had taken part as a correspondent in General Hancock's expedition against the Indians ill the great American plains. As a correspondent for the *New York Herald,* he also had gone to Abyssinia in 1868 with an Anglo-Abyssinian expedition sent to subdue King Theodore and to obtain the release of Consul Cameron and other officers and missionaries. The expedition was a success and Stanley managed to get his account to the *New York Herald* weeks before any other report appeared, and so he took rank with the best war correspondents. In 1869 he roved about the Mediterranean countries, doing special articles, before he returned to Paris to receive the Livingstone assignment.

After that great adventure he accompanied the British campaign against the Ashantees, in 1873- 1874, again for the *New York Herald;* and in 1875 the Daily Telegraph once more joined with the Herald to send Stanley to Africa on a new expedition, this time of discovery. The journey and the well-publicized reports that followed, were important in opening up Africa. The Daily Telegraph, in fact, was partial to expeditions of discovery. Acting independently, it had sent Mr. George Smith to Nineveh in June, 1873, and there he discovered missing fragments of the cuneiform account of the Deluge as recorded in the Bible. It likewise supported Sir Harry Johnston's exploration of Kilimanjaro in 1884-1885, and Lionel Decla's march from the Cape of Good Hope north to Cairo in 1899-1900.

Following Stanley's two sensational journeys, which occupied the journalistic spotlight, there were a number of wars of limited extent which attracted some attention. First was the Serbian campaign of 1876, followed by the Russo-Turkish conflict of 1877-1878, and other campaigns in the Balkans and the Near East, in which participated such famed war correspondents as Archibald Forbes, Januarius Aloysius MacGahan, and Frederic Villiers. The first two represented the Daily News of London, Villiers was a war artist for the *London Graphic.*

Some of the revelations by MacGahan of Turkish atrocities in Bulgaria in 1876 aroused vast indignation in Great Britain and elsewhere, and were almost as far-reaching in effect as William Howard Russell's Crimean dispatches had been twenty years earlier. MacGahan was an American and originally correspondent for an American newspaper, but most of his important work was done for the Daily News of London. Gladstone was greatly aroused by MacGahan's letters and, although Lord Beaconsfield tried to dismiss them as mere "coffee house babble," they were verified, and Turkish rule in Europe was circumscribed in 1878 by the Treaty of Berlin.

William Howard Russell, who left *The Times* several years earlier to edit the *Army and Navy Journal*, in 1879 was sent out to cover the Zulu War for the *Daily Telegraph*, an assignment notable because it is said to have marked the departure from a rule of anonymity for correspondents. Russell was given a "byline," that is, a signature with his reports.

It was at about this time, too, that Henri de Blowitz was making a reputation for himself and for *The Times* by his correspondence from Paris. He joined *The Times* in Paris in 1871 and continued there for many years. In addition to forestalling what was at least a possible war between France and Germany in about 1875, he attended the Congress of Berlin in 1878 and managed to obtain the Treaty ending the Russo-Turkish War and to have it published in *The Times* even before it was signed in Berlin.

There were Near-Eastern and Balkan adventures during the late years of the nineteenth century, in which Edmond O'Donovan, for one, took an active part. There were the Egyptian campaigns of 1883, in which some of the correspondents already mentioned again were active, and in which Bennet Burleigh of the *Daily Telegraph* and Moberly Bell, Egyptian correspondent for *The Times*, gained fame, among others. And there were more peaceful, but no less important exploits of other correspondents in the political realm.

The Boer War, or South African Wax, of 1899 to 1901, brought further reputation to Burleigh, and also to George Warrington Steevens, of the *Daily Mail*; Winston Churchill, then representing the *Morning Post*; and to one or two American correspondents, such as Julian Ralph and Richard

Harding Davis. *The Times of London* gave very fine coverage to that war, including an excellent series of letters from the besieged Ladysmith, an exclusive account of the signature of peace at Pretoria on June 1, 1902, and some special and excellent accounts of important battles. Earlier, the *Daily Mail*, through its representative, Edgar Wallace—later to become widely known as a writer of mystery tales—and thanks to an ingenious system of signals and cable codes, was able to announce that satisfactory peace terms had been concluded. This paper was two days ahead of all other news reports. Reuters' report of the relief of Mafeking, coming well in advance of any official announcement, was one of the great journalistic triumphs of the War and a great credit to the organization, although the name of the correspondent responsible is not known.

The Spanish-American Wax of 1898 had brought fame, among others, to Richard Harding Davis, James Creelman, Ralph Paine and Stephen Crane. The Russo-Japanese War of 1904 brought together again many of the correspondents who had covered the Spanish-American and the Boer wars. It was during the Russo-Japanese War, too, that Lionel James of *The Times* put wireless to one of its first important tests in news gathering.

The Balkan Wars were reasonably well covered, but it was the Great War that brought one of the greatest tests of the war correspondence system, and gave added luster to the names of Frederick Palmer and H. W. Nevinson, and world-wide reputations to such men as Sir Philip Gibbs, Sir Percival Phillips, and Edwin L. James.

Those wars which have occurred since the War of 1914-1918 have received uneven coverage. During the Manchurian campaign of the Japanese Army, and Japan's temporary occupation of Shanghai, the Anglo-American press, particularly, went to great lengths to cover it. On the other hand the Chaco War between Bolivia and Paraguay received relatively little attention from the press. Revolutions in South American countries were sketchily covered, except as they became manifest in Buenos Aires and Rio de Janeiro, where there was some measure of press organization. Italy's campaign in Ethiopia in 1935-1936, however, received a great deal of press attention, and correspondents went there in considerable numbers, but found the news so meager and so difficult to obtain that most of them left early in 1936.

The Spanish Civil War, again, presented unique problems for the press, beginning in the summer of 1936. It involved hazards for correspondents, censorship obstacles, a scattered news field, and it required mobilization of all facilities to give it coverage. What the wars from 1850 to 1870 did to stir newspaper enterprise was continued from 1870 to 1890 by the Stanley journeys into Africa, wars in the south of Europe, and by interests built upon expanding world trade and travel.

During the following twenty years, from 1890 to 1910, new wars were important in stimulating correspondence, but hardly more so than was the further extension of commercial enterprise and the fact that the development of a complete world system of telegraph and cable lines made communication easy and comparatively cheap. It was in these two decades, under Mr. Moberly Bell, that *The Times'* system of foreign correspondence was built to such notable heights.

Then came the busy years from 1910 to 1930, and since, with wars of previously unrivaled action on the broadest possible scale, with a succession of major and minor crises following. Beginning with the Balkan Wars and the Great War, the period was marked by a quick growth in all facilities and organizations for gathering news.

Post-war developments in the realm of news included aviation exploits, exploration stories, and crime stories. Transocean flights, beginning with Charles A. Lindbergh's New York-Paris flight in 1927, resulted in the expenditure of vast sums of money and energy by the press.

When Byrd, Wilkinson, Ellsworth and other explorers, went to the North and South Poles, press coverage followed them. The short wave radio began to play a part, particularly when Admiral Byrd went to the South Pole in 1929-1930. On that expedition he was accompanied by Russell Owen, reporter for the *New York Times*. It had cost the *New York Herald*, then in the forefront of newspaper enterprise, 62061971.25 gold, per word, to cable 2,000 words from Jamaica to New York, rushed at double the commercial rate, to gain precedence over other press messages giving details of the destruction of Cervera's fleet in 1898. This, in addition to the cost of the dispatch boats and ordinary cables, made war coverage very expensive.

The Times of London spent £50,000 during 1898 to obtain a satisfactory supply of foreign news, and a single telegram concerning a revolution in Argentina had cost £1,200. Although *The Times* is reticent as to its expenses, these figures were revealed in evidence given before the Select Committee in the Copyright Bill of 1898.

The *Chicago Daily News* won wide fame for its reports of the World War. How that service was organized, as described by Mr. Victor Lawson, the publisher, was printed in *Editor and Publisher*, and reprinted in Newspaper Building, by Jason Rogers, pp. 145-52. It describes the development of the *Chicago Daily News* foreign service from the time it was established in 1899 until 1918. During the first years of the Great War the service cost from Times, a two years' assignment called the longest in the annals of journalism, and an assignment that Owen covered so ably as to win the Pulitzer Prize for 1930.

In the century since 1838, when Mr. Bennett set up his skeleton foreign staff in Europe, it may be said that there has been a constant growth in the service of information provided for the public, especially by certain newspapers and press associations in Anglo-Saxon countries. The imperial interests of Great Britain, rapidly expanding, brought demands in that country for news on a world scale, and this was made possible by the advance in communication methods and the development of press associations such as Reuters, the Associated Press, Havas, and others of somewhat less importance, all coöperating in the exchange of information.

Scandinavian and Dutch newspapers never have been far behind in any forward journalistic steps, but either the available histories have been unfair to them, or they did not choose to attempt the more striking kind of enterprise, such as brought fame to English and American newspapers and journalists. In any event, details of their exploits are difficult to obtain. Nor were French, German and Italian journalists unheard of in the race for better news service, but the fact remains that the history of such progress appears to be almost entirely a history of the British and American presses.

By the time of the Boer War, the Spanish-American War, and the Russo-Japanese War more newspapers, and more press associations, were sending special correspondents afield. But it remained for the Great War and its aftermath to provide the more decided impulsion which virtually forced agencies and papers to establish permanent systems of correspondence covering the world. Able correspondents, especially trained, so far as possible, were sent to key positions in all important countries, and permitted to remain there. Much patience was devoted to organizing an almost faultless communications system, at the mercy only of cataclysms of nature or of censorship. It is such a system, somewhat humbled by years of economic dislocation and an increasing severity of censorship, that exists in these times.

4

The Purposes of the Media

THE THREE MAJOR FUNCTIONS

The primary purpose of a newspaper is to inform the citizenry, while the primary purpose of television and radio is to entertain the citizenry. Rivers, Schramm, and Christians claimed that through news bulletins or on-the-scene broadcasts or advertisements of opportunities, one of the chief functions of mass communication is to help us watch the horizon. Another is to persuade. Thus the media have at least three major functions:

(1) To inform
(2) To entertain
(3) To persuade

Information Function

This function is probably the most important of the news media, especially of the newspaper. It helps people learn about their environment. This function is primarily the "news" function of the media, especially of the newspaper.

But what is "news"? According to Thomas Berry, First, *news is any printable story which, in the opinion of the editor, will interest the readers of his paper* (or the audience of his broadcast). Second, *news is always completely true* or it is at least a set of facts that have been presented to the reporter as truth. Third, *news has a quality of recency about it.* Fourth, *news has an element of proximity about it. Fifth, news must have some element of the unusual about it.*

This information will, of course, vary from one time to another. For example, on a slow news day, some event may appear on the front page of a newspaper that, on a busy news day, would not run the story at all. This information will vary from one place to another, too. For example, some types of stories that appear frequently in rural newspapers would seldom make a page in a metropolitan newspaper. Furthermore, this information will vary in how it is handled by various newspapers. For example, several competing newspaper editors may agree that a given set of facts provides news, but they may disagree on the kind of news, facts to be omitted, and angles to be stressed. Such may be the case between a tabloid, a local weekly, and a daily and each's coverage of a murder. The tabloid would probably use large photographs showing the victim (and blood). The daily would probably stick to the facts and use a smaller photograph or no photograph. The local weekly would probably handle the story from a local angle, perhaps giving names of relatives, friends, and so forth, if the victim or perpetrator was a resident of the immediate area.

The treatment of information should be straightforward, factual, and impersonal — if possible. Of course, reporters have certain constraints regarding stories. For instance, most, if not all, stories that are written follow a particular formula. Other constraints include deadlines and even sources. Also, information seems to be getting more complicated because of jargon, technical terms, and government gobbledegook: thus, reporters sometimes have to interpret the news for the readers.

According to Curtis D. MacDougall, To interpret the news it is necessary to understand it, and understanding means more than just the ability to define the jargon used by persons in different walks of life. It involves recognizing the particular event as one of a series with both a cause and effect. The historians of the future, with their perspective, may be better able to depict the trends and currents of the present, but if the gatherer of information is well informed, through reading of history, the study of economics, sociology, political science and other academic subjects. and is acquainted with the attempts of other observers to interpret the modern scene in books and magazine articles, s/he will at least be aware of the fact that an item of news is not an isolated incident but one inevitably linked to a chain of important events.

But what about slanting and coloring? When the facts of a story are arranged so as to lead the reader to a desired conclusion, news is said to be slanted. In doing this, the reporter concerns himself with arrangement of facts. When some facts are stressed and others are made inconspicuous or omitted, news is said to be colored. In short, news is slanted when the writer has attempted to influence the reader by arrangement of facts alone; news is colored when the writer attempts to influence the reader by arrangement of facts and by choice of words.

The journalist should ask himself when should the news be slanted or colored? Or, more importantly, should the news be slanted or colored at all? The journalist must use professional ethics when answering these questions. According to Harold Lasswell, three important social functions are carried through the various levels of communication: Providing a watch on the environment and alerting the public to threats or problems developing in the world; Coordinating and categorizing the various elements of the social structure, so that members of the public can comprehend the forces with which they must cope to survive and prosper; Handing on from one generation to the next the knowledge and ideas that represent our cumulative cultural heritage.

Although Lasswell did not contend that mass communication media were fully responsible for carrying out these several functions, other media analysts, such as Schramm and DeFleur, have suggested that the media share increasingly in all three functions. As Hulteng put it, all of the various communication media are equally important to us in making sense of what William James called the "blooming, buzzing confusion" that surrounds us. By their headlines, by the placement and length of stories in the evening newscast, the media help to order in importance both events and personalities. They help us to categorize. Since we can't attend to everything that is going on, the media provides us with clues to those things of particular significance to us individually, so that we can focus on matters that affect us most nearly.

Concurrently, consumers of news use selective exposure. They reject what does not square with their individual views of the world. They use selective perception. They accept what they want to accept. They also use selective retention. They remember Information that enhances their own views and forget information that does not.

Maxwell McCombs, Edna Einsiedel, and David Weaver wrote, "Media messages are transformed by people's personal experiences, their motivations and interest in seeking additional information." In other words, how one interprets a message depends on one's experiences and characteristics. This, of course, includes selectivity as well as a host of other terms found in the mass communication, psychology, and sociology literature. The strengths and the weaknesses of the info0rmation function are presented later.

Entertainment Function

This function is served by mass media in various forms, such as comics, human interest stories, features, celebrity interviews, puzzles, and reviews in newspapers and magazines; soap operas, docudramas, movies, talk shows, game shows, dramas, plays, musical programs, and even news programs on television; music, Interviews, and news programs on radio; movies and plays in theaters; novels, nonfiction, and how-to books; and, of course, musical recordings of all kinds — from country and western to classical and opera. There are other forms of entertainment, particularly for television, but the primary concern here is the entertainment found in newspapers and the major television networks.

As mentioned, Rivers, Schramm, and Christians said that newspapers inform and radio and television entertain. Since newspapers have very little space after advertising, most of the holes are filled with informational pieces. These can be entertaining, but to publish entertainment pieces just because some people enjoy them is not a good enough reason. Certain newspaper readers desire more. Nevertheless, newspapers, in order to get those readers who read a particular entertaining columnist or a particular comic strip, will include them. After all, another subscriber means additional revenue from advertisers. Besides, newspaper editors realize that people do not like bad news all the time. The reader is actually enticed to most sections of the paper as a result. Thus, not only does the reader see or read the comics, features, and columns, he also notices the advertisements. And this is important.

The entertainment function, in addition to attracting certain readers and breaking up the paper, has to "be presented so as to be interpretable within the experience of the audience; It must appeal to audience needs and interests; and it must, so far as possible, be designed to avoid the hazards of noise and interference." As Rivers, Schramm, and Christians pointed out, receivers of entertaining stories must be willing to go along with the story or appreciate the character who never existed.

This may provide the clue to the late Erma Bombeck's successful transition from newspaper columnist to television celebrity; that is, her stories were basically the same funny segments of life that viewers of television, like readers of her columns, enjoyed. The entertainment function is an important one. It helps readers of newspapers, and it allows viewers to forget their problems while they watch others who have bigger problems.

Persuasion Function

The persuasion function, like the information and entertainment functions, has to get the message from the source to the receiver. But it has to do more. According to Rivers, Schramm, and Christians, it has to cause members of the audience to, in effect, change themselves. If people have preconceived notions toward something or about something, it is hard to change those notions or even get people's attention. But the mass media are supported by advertising; therefore, advertising of a persuasive kind has to be printed or aired. In addition to advertising, which is an obvious form of persuasion, the mass media may persuade people to buy or like or dislike something, even ideas, by other forms.

Most commercials are presented in an entertaining manner. Of course, audiences come with their guard held high. However, people working in the mass media realize that these people come with needs that have to be satisfied. All the people employed by the mass media have to do is make an attractive package. This process sounds simple, but it is not. Rivers, Schramm, and Christians pointed out that, usually, it means introducing information that causes the receiver to reexamine his environment and subsequently to reexamine his needs, relationships, and beliefs.

In other words, as ideas or products are introduced, the consumer should be questioning his environment, or his needs and his ways of meeting them, or his social relationships, or his beliefs and attitudes. There are other tactics that may be used to persuade. One is the threat, such as smoking cigarettes causes cancer. Unless this statement is supported by evidence — substantial evidence — people may not accept it. (And even if it is supported by documented evidence there will be those who do not believe it.) Of course, studies have shown that as threat increases, so does avoidance. In short, the reader or viewer does not want to be frightened, so he avoids the message; he avoids dissonance. Before persuasion can occur, however, defenses against change in attitudes and beliefs "must be breached and the process of reappraisal and reorganization of attitudes initiated."

Strengths and Weaknesses of Each Function

Information Function

First of all, I would like to take issue with Rivers, Schramm, and Christians's contention about radio and television programs. They said these media were designed to entertain.

Not necessarily. It is only because of entertainment being introduced on radio and television (and then eating most of the time each medium was on the air) that this became true. Today, Ted Turner, with his Cable News Network, has shown that people will watch news programs if they are packaged correctly — that is, presented in an entertaining fashion. After all, "action" stories are more likely to hold attention than "talking heads." And radio certainly uses "sounds" within a story to draw attention. This holds true for all-news radio networks. This author believes a medium's design is linked to what is first introduced in or on that medium, not the medium itself.

Rivers raises an important point regarding the information function. He wrote, all of us live in a synthetic world, and the synthesis is made largely by the news media. Even if we pay no attention to news reports, we learn from those who do. So awesome is the informing power of the news media that, when they are in error, few of us ever learn of it unless the media themselves tell US. It is the last sentence that is troubling. How many newspapers acknowledge their errors? Or if they do, where are the corrections printed? Because this function is so important — not only to the readers, but to the paper's credibility — errors, should be either corrected or acknowledged immediately. Article IV — Truth and Accuracy of the "Canons of Journalism" should be remembered by the editor.

But reporters and editors have another problem, a problem that confronts them every day: what event to cover or write about, and which of the many stories to publish. As mentioned by Rivers, journalists cannot reach everyone with single reports; they must provide a wide range of reports. Consequently, they have to ask themselves, "What kinds of information do the American people need to promote and protect their own legitimate interests and to function as effective citizens?" In order for journalists to answer this question, they "must recognize the degree of diversity in ability to understand and absorb information — and, of course, the degree of *interest* among individuals."

Unfortunately, when journalists and editors try to answer this question, they sometimes forget about accuracy. In his book, *Between Fact and Fiction: The Problems of Journalism*, Edward Jay Epstein wrote, journalists are rarely, if ever, in a position to establish the truth about an issue for themselves, and they are therefore almost entirely dependent on self-interested "sources" for the version of reality that they report.

The reasons for this are:

(1) Newspapers have strict deadlines, which limit the time that can be spent investigating a story.
(2) A restricted number of news holes, which limits the space that can be devoted to elucidating the details of an event.
(3) Fixed budgets, which limit the resources that can be used on any single piece of reportage.

As Epstein pointed out, "it would be unreasonable to expect even the most resourceful journalist to produce anything more than a truncated version of reality." Journalists, therefore, are trapped, so to speak. For example, they cannot compel a witness to furnish them an account of an event. Witnesses need only tell reporters what they deem is in their own self-interest, and then they can lie or fashion their story to fit a particular purpose without risking any legal penalty. Nor can a journalist test an account by hostile cross-examination without jeopardizing the future cooperation of the witness.

This happened in 1969 when reports concerning Black Panther violence were published. The Black Panthers claimed that an organized campaign of genocide had been waged against them. The reporters closest to the group could not dispute this claim because it would jeopardize their access to certain Panther spokesmen.

Journalists also lack certain technical information, which forces them to rely on authoritative reports or so-called experts for their information. Journalists cannot always identify their sources. When this occurs, they cannot necessarily document their sources' claims. Thus, their stories may not be corroborated by other so-called experts. Consequently, egregious errors may occur or remain. In essence, "daily journalism is largely concerned with finding and retaining profitable sources of prepackaged stories." This was true even in the case of Watergate. For example, the press did not assemble the evidence; investigative agencies of the government did. Then it was deliberately leaked to the press. The dependency on leaks therefore causes most of the problems in reporting. Since a reporter does not have the time to verify every piece of information, conflicts and disputes may develop. Thus, the reporter's and the newspaper's reputation become questionable.

Epstein wrote, Journalists . . . are caught in a dilemma. They can either serve as faithful messengers for some subterranean interest, or they can recast the message into their own version of the story by adding, deleting, or altering material. The first alternative assures that the message will be accurately relayed to the intended audience, although the message itself might be false or misleading. The latter alternative, while lessening the source's control over the message, increases the risk of further distortion, since the journalist cannot be aware of the full context and circumstances surrounding the disclosure.

According to Epstein, the tension in the dilemma could be alleviated to some degree if journalists gave up the pretense of being establishers of truth, recognized themselves as agents for others who desired to disclose information, and clearly labeled the circumstances and interests behind the information they reported so that it could be intelligently evaluated.

Of course, the mass media's information function does have positive attributes. Namely, it does provide information of some kind. Even if it comes from other agencies, it keeps people abreast of what is happening. Unfortunately, people have to realize that what they read, see, or hear is what a particular newspaper, television station, or radio station wants them to read, see, or hear. And what that newspaper, television station, or radio station has presented to the public has been provided by a source. The journalist did not come up with it on his own.

Entertainment Function

The mass media provide entertainment in various forms, including news stories, and this entertainment serves an important recreational function. As Ray Hiebert, Donald Ungurait, and Thomas Bohn claimed in their book, *Mass Media II*. "They (mass media fare) provide emotional escape, create fantasy, and allow for physical catharsis necessary to renewal of the human spirit."

Furthermore, audiences of the media "use music, film, television, novels, and magazine literature to meet their need for art; and this art literally improves the quality of life in our intense, crowded, increasingly urbanized society. Art brings 'beauty' to mankind."

In newspapers, entertainment helps support a page. For example, instead of having a solid page of straight news, which would probably dull the reader's senses, editors try to incorporate features, amusing sidebars, human interest stories, and fillers. Even news stories can be made entertaining by a different writing style. Entertainment, whether in newspapers or on television, can inform to a certain extent. For example, a specific columnist in a newspaper or a miniseries such as "Roots" on television informs the reader or viewer. The latter, for instance, provided information about the history and problems of African Americans. Editorial cartoons entertain as well as "take positions on issues, analyze and interpret events."

Entertainment can help persuade. As Hiebert, Ungurait, and Bohn pointed out, "One must attract and hold public attention in order to persuade, and entertainment is often more effective than information in winning over an audience." Of course, the point should be made that the function performed is often determined by the receiver. What is entertainment to one person may be information to another. However, it must be remembered that whatever is presented in the media, the reader, listener, or viewer did not make the selection; the employees of the media did.

Newspapers, for example, use the smallest amount of pure entertainment. Nonetheless, it is an essential part. The *Washington Post*, as it has been pointed out, "for years published the largest number of comic strips of any newspaper in the country." The primary reason: to help build its circulation. Television's content is dominated by mass culture, or the more than 75 million American households that own a set. Therefore, since so many Americans want to be entertained, and since these people purchase advertisers' products, television's course has been charted.

The entertainment function is not without criticism or weakness. For instance, there is the question of whether entertainment — some of it, at least — caters to the lowest common denominator in the mass audience. If so, it may have a degrading effect on our culture. Of course, whether a person believes this to be true depends on his perspective at the time.

Persuasion Function

Each person interprets differently what he sees, reads, or hears. Therefore, in order to reach some consensus about truth, a free exchange of these interpretations must exist. This is the principle upon which our press is based. Unfortunately, because of the press's structure — cross-media ownerships and conglomeratesthis is hard for Americans to do.

As Hiebert, Ungurait, and Bohn pointed out, The growth of mass media as powerful and complicated institutions has made it increasingly difficult for individuals outside the media to protect themselves from massive propaganda and to raise their voices to persuade others. Must those who do not have access to the mass media be denied the right to influence others? Must they content themselves with being victims of the persuasive force of those who do have such access? This question poses one of the basic dilemmas of modern democracy.

The persuasion function is strong and can be seen in any periodical or newspaper or on television, and heard on radio. The mass media are used by politicians to persuade the public to either vote for them or accept their ideas. Persuasion is presented in stories related to business, government, hospitals, schools, religious organizations, and even the mass media. In short, stories, programs, and advertisements have elements of persuasion.

Since "some studies of some media have shown that more than 50 percent of the editorial matter originated in press releases or promotional material," it is little wonder that much of what is published is "puffery, self-promotion, or a cover up of damaging facts." In the March/April 1980 issue of the *Columbia Journalism Review*, Joanne Ambrosio revealed that in the *Wall Street Journal*'s October 4, 1980, issue, "eighty-four stories were based on press releases . . . 45 percent of the day's 188 news items" In addition, "in thirty-two of these examples, the releases were reprinted almost verbatim or in paraphrases."

What kind of reporting is this? And if this is a common practice of the *Wall Street Journal*, what about other newspapers? Do they readily publish news releases put out by companies? Or do they question, then investigate? Of course, this practice is questionable and certainly needs to be examined at great length by every managing editor. After all, their newspaper's credibility will be questioned, especially if the information presented is merely favorable publicity for a company. On the other hand, leaders of businesses or governments may manipulate the media — they have in the past — to shape public opinion. In either case, false or biased information — no matter who was responsible may persuade the public to believe an untruth to be true.

Perhaps the persuasion function of the press has gotten out of hand. Indeed, the press needs to examine its responsibilities to the public. An objective story may be impossible, but journalists could strive for a fairer, more balanced story than they are writing.

Entertainment — The Best Fulfilled Function

The mass media undoubtedly fulfills the entertainment function the best. Not only does the media, especially radio and television, include entertainment in abundant supply, it is diversified. There are comics, editorial cartoons, satiric columns, advice columns, features, human interest stories, and more in newspapers. There are dramas, soap operas, movies, game shows, and more on television. In fact, most of television's programming is entertainment. And for the person who likes nothing but movies or music, there are special cable networks to which he may subscribe. In fact, as cable and other forms of satellite communications technology develops, entertainment will fill people's lives even more than it does now. On radio, entertainment fills the air waves. From music programs to celebrity interviews, entertainment occupies most of a station's air time. And in order to compete with other AM or FM stations, other program formats will be developed.

Information — The Least Fulfilled Function

The mass media fulfills the information function the least. As shown, this function is not necessarily fulfilled by the media as much as it is by those who supply the media with information. In other words, the media seldom get a story; it is usually given to them by some person who hopes to gain something. For example, a politician may grant an interview regarding a bill. Although the media get the politician's points of view on the bill, he has received free media coverage, which may help him in the polls, especially if the audience likes what he said.

Another point is the failure to check news releases for inaccuracies or to paraphrase them. A third point is the failure of reporters to write in a straightforward, stick-to-the-facts style. Often, they are obligated to their editors and publishers to slant a story a certain way. This can cause problems; the reader or viewer may question the story's accuracy or the reporter's interpretation of the facts. Of course, there are other "wrongs," but many have been mentioned.

5

New Media Technologies

When we refer to *new media*, we often mean applications of microelectronics, computers, and telecommunications that either offer new services (e.g., mobile cellular telephone) or enhancements of older ones (high definition television). Indeed, many of the new media are not so new as much as they are extensions of older forms, as in cable television services, computer communication networks, or facsimile transmission (fax). As social scientists, we typically are not as concerned with technological innovations themselves as we are with how individuals, groups, or organizations change their patterns and capabilities for communication by uses of new media. Ultimately, our concern is more with the human and social impacts than the technology itself.

Despite this avowed objective, those of us who do new media studies are often accused of not being sufficiently theoretical in our research. This is partly true, but in most cases there is good reason for it. New media technologies are changing so rapidly that just gaining a suitable level of description in research is sometimes a challenge; such description is a necessary precursor to moving on to levels of explanation, understanding, and prediction. On the other hand, as we are able to gain a "fix" on social aspects of new media applications, existing or modified theory can be of great advantage in generalizing about social uses and consequences. In this chapter, we illustrate this point with several different surveillance. Later refinements of the approach acknowledge that audiences are fluid constituencies, occupying various "social positions" or roles at different times of day and in different settings. With these refinements in mind, recent uses-and-gratifications research has sought to better specify the nature of very specific audiences in order to better understand the linkage between social characteristics, context, media use, and gratifications.

General Applications to New Media

How do gratifications obtained from new media differ from those experienced via conventional media? New communications technologies generally offer users or audiences (a) more (and complex) choice in how they see or hear media content (e.g., cable television expands viewing options and possible sites for media consumption), (b) new opportunities for altering the message directly or upon replay (e.g., eliminating commercials from off-air taped television), (c) the ability to "time-shift" or reallocate time for certain media experiences, notably broadcast television and movie viewing, and (d) chances to interact with other audience members (computer conferences, telephone "chat" lines). Communication systems such as the VCR, cable television, and personal computers fundamentally expand the repertoire of media available to people, and in so doing fragment the "mass" audience into narrower viewer/user groups or cultures. The current research on cable television audiences, much of it undertaken from a uses-andgratifications perspective, illustrates the range of social effects, and especially gratifications, one might observe with various communication technologies.

Applications to Cable Television Use

Early research on cable television focused largely on ascertaining why people subscribed to cable, and it was assumed that the answers to that question pointed to the gratifications people obtained from cable. Such studies relied exclusively on self-report measures. For example, work by Becker, Dunwoody, and Rafaell (1983); Jeffres (1978); McDermott and Medhurst (1984); Ducey, Krugman, and Eckrich (1983); Metzger (1983); and others explained subscription behavior by identifying peoples' interests in obtaining improved television reception (especially in more rural markets) and more variety in programming from cable television. These were the two leading reasons cited for subscribing. The desire for variety is sometimes associated with *specific* programming interests and hence with gratifications sought by the subscriber.

For example, some studies report that the "variety" cable subscribers are interested in obtaining amounts to an appetite for movies, sports, news, and religious programming; hence, one might infer that the gratifications associated with viewing cable television are entertainment (illustrated by interested in movies, sports), surveillance or information (illustrated by interested in news programming), and personal identity (illustrated by interested in religious programming).

Nevertheless, people express contradictory reasons for actually watching cable television. Simply put, people have different reasons at different times for doing what they do. Some of the investigations into television viewing styles and content preferences are illuminating on this point.

Zillmann and Bryant (1985), Rubin (1984), and Heeter and Baldwin (1988) examined relationships between reasons or motivations for television viewing and specific program choices. Zillmann and Bryant, for example, found that distressed individuals were most likely to watch soothing television programs lacking any jarring emotional content. Rubin distinguished between ritualized and instrumental television viewing in hypothesizing that there were two dominant styles of watching television; he positioned ritualized viewing as habitual and frequent television use in search of companionship or a way to pass time, whereas instrumental viewing is highly selective and purposeful. Building on such investigations, Heeter and Baldwin's study on cable television users reported that the additional program variety available through cable allowed certain viewing patterns to dominate. Given the program variety on cable television and, in particular, the opportunity to view certain channels that are consistently of one program type (allmusic channels, all-news channels, all-weather channels, all-sports channels, etc.), cable affords ample opportunities for viewers to adopt specialized viewing patterns representing significant relationships to content types. For example, the increased presence on cable television of "browsing" low-involvement channels suggests an increase in opportunities for viewers to pass time with the television. There is ample anecdotal testimony that people use MTV much as they use radio, namely, for background music, a "ritualized" use category.

Addressing the realm of news (e.g., CNN) on cable, Heeter and Baldwin's (1988) analysis has unique implications concerning information content. They hypothesize that cable television may draw people away from news programming and toward entertainment, and that many cable users seem to be actively selective in their viewing. This is illustrated by the frequency with which they change channels during viewing sessions. To use Rubin's terms, cable television (and remote control devices) can facilitate instrumental viewing by maximizing choice and providing consistent, predictable fare on horizontally programmed channels (movie channels).

Other research on specific cable content and audiences has focused on the impacts of either news services such as CNN or music video channels such as MTV. Whereas numerous content analyses of MTV's fare have documented its range of sexual and violent music videos, studies of the news services such as CNN predictably have sought to assess the impact of cable services on presumably entrenched news viewing habits, and the social correlates of watching news. White (1988), for example, found that viewing local access services available on cable television was positively related to feelings of attachment to the community. Baldwin, Heeter, Anokwa, and Stanley (1988) found that cable subscribers paid little attention at all to networked cable news services (e.g., CNN), leading them to speculate that local news remains important even when national news alternatives are available. Such findings cannot comment on the attraction of a service like CNN on extraordinary "breaking news" occasions-CNN's coverage of the Gulf example, attracted huge and dedicated audiences. It may be that cable channels function as "additions" to the normal complement of news available to subscribers from other sources, and may actually enhance attention to local news as a function of attention to *all* news.

Another category of research on cable television seeks to document the demographics of the cable subscriber compared to the nonsubscriber. That research yields a portrait of the typical cable subscriber as younger, middle class, having children, being more educated, and somewhat wealthier (Greenberg, Heeter, D'Alessio, & Sipes, 1988; Webster, 1983). In addition to offering information concerning the mesh of this technology with the social structure, such studies hint at the possibility of linking socioeconomic characteristics with viewing typologies. Although such research to date has not employed uses and gratifications approaches, it has led to notions about the uses to which subscribers put cable television. The attraction of additional children's programming available on cable to families with children provides an obvious example of such linkages. Current research, however, is unable to establish any stable relationship between subscriber status and particular viewing "styles." Simply interacting with one particular communication technology does not *automatically* denote marked gratifications shifts.

Finally, a discussion of cable television that neglected to note the way in which certain programming services have created national constituencies or audiences would be remiss. On a more macro level, it is clear that cable television has had broader social and cultural impacts that cannot be apprehended well by uses-and-gratifications perspectives. For example, when the Chicago-based superstation WGN attained broad distribution, Cubs fans proliferated throughout the country. "Fandom" was no longer limited to the immediate Chicago vicinity. Similarly, when a new music video ascends in popularity, fashion trends quickly incorporate the mode of dress represented in the video. So-called Madonna "wanna-bes" are a product of the interaction between audiences and specific programming fare, abetted by a willing fashion industry. This is an aspect of cable television's ability to narrowcast to highly targeted audiences that uses-and-gratifications researchers such as Lull (1985) are only beginning to recognize and investigate.

As media systems such as cable TV or personal computers create new, nongeographically based communities, the uses-and-gratifications approach can be helpful in exploring the relationship between technologies and people and in identifying how people negotiate their identity, their social position, and their emotional lives in an increasingly technologically mediated world.

CRITICAL MASS: ELECTRONIC MAIL AND MASS MEDIA

In studying new media technologies it is important to recognize that just as the technologies may have social impacts, a variety of social factors impact the diffusion and subsequent effects of these technologies. One factor of interest in current studies of new media is the concept of "critical mass." For physicists, a critical mass is the amount of radioactive material necessary to sustain a chain reaction. The term has been adopted by social scientists to refer to the number of individuals who must be involved in a social movement before it may "explode" into being (Oliver, Marwell, & Teixeira, 1985). Adoption of a new media technology is one such social phenomenon that offers an excellent example of the critical mass process. At a certain point, adoption of the technology begins to "take off" dramatically.

In examining this phenomenon, Markus (1987) developed a set of propositions relating to the critical mass for *interactive* communication technologies. First, she indicated that, within a community, adoption of a technology such as the telephone or electronic mail is an "all or nothing" proposition. If a critical mass is achieved, all individuals in the community will eventually adopt the technology. But, if the critical mass is not achieved, usage will drop because of the lack of reciprocity, and eventually no one will use the technology.

Other propositions relate to the resources of the individual and the community. Markus indicated that the fewer resources, that is, time, money, or skills, an individual is required to engage in using a technology, the greater the likelihood of achieving the critical mass leading to universal access. In discussing the distribution of resources throughout a community, she also indicated that greater heterogeneity of resources within a community, as well as early adoption by "high resource" individuals, will increase the likelihood of achieving a critical mass.

Application to E-Mail and Facsimile

In applying this concept of the critical mass to electronic mail, Rice, Grant, Schmitz, and Torobin (1990) observed the relationship between an organization's communication network and the manner in which electronic mail was used by employees of the organization. After surveying all employees of the organization regarding the frequency of communication with each other member of the organization, network analysis was used to determine the underlying communication structure of the organization. Simple inspection of the patterns of adoption within these groups provides a clear indication of the process discussed by Markus (1987). The analysis indicated three distinct subgroups among the 36 employees included in the study. Within two of the three subgroups, all but two individuals were users of the electronic mail system, whereas no one in the third group adopted the technology. This analysis also reported a significant individual-level critical mass effect in which the combined adoption pattern of each person's communication partners, weighted by the frequency of communication, proved to be a significant predictor of whether an individual adopted the technology.

One of the best examples of the workings of critical mass in the new, interactive communication technologies is the facsimile or "fax" machine. The first facsimile machines were developed in the mid-1800s and were used for a century for transmitting pictures and maps over telephone lines. In the 1960s, standards were developed to ensure that machines made by different manufacturers could communicate with each other. But the technology did not become popular as a means of interorganizational communication until the mid 1980s, when enough organizations had adopted the technology. Suddenly, it seemed as if "everyone else" had a fax machine available.

The interactive critical mass point had been reached and the technology was well on its way to universal adoption within business organizations. As the diffusion curve of the fax machine within the business community levels off, adoption of fax machines for residential use is beginning. The large number of fax machines already in use by businesses will contribute to the critical mass for residential fax machine use. An application of Markus' (1987) theory of critical mass suggests that fax machines may one day be as common as telephones in our homes. One social impact of this type of adoption suggests an important corollary of this critical mass theory, namely that people may be forced to adopt a communication technology, with all the benefits and drawbacks that go along with it, simply to maintain their current communication networks.

Application to Mass Media

The preceding discussion dealt exclusively with the critical mass for interactive communications technologies. For mass communication technologies, there are two different sets of critical mass concerns, relating first to the provision of the technology and second to the actual adoption of the technology. Grant (1990) explored a critical mass of organizational functions that must be served before an individual can adopt a mass communication technology. His analysis indicates that, before the first consumer adoption of a new mass medium such as HDTV can take place, a number of organizational functions must be provided. Production hardware use to develop the messages (software) must be manufactured and distributed. Software must then be manufactured and distributed, usually through a system that includes a sequence of national and local distribution. The reception hardware must also be manufactured and distribution, again through both national and local channels of distribution. Finally, after each of these functions is served, consumer adoption may begin. Grant's discussion indicates that technical standards, vertical integration, and compatibility with existing technologies are factors that aid in the achievement of this critical mass, termed the *diffusion threshold*.

The videocassette recorder (VCR) provides an excellent example of how the diffusion threshold works. Before the first consumer VCR purchase could be made, technical standards had to be developed and someone had to manufacture the VCRs. Then, these VCRs had to be distributed nationally (through wholesale operations) and locally (through retail stores). Because the first VCRs were manufactured by the same companies making television receivers, these companies could rely on their current national and local distribution systems to make the machines available to consumers. Early consumer VCR purchase was also dependent on the availability of software. Because VCRs could be used to "time-shift" (record programs off the air), software was already available and distributed nationally through television networks and locally through local television stations. Thus, because VCRs were compatible with the existing television distribution system, the "diffusion threshold" was reached more quickly. Once a large number of VCRs had been sold to consumers, a new software manufacturing and distribution system to produce prerecorded tapes was economically practical and video stores began appearing throughout the country.

Compared to most other mass media, initial adoption of the VCR was a relatively simple process. With many mass media, once the "diffusion threshold" is achieved, adoption of a mass media technology is still not guaranteed. In a capitalist society such as the United States, the fact that most mass media are advertiser supported provides a further barrier to the diffusion of a new mass medium. Because there are so many media channels for the dissemination of advertising messages, a new medium is at an extreme disadvantage. The medium must prove that it has an audience before earning substantial advertiser support, but, without income, the programming provided by the new medium is likely to be inferior to that provided by existing media. Although this relationship may, at first glance, appear to be a "chicken-and-egg" question, the answer is as simple as it is costly. A new mass medium must have the financial support to produce programming to attract an audience, and then the advertising dollars follow. The attainment of a large enough audience to sustain the medium through advertising revenues may be considered yet another element of critical mass.

The challenge of attaining this type of critical mass is complicated by the continuing proliferation of mass media channels. Neuman and Pool (1986) indicated that as the number of media channels and media messages increases, audience resistance to new media increases proportionately. Although they indicate that total media message consumption has increased moderately, the increase in the number of media messages targeted at each individual has increased much more dramatically. Rather than divide their time equally among the abundant media options, individuals are more likely to concentrate their efforts on the media outlets with which they have developed a relationship. The attainment of a critical mass for a new advertiser supported mass medium is therefore an extremely difficult proposition.

One example of this process is the adoption of FM radio. FM broadcasting was approved by the FCC in 1942 (with stereo broadcasting approved in 1961). However, for the next 30 years, the majority of the radio audience ignored this channel, even though it provided far superior sound quality to AM radio. But, as time passed, more and more people began listening to FM radio, and, eventually, advertisers began pumping money into FM radio stations and programmers started programming their FM stations to compete with the most popular AM radio stations. By 1979, FM audience share overtook AM radio's share and, today, FM radio stations garner the majority of the radio audience and radio advertising dollars (Smith, 1985).

Diffusion of Innovations: Telephone Services

Diffusion of innovations has long been a general theory of how new ideas or technologies are communicated, evaluated, adopted (or not), and reevaluated. The major source of information on this topic has been in the work of Everett Rogers and his colleagues (cf. Rogers, 1983, for an overview). The theory has been applied to everything from agricultural methods, to family planning, to adoption of personal computers. Moreover, Rogers and others have devoted attention to its applications regarding adoption of new media.

Basically, the theory holds that the diffusion of innovations is a process through which ideas are communicated through various channels, over time, among people who belong to a given social system. Whereas uses-and-gratifications theory focuses mainly on how certain social and psychological needs may be fulfilled by media uses, diffusion theory encompasses a focus on communication channels, stages of awareness and decision making, criteria for decisions, characteristics of potential adopters, likely advantages of the adoption, complexity of what is being adopted, costs (relative and monetary), and who, if anyone, is promoting the adoption.

Some of the more process-oriented aspects of diffusion study include the differentiation of people by personality type, experiences, and education (to name a few characteristics) who may be characterized as "early adopters" as against slow adopters. Communication channels that carry the new information are often contrasted as public and mass oriented as against interpersonal. Studies have often revealed that public communication may often be the vehicle for communicating information that leads to the awareness of ideas, whereas interpersonal communication may be more crucial in the person's decision making. The diffusion process may be summarized in the following steps (with a focus on new media studies):

1. ***Knowledge.*** The individual or group gains an awareness of something new, such as new computer software, cellular telephone service, or a personal computer in the home. However, the potential adopter has not yet formed an opinion about whether that idea would be valuable.
2. ***Persuasion.*** In this step the potential adopter makes attitudinal evaluations of the idea. Will the new E-mail system benefit this office? Will my family enjoy a compact disc machine? Can I use fax to advantage? These are not only evaluative opinions about the ideas, but also are personally associated with the individual or group. They form the necessary basis for whether the innovation is to be adopted.
3. ***Decision.*** This is the point at which the innovation is either adopted or rejected; the new idea is tried or avoided. Communication in the diffusion process typically propels the adopter toward a decision, so that the individual has to take action even if it is rejected. Communication does not stop after the decision is made, because the individual may continue to react and reevaluate the decision.
4. ***Confirmation.*** Further communication is used to evaluate the decision that was made and the consequences of the decision. Were the benefits of a new office computer network actually realized? Is office productivity improved? Am I less competitive because I did not make the adoption? In this last instance, there may be pressure to reverse a formerly negative decision.

Adoption of new media technologies has been of late a burgeoning subject for diffusion research. The practical question has been whether traditional models of the diffusion process apply to new media, for example, as in the adoption of VCRs, personal computers, facsimile machines, cellular telephones, and the like. A more theoretical question concerns whether the process itself may have some special social or psychological implications because of the nature of many new media. One example of this concern reflects the interactive quality of many new media (electronic mail, new telecommunications services) and even some older ones (e.g., the telephone). Adoption of the telephone, for example, was motivated not just by its availability to a single user, but also by how many other users could potentially be contacted on the network. (Having a telephone is hardly valuable if there is no one to call!) As we saw earlier in this chapter, the idea of "critical mass" has become important in theorizing about the adoption of new media, at least those media where a growing universe of users is involved.

There are also many other factors potentially relevant to the adoption of new media technologies and services. Next we explore examples reflecting telephone services (one category of innovation) and then ask ourselves how beneficial the theory of diffusion of innovations is for this topic.

Modified or Enhanced Telephone Services

The following example of the adoption of telephone services was a problem area that benefitted by interpretation relative to the theory of diffusion of innovations (drawn in part from Williams, Sawhney, & Brackenridge, 1990, and briefly reviewed in Williams, 1991). Over the years telephone companies (we will use United States examples here) have steadily sought to improve basic telephone services and, particularly since the divestiture of American Telephone and Telegraph in 1984, to introduce new services that would yield additional revenues. Typically in the business, "POTS" refers to the level of "plain old telephone service," and all enhancements build on this.

The mostly "basic" service modifications, like getting private lines or "emergency" service like 911 calling, are not mainly an individual or group adopter phenomenon. Instead, they have been brought about more by the regulatory forces in telephony when public utility commissions, together with cooperating telephone companies, decide that services enhancements are worth the public investment. These are a part of so-called universal service, to which everyone is entitled. Still, however, a customer may have the option of deciding whether to stay on a party line, or pay a few more dollars for a private one. This, then, is more or less an "adoption" issue. The availability of "custom calling" and the newer "enhanced" services were initially a function of telephone switching technology. The coming of electronic switches in the 1960s made tone dialing and custom calling features available (e.g., call waiting) as an optional service, and digital switches support the newer enhanced services likes "caller identification." These are all optional services; that is, they require individual purchase and extra payment beyond basic service.

Typically in the telephone business before 1984, new services were introduced with a minimum of fanfare. The business was heavily regulated, meaning the Federal Communications Commission and state utility commissions controlled profits, so the motivation for aggressive marketing campaigns was limited. New services were announced as "trials," sometimes modestly advertised, and the public was left to adopt or reject. If customers picked up on the services, the services were retained; if not, they were dropped or their introduction elsewhere postponed. There was not much interest in the process of diffusion or the adoption behaviors of customers. This pattern began to change after the intentional introduction of competition into the telephone business, a phenomenon that was growing in the 1970s with the introduction of competing long-distance services, and was unleashed as policy with the breakup of AT&T in 1984. This policy shift was initiated in part to encourage introduction of new services into the telephone business; some of these services would eventually become unregulated, meaning that they could become new profit centers for telephone companies.

Examining Customer Attitudes and Behavior

The move from regulation to competition in the telephone business has brought a much expanded interest in customer attitudes and behavior, and for this purpose some social theory has been useful. As introductions of new services move from being "take it or leave it" trials to marketing campaigns, it becomes important to understand the behaviors of potential adopters.

One theory useful in this regard is uses and gratifications such as discussed earlier relative to cable television customers. Although there has been some progress in assessing gratifications associated with telephone use (see Pool, 1977, 1983; some studies reviewed in Williams, 1991), our focus for the present illustration will be on diffusion of innovations. The examples are drawn from several unpublished proprietary studies as well as a more recent study of rural Ohio telephone customers (Williams, Sawhney, & Brackenridge, 1990).In the latter study, conducted in the summer of 1990, the United Telephone Company of Ohio was interested in rural customer attitudes and behaviors regarding residential services. First, it was clear that most of the residential customers in the study fell into one of three categories r elative to service adoption. Briefly, these were as follows:

- ***POTS Residential.*** These are customers with no immediate need or interest in anything other than maintaining basic telephone service and costs at their present level.
- ***POTS-Plus Residential.*** These customers have typically purchased some extra or custom services related to family use, such as an extra line for children, or call waiting.
- ***Residential Doing Business.*** These customers bought extra lines for services because they were doing part or full-time business from their home.

Second, we can examine diffusion steps relative to these customer differences; for example:

1. ***Knowledge.*** The POTS residential customer had little interest in, or knowledge of, additional or enhanced services. An exception might be awareness of a discount long-distance service often offered to the customer via a telephone sales pitch, but promptly

rejected. The POTS-Plus customer, may have a passive awareness of new services, having seen advertisements or read descriptions enclosed with their monthly phone bill. But he or she is not actively seeking this knowledge unless there is an immediate, pressing problem to be solved. By contrast, the Residential Doing Business customers are the most active knowledge seekers, presumably because they cannot be effective in doing their business without them.

2. ***Persuasion.*** The POTS Residential customer has already often built defenses against persuasion regarding new services, whereas the POTSPlus customer might be alerted to a possible purchase if the connection is made with some existing problem (teenagers tying up the sole phone line, for example). Residential Doing Business customers seem more open to persuasion, because they are information seekers for anything that will benefit their occupation. They may be interested in a wide range of details, along with suggestions of business or personal productivity improvement.
3. ***Decision.*** The position to reject new services is mainly reinforced in the POTS customer when there is any attempt at persuasion. (Interviews with such customers often turn up anecdotes of rude telemarketers, or "hang up" reactions, all mostly negative.) As mentioned, POTS-Plus customers may be easily on the verge of a decision if they see a solution to a pressing problem. However, these customers may review their needs when moving into a new dwelling; enhanced phone services can "fit" into a wide range of new purchase decisions-for example, along with a new television set and cable service. Enhanced service decisions by the Residential Doing Business customer is like his or her other business decisions; if not solving a problem, they look for new cost-benefits, productivity, business opportunities, and the like.
4. ***Confirmation.*** Only Residential Doing Business customers seem interested in further communication

regarding decisions they have made. They may seek reaffirmation of their business decision as a part of seeking new alternatives. On the other hand, POTS and POTS-Plus customers have no or little interest, respectively, in further communication or activity regarding the decisions they have made to adopt or reject.

Although the foregoing type of study surely offers no earth-shattering insights, it does serve several ends. First, from a theoretical standpoint, the growing innovations in telephone services, coupled with the move to competitive marketing in this business, provide a current context for reaffirming the utility of applying the diffusion of innovations paradigm. Second, the types of generalizations given above, if examined in more detail, form an excellent basis for planning differentiated marketing strategies for categories of residential customers.

Expanding the Level of Analysis

Although the foregoing sections illustrate how social scientific theories can usefully be applied in the study of new media, it is important to consider broader perspectives than "one theory-one medium" examples. Like the "critical mass" phenomenon discussed earlier, there are further, expanded levels of analysis to be considered. For example, we can consider at least two sets of structural variables in new media study and theory. The first concerns the network of relations among potential adopters and/or users to ascertain social information factors, adoption patterns, and boundaries of adopting communities. The second set of structural variables includes the external environment, including competition, general economic factors, interorganizational relations, regulatory factors, and policy factors, to name a few.

Additionally, the preceding discussion of critical mass factors illustrates that analyses of new media technologies can take place at multiple levels, from individual and group to organizational and system levels. Just as there are reciprocal impacts between a technology and society, factors at each level affect and are affected by each other level. In searching for a body of theory to apply to the study of new media technologies, some importance may be placed on a theoretical framework that operates at multiple levels of analysis. We close with two examples.

Media System Dependency Theory

One such theoretical framework is Media System Dependency Theory (Ball-Rokeach, 1985, 1988). This theory suggests that in order to understand media-related phenomena, it is important to analyze dependency relationships within and across levels of analysis. The theory states that the power of media is a function of the dependencies of individuals, groups, organizations, and systems on the scarce information resources controlled by the media. Thus, media content (and any related media effects) is a product of a variety of dependency relationships operating at multiple levels of analysis.

A good example of how these dependencies interact may be found in an analysis of the television system in the United States. To understand how television might be adopted by or have an effect on a specific individual, it is important to note that the medium is dependent on advertisers for revenue, the government for the right to broadcast, and the individual viewer for continuing to use the medium and provide a "product" for sale to advertisers. In turn, advertisers, the government, and individual viewers are each dependent on television in one form or another. Media system dependency theory states that because all of these dependency relationships affect each other, an analysis of the role of a medium in society should examine these dependency relationships across levels of analysis.

The theory explicitly addresses the relationship individuals have with the media (Ball-Rokeach, 1988; Ball-Rokeach, Rokeach, & Grube, 1984), indicating that, over time, individuals develop a dependency relationship with a medium to fulfill specific goals of play, orientation, and understanding. Although an individual's dependence on a specific medium is expected to be comparatively stable overtime, Ball-Rokeach (1985) indicated that, in times of ambiguity or threat, dependency on mass media increases as individuals seek additional information to help them in their daily lives.

Media system dependency theory is one of many theories that provides insight into the complexity of new media technologies. By integrating this theory with others, such as the diffusion of innovations, social information processing, uses-and-gratifications notions, and critical mass theories, a more accurate picture of new media technologies may be possible than by simply using a single theory.

Social Information Processing Theory

How people choose among competing media introduces the subjectivity inherent in the evaluation of new media technologies. One especially illuminating perspective in this regard is the "Social Information Processing Model of Media Use" proposed by Fulk, Steinfield, Schmitz, and Power (1987). This model premises that, rather than engage in an objectivity rational process in which new media are evaluated based on their characteristics, individuals engage in a process in which the evaluations of others (social information) is crucial in choosing among competing media.

As applied by Fulk et al., the social information perspective suggests that the attitudes, statements, and behaviors of others are more important in media choice and evaluation than the inherent attributes recognized by the users. Fulket al. indicated that the media choice process remains a rational one, but stated that the rationality is influenced by past statements and behavior as well as social norms rather than by a matching of media attributes with task requirements.

In their assessment of electronic mail, Riceet al. (1990) found moderate support for the role of social information processing variables in predicting the adoption, usage, and evaluations of the system. Schmitzand Fulk (1991) provided similar evidence for the role of social information in the evaluation of electronic messaging.

The above discussion of social information and critical mass provides some important directions for the study and understanding of new media technologies. First, and most important, it suggests the interaction between the technologies and the social environment. Just as the technologies may have social impacts, societal factors, in turn, impact the manner in which new technologies are adopted, used, and evaluated. Analysis of these technologies is further complicated by the fact that evaluations of these technologies are based on subjective social information. It is not enough to understand the features of a communication technology; the perception of those features (and the wide variety of factors influencing those perceptions) must be understood as well.

6

THE NEWS AS SOCIAL CONTEXT

It is the form of news as it is currently reported—its definition of an event and its use of "attribution" by officials—that this work examines in an attempt to understand the effect and limits of its rules. The central argument will be that contemporary journalism has at its base one or more innate, institutionalized biases or structural flaws. These flaws may result in political or informational biases, but they are primarily rooted in the textual structure of the generally accepted narrative style that reporters use to describe specific events. To be more explicit, the hypothesis states that even when all the facts of a story can be shown to be correctly reported, it may still be so slanted, so incomplete in its choice of fact or inaccurate in its manner of presentation as to be propaganda and not objective news.

Indeed, it is through this "facticity," the accumulation of officially sanctioned, partial quotes about events whose boundaries are narrowly and arbitrarily prescribed, that contemporary news daily and consistently abdicates its promise. The question is not one of the competence or ability of a specific reporter or editor at any one newspaper or in any one situation, but rather the issue of an institutionalized bias at the heart of the concept of news today. Others who in the past have criticized the news as an information system have focused their analysis on the composition of a television news program or a newspaper's bureaucratic structure. Rather than attempting an analysis at that level, this work focuses its attention at the level of the narrative, the news text itself.

Others have argued that bias enters news as a result of organizational socialization, as a function of capitalist hegemony, through "gatekeepers" within each organization, or what Gaye Tuchman calls "rituals" of objectivity and performance. Failures of objectivity in journalism have been blamed on the physical limitations of print media, the economic considerations that bind industry managers, and even the fantasies that professionals bring to their work. Each of these views has its defenders and detractors. It is not the intention of this work to enter directly into debates on the sociology of the newsroom, the psychology of the journalist, or the issues of newsroom economics. But to the extent that a structural bias or flaw can be described as occurring within the narrative form of the news, the argument will be that these other factors may be the result of and are certainly dependent on the nature of that textual pattern.

This work examines the narrative form itself, the generative rules of news writing as they are used in mundane stories. It is believed that to the extent that a narrative bias exists, its description may embrace the mechanisms of hegemony and the form in which those who believe they are performing an objective function present, instead, biased and incomplete reports. These result from the text, outgrowths of what is at base a narrative practice that has not been adequately studied. The argument is that the problem of facticity and false truths exists first and foremost at the level of the structure of the text itself. This study focuses its efforts at that level and only later attempts to integrate its findings into the political, sociological, and psychological debates.

Thus there is no attempt to interview or investigate the actors in the Hawaiian drama centering on Judge Shintaku's injuries. Issues of responsibility among the news directors editors, and reporters who covered the Oahu story are irrelevant, at this remove, to the stories themselves. They are the traces remaining of that complex of a 1981 event bundle. The value of the Hawaiian case is, in fact, precisely in its narrative reliance on the accurately reported individual "facts"- the attributed statements by police, prosecutors, physicians, and other officials. The impression and conclusion, however, was either demonstrably false or, at the very least, suspect from any but the officially sanctioned perspective. The inaccuracies, which should have been evident to a first-year medical student, were never addressed by reporters or questioned by editors. What was said the "facts" of the story, are what stood and stand as a record that lives in our present.

To the extent that this can be shown to be a typical result of the narrative form used by contemporary reporters, the result is that North American journalism appears, because of its flaws, to become what it purports to most despise: a powerful propaganda tool for the maintenance of the status quo and an organ of the literate and elite. Because of its structural flaws it is too rarely a vehicle for the dissemination of balanced, unprejudiced information or a force for social change.

Thus this work takes the political, sociological and economic criticisms of the press and reformulates them at the level of the narrative mechanism. It seeks a position in the dialogue on the nature of journalism that begins with the technique of the narrative irrespective of its subject. This will require, first, the search for and description of a consistent, narrative pattern in contemporary journalism. That, in turn, requires the analysis of specific news stories as if they were exotic artifacts from a distant culture and not items of such familiarity as to have a form whose rules appear self-evident or natural. The form in which news is written has such consistency and ubiquity as to be part of what phenomenologists have described as the "taken-forgranted world." To be so accepted means, often, not to be seen, and if news is to be studied for potential structural deficits, it must be taken from the assumed world and placed within that of the exotic. Just as Roland Barthes used his semiologic system to examine the content of French cultural artifacts ranging from movies to magazine text, so must news be seen as a systemic artifact in which the assumptions inherent in the form can be made overt.

NEWS AS FACT

Contemporary journalism presents itself as offering a record of reality that is as unbiased and as complete as possible. Individual newspaper, newsmagazine, and broadcast stations each maintain a formidable system of editors, reporters, artists, and technicians whose job it is to gather, prepare and present periodic collections of nonfictional stories that mirror as closely as possible the unbiased-if editorially selected—facts of existence within their circulation worlds. Daily and weekly news organs promise, in North America at least, the description of discrete and discontinuous events of presumed relevance to the lives of their auditors, those readers or viewers who choose to read a newspaper or magazine report, listen to a radio broadcast, or view a television news hour and accept it as a representation of shared reality.

Daily journalism, to put it another way, is supposed to be an unreflective exercise in which facts are presented in a specialized form without overt interpretation in as tightly written, legible and cohesive a manner as possible. Were it reflective it would be not news but "commentary" or "opinion." This is what Graham Murdock calls the "canon of objectivity":

The canon of objectivity requires that news should offer as complete a capture of events in the world as possible, and that the presentation of those accounts should not be shaped by the personal values or commitments of the journalists involved. The ideal of objectivity, then, rests on the claim that the news is accurate, comprehensive and neutral, and consists of independently verifiable facts that are clearly separated from expression of opinions or values.

Fact and Propaganda

In theory the news story—the objective description of an event in the world—should be easy to describe, analyze, and distinguish from its cousins, advertising and propaganda. Advertising is the presentation of facts or perspectives with the express purpose of selling or promoting an article, position or belief. Propaganda refers to the selective presentation of possibly spurious facts to advocate a political position or point of view in reality, however, these are enormously plastic concepts whose boundaries shift from generation to generation and from writer to writer. It was once common in the British press, for example, to pay reviewers to cover new theatrical productions. Today, however, the payment to publications or reporters for information on a new show is advertising and the acceptance of money for a review would be viewed as immoral and grounds for the writer's dismissal. It remains common, however, for newsmen to use information distributed by a corporation's paid public relations functionaries whose job is the selective presentation of information ("news releases") favorable to their employers.

The relation between contemporary journalism and propaganda is at least as equivocal. Propaganda is both "the systematic propagation of a given doctrine" and "material disseminated by the proselytizers of a doctrine". It can be argued that American news broadcasts and periodicals, despite pretensions to value-free reportage, regularly fulfill the first and almost certainly the second definition. Todd Gitlin, for example, describes the "dominion and continuance of an ideology through the news" as an unspoken, unacknowledged, persistent process by which large amounts of information are daily sifted into a single, journalistic perspective that adopts a single, official point of view. The "frame of the news," the context in which stories are chosen and presented, is dominated by the quotes and observations of officials and accepts, usually without question, the official perspective of moderation as opposed to extremism, individualism as opposed to collectivism, gradual reform as opposed to radical change.

The result is a news context that "precludes a full explanation of dissenting views."

The domination of the news by official policy makers has been described frequently, but it is so crucial an element in our argument that it deserves one more exposition. One survey of 2,850 stories in the *N.Y. Times* and *Washington Post* found that almost 80 percent of the stories in both publications were based on the official pronouncements of public officials. Another study of 2,500 stories in those papers found that 78 percent of the articles were based on statements by public officials. These stories, an overwhelming majority, typically present as fact and without critical examination the statements of officials with a vested interest in a single position or policy. The poor, the black, the disenfranchised, and the unemployed, on the other hand, tend to make the news only when they appear to threaten or confound the known values and established order. As Chomsky has shown, the result, at least in terms of United States reportage of foreign affairs, leads to a consistent exclusion of facts unacceptable to U.S. officials and a consistent bias supporting official U.S. positions.

As Lewis H. Lapham notes succinctly: The American press is, and always has been, a booster press. Its editorial pages characteristically advancing the same arguments as the paid advertising copy. Together with the teaching in the schools, the national media preserve the myths that the society deems precious, reassuring their matrons . . . that all is well, that the American truths remain securely in place, that the banks are safe, our generals competent, our presidents interested in the common welfare, our artists capable of masterpieces, our weapons invincible and our democratic institutions the wonder of an admiring world.

In short, American newspapers can be seen as presenting "the systematic propagation of a given doctrine"; the dictionary's primary definition of propaganda. It is precisely for this reason that critics, like Chomsky, argue that "the media's purpose in a free society is to manufacture consent among the governed, rallying the population to endorse elite decisions. Propaganda, in effect, is for, 'a free society what force is to dictatorships."

Pravda. Ibis is the way news has come to be. It is not a necessary pattern. The Soviet news system, to take one contemporary example, is characterized by a very different balance between official and civilian views. Despite a near-universal North American assumption that the "free press" is unbiased and populist in comparison with the presumably elitist and propaganda-laden Soviet news, a 1988 report in *Editor and Publisher* (a newspaper trade magazine) revealed that over 79 percent of the official Russian newspaper's content originated not from press conferences or official statements but with citizen complaints, queries, revelations, and observations. *Pravda*'s staff devoted the majority of its time to investigation of these reader tips and not to slavish coverage of Kremlin views. Finally, one presumes, although the story did not report, that the degree of *Pravda*'s copy that is official in origin is overtly so and therefore easy for a skeptical reader to discount. It is at least theoretically possible to argue that the form and pattern of news in *Pravda* (*Isvestia*. etc.) is more responsive to Soviet readers' concerns than the *New York Times* or the *washington Post* is to those of their respective clientele.

Sports. For sports "news" reportage, the lines between news, advertising and propaganda are even more blurred. Television networks bid, for example, for the exclusive right to televise Olympic games and present them, at least in the United States, as news. Both broadcast and print Journalists create, every four years, through supposedly unbiased reportage of an international event, a dramatic contest between U.S athletes—heroes—and "foreign" competitors who were "challengers." Advertisers queued for the right to pay to be "Olympic sponsors" in Los Angeles in 1984, using the game's logo and prestige (with contestants sometimes wearing their corporate symbol) in return. The name of a gold medalist may be news, but the format and thrust of Olympic television coverage is demonstrably advertising and nationalistic propaganda.

At the 1984 Summer Olympics in Los Angeles, California, Canadian broadcaster protested the degree to which American television coverage focused on U.S. athletes to the virtual exclusion of non-U.S. participants. U.S. news coverage was seen by the Canadian Broadcasters (who shared broadcast markets in trans-border regions) as so slanted and biased as to prejudice their attempts to report shared events, Reportage of actual sports events, commercial advertising by official sponsors of the Olympics, and nationalistics propaganda-the assertion of U.S. supremacy and the U.S. socio-economic system-all were hopelessly confused in the television coverage of those games.

FACT AND BIAS

Despite these inconsistencies, daily journalism purports to present "real facts." At least in theory, the essence of the news as it is both taught and practiced today is the presentation of objective, unbiased information free from the taint of slander or libel: someday died, somebody was jailed; the speech of an official was heard and is presented to the readers or viewers as a news. Daily stories are defined, as they were in the Shintaku reports, by the ability of a reporter or news organization to prove, if questioned, that the journalistic narrative offered without malice an accurate if selected trace of single event. This is the basic conceptual framework with which sometimes complex processes are distilled and aspects of them isolated to fashion distinct news stories measured, professionally, in column inches or, in a broadcast format, second of time modern news folk, at least in North America, stand by the "'journalistic method,' i.e. the modern reportorial stance-probing, fact-obsessed, " objective"-which evolved through the 19th century" and has become, in the later part of the twentieth century, an unexamined given.

One problem with this perspective is that the general public does not, in the United States at least, appear to hold the success of that Exercise in great esteem. Polls since the 1970s have consistently Shown public confidence in journalism on a par with confidence in Politicians and significantly behind that accorded school officials. More than 70 percent of those surveyed did not trust either the politicians who are a newspaper's primary source of information or, not surprisingly, the periodical itself, which provided a primary arena for the politicians' views. It is with some chagrin that news people find that viewers and readers do not maintain a high estimation of either the daily content or the general perspective of most contemporary news organs. Public opinion surveyors periodically check and recheck the degree to which Americans believe or trust their domestic news sources. The logical conclusion, that the most readers and viewers assume news is not an unbiased, accurate, germane representation of the world, is a continuing source of concern to many professionals.

Articulate and educated Individuals, including some journalists, argue generally or anecdotally that news is persistently slanted, inaccurate, or incomplete. For example, playwright Arthur Miller, who had extensive experience as the subject of many news stories, suggested that the problem was systemic, rising from the necessity of newspapers and magazines to publish consistently and rapidly. Summing up press coverage of Marilyn Monroe, Miller said: You know, journalists usually come around with an angle. They have to. They simply never get the time or the opportunity to hang around long enough to decide anything. Over the years, that angle becomes the easiest [if prejudicial] thing to do, and its gotten, in Marilyn's case, to be very fruitful in terms of copy. And they keep pounding on her all the time until the thing becomes reality.

Poet Robert Frost was even more succinct in his view of journalists. It was the paraphrase, the attempt to summarize what for Frost could not be condensed, that infuriated him. As he said of one reporter: "My grounds for wanting to let him have both fists in succession in the middle of the face are chiefly that he stated me so much worse than I know I state myself." Such condemnation by poets and writers may, perhaps, be expected and yet remain worrisome in light of generally declining public esteem. But veteran reporter Mark

Harris admits to urging his friends not to read newspapers and to spurn television news as limited, ephemeral and unreliable. He thus echoes Thomas Jefferson who was, I believe, the first to argue that a man who did not read might be better informed than one who did because the potential for less information also meant the certainty of a decreased amount of disinformation.

Reaction by contemporary news professionals to such attacks typically has been to investigate individual incidents of alleged bias but not to question the general framework or organization of the news story as a form of information itself. When a CBS documentary charging that U.S. Army Gen. William C. Westmoreland falsified accounts of enemy troop strength in Vietnam resulted in a $120 million libel action, for example, intense and involved studies—by CBS and by others—were begun into that specific story's generation. Unquestioned, however, was the general narrative structure of the story itself, the format of Its copy, and the wisdom of its editorial reliance on disparate "facts" to organize the information that was the framework of that show.

NEWS AS A SOCIAL CONSTRUCT

News is a social construct empowered by a cultural history and a tradition of institutional practice based on material and cognitive realities. As such it has, in Western's words, the "power of definition." While it may not mirror reality—the omniscient eye—it becomes a record of and the accepted version of past events. As Tuchman puts it, "the act of making news is the act of constructing reality itself rather than [simply] a picture of reality." Thus any report, whatever its inherent bias or failings, confirms an occurrence and simultaneously changes it into an event by placing it in a specific context:

News is a window on the world . . . but like any frame that delineates the world, the news frame may be considered problematic. The view through the window depends upon whether the window is large or small, has many panes or few, whether the glass is opaque or clear.

OBJECTIVITY

Others have commented on the degree to which a social context defines, politically and socially, the information that will be presented. The frame offers an encoded "preferred reading." Given possible multiple readings of mass media, the power of the news lies in its ability to ensure that readers or other active users are presented with the same or similar bureaucratically created and ideologically embedded accounts. Hence the frame may be more important than the specific details it organizes.

The assertion that all news functions as the frame or context of an event, thus distorting by the act of selective description, affirms the proposition that real objectivity is a chimera, a false Grail that all observers may seek but which remains unobtainable. In physical science this has become a central truth of physical reality. and in social science it is an equally accepted, if more bitter truth. By being involved in an event—even as recorder—we influence it. As Max Weber argued and David R. Caploe restates, it is manifest "that even the most apparently simple 'description' is, in reality, highly dependent on a whole series of major and fundamental analytic assumptions that are usually implicit." "The facts"—or any fact—cannot and do not stand alone but are mediated through a complex of bias and assumption that can and must be made overt before information can be assessed. Journalism is not unique in this regard, although it is unusual, perhaps, in its members' resistance to the self-reflective analysis of its prejudices and preconceptions.

If news is not and, indeed, cannot be objective (free from bias and individual perspective) what can be said about it? First, it can be shown to be consistent, following a general pattern of presentation accepted, usually without question, by journalists and readers alike. From its grammatical structure to its choice of topics, the news follows a specific pattern that can be examined and discussed. The use of the English language, choice of paragraph styles and definition, techniques of opposing paragraphs for balance are, for example all aspects of a reportorial style currently accepted by television, radio, newspaper, and magazine reporters writing for local, regional, or national presentation.

Further, mainstream journalism in all its forms is highly predictable in the way it organizes information. News professionals (radio, newspaper, newsmagazine or television) can be expected to cover most classes of occurrence—murder courts, and natural disasters-in set ways. As Joseph T. Scanlon and Suzanne Alldred noted: The mass media behave roughly the same way when responding to all major events whether these are natural or man-made disasters, criminal occasions such as assassination attempts, hijackings, hostage takings or other acts of terrorism or simply major, unexpected events.

This is not a new or radical view, although it may be an uncomfortable one for those who wish published or televised reports to mirror precisely the apparent uniqueness of the events they choose or are assigned to cover. But for coverage to occur, consistency and predictability are both a virtue and necessity. The world must be "tamed to meet the needs of a production system in many respects bureaucratically organized."

Structural analysis provides one method by which one can attempt to understand the way the world is ordered. It assumes a series of principles that can be made overt and whose description makes clear elements of the whole. It is therefore integrative and hierarchic. As Roland Barthes stated: "In order to conduct a structural analysis, it is thus first of all necessary to distinguish several levels or instances of description and to place these instances within a hierarchic, integrationary perspective."

Structurally, one is interested in the form as well as the specific datum of any story. To the degree that the structure is both consistent and predictable, one should be able to analyze specific stories as examples of broader, narrative classes and say: What is true of A is true of $A_1 \ldots\ldots A_n$. This is to say that an examination of the news for inherent bias and systematic exclusion must be structural and can be carried from one to another level of journalistic output at stages of story generation, research, and production. But any such analysis must begin at the basic level of the grammar of news, the structural characteristics of its text.

The concept of a frame in journalism typically refers to social and political perspectives or constraints that reporters, editors, and producers bring to or have imposed upon their work. Here the "frame" will be taken to mean the narrative form itself, the pattern of words that create the copy that becomes the news. Issues of information, bias, and social content raised by others result from the text, and it is in the domain of the text that the mechanisms of embedded meaning must be found.

NEWS AS MYTH

Practitioners insist that news reportage is neither propaganda nor advertising. It is, most argue, as objective as possible a description of discrete and discontinuous events. Reporters, from this perspective, are not writers or thinkers participating in the event itself but recorders whose function it is to capture the speech and actions of a specific time and place so they can be disseminated to a wider audience. Like Lévi-Strauss's anthropology, reportage becomes at its best a *technique de dépaysement* and the best reporter, like the consummate anthropologist, is not simply a neutral observer but a man distanced from his subject and in control of that alienation.

Clearly this is the exception rather than the rule, in news reportage at least as much as anthropology. Reporters are not impartial observers, and their stories do not necessarily define accurately or completely the discrete events they purport to cover dispassionately. While Johnsonian techniques of editorial involvement were used to paint a portrait that all agree is true, the reporter/writer was castigated for transgressing assumed bounds and rules. The lines between news as a *technique de dépaysement* and as a *technique de politique* are, as Chomsky, Gitlin, and others have pointed out, continually blurred or blurry.

"If you can't put the news in perspective," argues one journalism instructor, "you're not a Journalist—you're a tape recorder." The baggage of personal history, Individual or cultural perspective, and professional background all newspeople bring to the coverage of any event mediates their reports. Tape recorders, for example, have a clear function, and while tapes can be modified and edited, at least their function and limitations are clear. Sounds of a specific range and intensity when emitted within the range of an activated microphone are picked up indiscriminately and held on tape until altered or erased.

The reporter's role is more equivocal. A two-hour speech is condensed to perhaps a forty-five second radio report or twelve inches of newspaper copy. He or she cannot tell the proverbial "truth, whole truth and nothing but the truth." There is not time enough on television or space enough in the newspaper for even a tithe of that complex truth. Nor can any newspaper or broadcast station deliver what the *New York Times* promises: "All the News that's Fit to Print." Even if one could describe what is and is not "fit to print" by some objective standard, there is no room for so much data and there are not enough writers to fashion it. If the reporter's job is to selectively describe an event, the questions multiply Immediately—what event, based on what subjects, and for whom? Is the report fashioned for some amorphous public at large or to satisfy the editor who sent the person out? Who judges the story—the reporter, members of the public, or one of a pantheon of editors whose job is to assure that appropriate stories march through a television news hour or across a newspaper page?

The ultimate purpose of a recording machine is clear—to capture sounds indiscriminately within a certain decibel level issued within the range of its microphone—but the ultimate service of a newsperson is more equivocal. Newspapers and television and radio stations serve first and foremost an economic function. They exist to create profits and make money for the owners through the sale of individual copies and of space within the publication or news broadcast to advertisers.

The latter are not primarily interested in public service but rather in advertising products to increase profit margins. Thus the newsperson works for a corporation whose primary purpose is the return of capital to the corporation owners. The corporation's critical clients are a group of other corporate entities who buy space or time slots abutting the news in the hopes of selling more of a specific product and thus of increasing their profits as well.

The extent to which these realities limit or define the news reportees job and the degree to which they shape editorial perspective is unclear. At one end of the debate is Mark Crispin Miller, who said of television reporters simply that they "serve commercial television. Their aim is to boost ratings: They always tell the people what they think the people are already thinking." At the other end of the spectrum is the news professional's insistence taught in schools of journalism, that news is absolutely separate from economic consideration, that issues of advertising and economics never affect a story's content. Between them, perhaps, lies the measure of truth. News is a mediated, synthetic product, and the best indication of its warring factions may be the story itself. There in the narrative of specific stories are the traces of decisions, judgments, selections, and battles. There is where we will soon have to begin.

Semiology and Myth

To understand this problem at the level of the text it may be helpful to consider a specific vocabulary with which reportage can be analyzed anew. The French structuralist Roland Barthes offers a paradigm called semiology. It promises one way out of the maze, allowing the narrative form of news reportage to be described as a category of myth. Myth does not, here, mean a fairy story or ancient tale told long ago around camp fires in early or preliterate worlds. Myth describes, in Barthes's language, a consistent system of narrative representation in which symbols (words) have cultural and contextual relevance. Myth is an attempt to describe the cultural context of specific human events, actions, or artifacts using a structuralist perspective that is linguistic in origin.

To say that news reports present a mythic, narrative system is to say that it describes signs (actions or events) that are presented through a series of cultural filters which include values of the reporting and reading culture. News reportage thus takes the raw events of our world and places them in a unifying context, a translation that renders them comprehensible and safe to readers or viewers, who can disregard that system of presentation just as readers of this passage do not stop to think of the degree to which the language (English) and style (academic-narrative) that order these words as I write also define and limit my mode of presentation.

An example Barthes uses to make overt how this mythic system functions as a frame is the cover photograph of a *Paris Match* magazine showing a young black soldier in a French uniform saluting, with his eyes uplifted, the French tricolor flag. The photographic image is sign (a man stood for an instant at a time and place and his image was captured on film using an indelible chemical process). What he signifies—the meaning carried by the image itself and the source of its power—is France as empire with all its citizens (of all colors and in any location, even, perhaps, Algiers) faithfully serving the fatherland. At a second level of meaning this signifier, a black soldier giving the French salute, brings together ideas of race, nationality, colonialism, and imperialism simultaneously. Finally, what is signified, the underlying imperative, is hidden by the sign itself. Here it is, the photo says, the French empire with the ideals of liberty, equality, and fraternity turned out in imperialistic or at least military splendor.

Barthes's system of meaning thus describes an information system imbedded in the narrative. In this case the sign was a photograph that pictured an individual saluting. The photograph captured and emphasized details of an "objective event" that signified simultaneously certain social and political messages. The photograph was placed in a magazine (or run in the newspaper or used on television) where its political message resonated from but may have been obscured in the sign—a photographic image presented in a national paper whose reproductive screen is perhaps 350 dots per inch. The editor's selection of the photo, one of presumably hundreds he had to choose from, was based not merely on aesthetic value or abstract composition, but ultimately on its mythic value: the interplay of sign, signifer, and signified which together loaded the original signifer with meaning. It is myth precisely to the degree that this interplay occurs and seemingly isolated signs are taken over by cultural meaning and messages. Thus it is not a harmless and value-free record of a moment in time at a single place, but an encoded statement of politics, empire, race, and allegiance.

Sign, Signifier and Signified

While the language is specific in Barthes's analysis, others have commented on the three legs that must inform all opinion. More than sixty years ago, Lippmann noted that "the analyst of public opinion must begin, then, by recognizing the triangular relationship between the scene of action, the human picture of that scene and the human response to that picture working itself out upon the scene of action." His observations, prescient and penetrating for the time, dealt with the general problem of the objectivity of the observer and not the issue of the way in which meaning was imbedded into the narrative form. In the intervening sixty years, techniques of linguistic analysis, structuralist theory (in social science and well as linguistics), and content analysis have been devised to allow one to see the specific datum as a part of the whole and the individual, apparently banal rule as part of a larger social structure.

"Joe Died." Seeing news as a structural system of representation provides a certain distance and a perspective of its own which Barthes's semiology can analyze. His system, ultimately, allows the reconciliation of the traditional view of reportage—"the description of discrete events"—and the criticism of individuals such as Chomsky that "news is propaganda." This becomes clear in the general structure of

the attributed newspaper sentence. Consider, for example, the information for a story describing the death from heroin overdose of an individual whom the police suspected of trafficking in drugs. It begins with an event (Joe died), which is placed in official context (Joe died, the police said) and given import by the police suspicions (Joe, a suspected drug dealer, was shot Thursday, police said).

The death, the event of Joe's demise, can become a sign to be treated by the reporter. But what is to be signified by that death (Joe represents an illegal, antisocial activity requiring police intervention) comes not from the event itself but rather from the officials' involvement (he died unnaturally, else why would they be involved?). Finally, the implicit message (drugs are evil and police fight evil drugs) is far removed from the sign and subsumed in the political war against the use of controlled substances, which may have, in the end, little to do with this specific death.

"Myth hides nothing and flaunts nothing: it distorts: myth is neither a lie nor a confession: it is an inflection," Barthes argues. Thus news as myth distorts not consciously or dramatically—as many presume overt propaganda must—but by "inflection," by choice of sign and level of attention. Do we quote Joe's grief-stricken mother who says he was a good boy accidently addicted to drugs while being treated at a Veteran's Hospital where the standard of care was abysmal? Does the reporter credit Joe's girlfriend who says Joe was in fact no longer using drugs (and thus his death was related to some other complex of events)? Or do we accept the police report and base the narrative on its official view moralizing, at least by inference, that drugs always lead to an untimely end?

Normally we simply quote the police, who signify authority, professionalism, social consensus and investigatory prowess. To a newspaper of record they are the record, signifying the judicial system that is America's guarantee of fair treatment, equal protection under the law and so on.. News's relation to myth is, as Barthes argues, not one of truth but of use. The truth of Joe's death is not necessarily informed by the police offlcial's statement. It tells us less than nothing about the man, the degree of his drug use, or the reasons for it. It is useful for contemporary politicians to say that cocaine (or heroin or marijuana or crack) is a scourge but that does not mean, necessarily, that it is true. Pharmacological literature has consistently described cocaine, for example, as neither physically addictive or biologically harmful except when used in massive amounts. Cocaine is far less physically damaging to humans than state-subsidized drugs-tobacco or alcohol — but promulgation of this fact is not politically or culturally useful at present and thus generally ignored in all but the most technical of biochemical literatures.

In Barthes's language, myth is "depoliticized speech" that reflects a bourgeois ideology born in the Nineteenth century. It "records facts or perceives values, but refuses explanations; the order of the world can be seen as sufficient or ineffable, it is never seen as significant." This is precisely why the police investigators and not Joe's mother would be quoted. The police's and therefore the reporter's interest and perspective is bounded by the judicial system, which does not seek the context of the event or the significance of an individual life. Rather, it allocates an event's place within proscribed rules of socially sanctioned right or wrong. Reasons and explanations, antecedent contexts, and mitigating circumstances do not require, in this model of myth, interpretation or assessment.

The apparently simple, declarative statement that Joe died, according to the police, can be passed off as sufficient. It says nothing, in the end, about Joe—his life, his possible habituation or the context of his demise. It is sufficient and insignificant, part of the daily dross of a police reporter's beat. Overtly it says nothing about drug use, drug abuse, the specific causes, or social effects of chemical habituation. It says a great deal, however, by inference and exclusion. Like Dragnet's Sergeant Friday, reporters can insist on "just the facts, Ma'am," and deny their brief reaches beyond the role of record and into the complex of inference and social order.

Unary Transformations

The levels of imbedded meaning, the progression from the original sign to the affirmation of the final myth is clear. There is little ambiguity in its message and little room for a reader to ponder its meanings or nuances. It is, borrowing from the language of generative grammar, unary in the progression from original signifier (Joe in physical extremis) to final signifier to final sign: A transformation is unary if, through it, a single series is generated by the base: such are the passive, negative, interrogative and emphatic transformations. The Photograph is unary when it emphatically transforms "reality" without doubling it, without making it vacillate (emphasis is a power of cohesion): no duality, no indirection, no disturbance. The unary Photograph has every reason to be banal. . . ."The subject," says one handbook for amateur photographers must be simple, free of useless accessories; this is called the search for unity."

This, Barthes argues, is a typical quality of the news photo and, I will argue later, equally typical in journalism's written form. The photo of the French soldier saluting was effective precisely because it lacked resonance. Its emphatic refusal to describe events outside a series of socially accepted precepts led the viewer (or reader) to a political position and statement. It insisted on a specific meaning while it trumpeted what appeared to be a picture or story filled with content. In photography, one is reminded of *Life* magazine's decision in 1937 not to use photographs by Andre Kertdsz because his images "spoke too much" and opened the doors to shifting references, which its editors did not want.

In the story of Joe's death, a similar series of transformations occurs, leading without question to a specific cultural message. The signifier in this generic story depends not on the events of Joe's death but on what police say are the circumstances. The reporter quotes the police officer, who says Joe was being investigated for drug dealing, perhaps adding with a sigh that Joe was "another victim of cocaine." Had the investigation continued perhaps it would have been shown that Joe was in fact neither selling nor using drugs at all. The headline reads "Another Victim of Cocaine" and the meaning, whatever the facts of Joe's life may have been, is set in the story—by "fact" and in narrative context—forever.

Myth and Reality

Thus the news as myth gives a "natural image of this [culturally defined] reality," forming an umbrella and overview that can shelter both Chomsky and other critics from the rain of complaint by those who argue as an article of faith that news is truth. This inherent value system—the mythic language—describes a reportorial perspective in which events consistently are mediated through a single complex of cultural values. Two examples used by Chomsky and Accuracy in Media, a watchdog group, will suffice to show how structurally similar events are described differently when mediated through this mythic lens.

The 1986 Russian downing of an off course, Korean passenger airplane near its coast was editorially condemned in the United States as an "unforgivable act." In 1988, however, the U.S. military's destruction of a nonmilitary passenger airplane on its appointed course in the Persian Gulf was generally described in the U.S. news media as a tragic but understandable accident resulting from then current hostilities in that geographic region. Similarly, Russian involvement in an Afghanistan civil war was decried as adventurism by U.S. news organs, which in the 1960s and early 1970's, had supported an equivalent American involvement in the Vietnamese civil war.

Structurally, both sets of events were separately consistent. Both countries claimed, in their respective incursions, to be present at the legitimate request of a recognized and sympathetic government fighting rebel forces in a civil war. In each case an unarmed, civilian airplane was shot down by the respective super power. But the structural similarities between these events—East and West—were largely ignored or denied by American journalists because they were not in accord with the prevailing sociopolitical perspective that pits

American virtue against Soviet evil. After all, as then President Ronald Reagan was fond of pointing out, the U.S.A. was a light to the world while the U.S.S.R. was an "Evil Empire". Thus in their reportage of these two structurally similar but politically different events, U.S. media followed the prejudices of their national leaders. The similarities and responsibility for lives lost was not, really, the point because, as Barthes noted, "men do not have with myth a relationship based on truth, but on use." Use is defined in news by the sources a newsman chooses and, as we have seen, these are largely official. Truth is who reporters quote—"PresidentBush said," "Police Chief Keala said," "GovernorAriyoshi said." Thus news reports become, as Chomsky suggests, propaganda. It is not the work of a perfidious cabal, however, but a banal and unconscious reflex, the sum of assumptions that pour through at the level of the sign.

If news is myth, however, it cannot operate simply in the domain of political reportage. That would be too limited and would set apart reporters, editors, and readers of international affairs from the general newsroom group. In most city newsrooms the same editor who lays out a page of local copy also handles international reports. The style of news runs seamlessly across the page from political to economic to city beats at the scales of international, national, regional, and local reports. If news is myth, then its bias must pervade the form of mundane reportage as well as international stories. One can postulate generative and "taken-for-granted" rules, by which the social bias is inserted into mundane descriptions of real-time reports, "depoliticizing" as it transforms complex events into a publishable form. The means by which this occurs is explored in the third chapter, which analyzes a category of apoliticized reports of real-time events.

Thus to the extent news can be described as myth, it presents as objective "truth" a specific and proscribed reality that is based on a cultural inflection. The question is how one can study this "inflection" in contemporary news. If it exists as a structural pattern it must be pervasive in not only political and international reportage but mundane stories as well.

7

The Object of Journalistic Objectivity

When journalists and journalism scholars write about "objectivity," they often disagree, sometimes quite radically. For instance, Denis McQuail (1984, 108) says objectivity is "both necessary and impossible," and J. Herbert Altschull (1984, 128-34) says that even discussions of objectivity are useless. Donald McDonald (1975, 87), however, claims that objectivity "is well within the possibility of the mass-communications media despite many practical difficulties."

Beginning in 1926 and through revisions in 1973, 1984, and 1987, the members of the Society of Professional Journalists included in their Code of Ethics the statements that "Objectivity . . . is a standard of performance toward which we strive. We honor those who achieve it." But in the 1996 revision of the code, the word "objectivity" disappeared entirely. What are we to make of this? These and other commentators seem reluctant to explain what they mean by the term. Thus once again, we need to look beneath the term itself and attempt to locate some of the realities to which it refers. We are not discussing "objectivity" in any universal, unqualified sense. Rather, we want to consider only how the concept applies to journalism. Moreover, since objectivity is almost always discussed in reference to news (rather than to interpretation, evaluation, or persuasion), it is best if we further narrow our focus to that single alley of journalism that deals with news gathering and news dissemination—to what is frequently referred to as objective reporting.

At this point, the first question we must examine is whether objective reporting can be, in any way, possible. If there is no way in which it is possible, we can close the book on the subject, for, as Aristotle pointed out long ago, "Concerning things . . . which cannot possibly exist or take place, no counsel can be given" (1:4, 1359a).

Some Impossibilities and Some Possibilities

Those who say that journalistic objectivity is impossible because we cannot know the *whole* truth about any event, person, or circumstance are, of course, correct. None of us is omniscient. We see a man take a step toward the street. But we do not know the whole truth about him or this event. We do not know the clothing he might be wearing under the clothing we see, nor do we know the number of threads or stitches in any of it. We do not know the number of hairs on his head. We do not know where he is going or why he is going there (perhaps even he doesn't know). We do not know what effect that one step has on his muscles, his blood pressure, his nerves. Our knowledge of even this one, simple event is enormously limited.

Since we cannot know everything, we cannot report everything. More than that: it is quite likely, because of lack of space, time, pertinence, and other factors, we will not report everything that we *do* know. If this is what is meant by those who deny the possibility of journalistic objectivity, they are correct, but they are also missing the point. It is true that we cannot know and convey the "whole truth" about anything. That, however, is not what journalists are trying to do. They seek to mine a limited piece of land. The task of journalism reporters is to obtain and communicate only the knowledge that would be practically useful in enabling people to decide what to do or avoid doing in the situations in which imminent choices need to be made.

Most reporting involves gathering and conveying knowledge about events, persons, or situations that are outside the reporters. Instead of gathering information about and writing about themselves, reporters usually attend to persons, activities and situations that exist independently of them, to something that for reporters is "out there."

Here we must confront two closely related questions. First, is it possible that reporters can ever know anything outside themselves as it really is, unencumbered and unaffected by the fact that it is they who know it? Second, is it possible that reporters can be sure that what they think they know outside themselves does, in fact, really exist? Perhaps a single example will answer both questions.

If one were a reporter covering a joint session of Congress on Tuesday, January 23, 1996, and a person who has been introduced as the President of the United States is speaking and says, among other things, "In our schools, every classroom in America must be connected to the information superhighway, with computers and good software and well-trained teachers," and no one has claimed that the person speaking is not really the President of the United States, and no one is claiming that what he is saying is something he would never say, is it possible that no matter what the reporter thinks of President Clinton, the Congress, computers, schools, the weather outside, the reporter's own family relationships, and much more—is it *possible* that the President is indeed speaking before a joint session of Congress? And is it *possible* that he is indeed saying, "In our schools, every classroom in America must be connected to the information superhighway, with computers and good software and well-trained teachers"? And is it *possible* that the reporter can know that the President is speaking these words? And is it ever *possible* for the reporter to communicate at least what the President is doing in such a way that what he says corresponds to what he knows, which, in turn, corresponds to what is "out there"? None of the critics of journalistic objectivity denies those possibilities. In fact, they might point out, unless there really are some things outside ourselves and unless we can really and truly know at least some things about those things and at least sometimes accurately state what we know, there would not only be no need to discuss objective reporting but also no need to discuss journalism itself. Or at least there would be no point in discussing journalism as it has now been frequently defined. The definition declares that there is such a thing as knowledge, that at least some knowledge conforms to reality and, once known, can help people make good practical decisions. If such is not what journalism is, those who say otherwise must furnish a new definition.

So far, therefore, we can say this much about the realities that underlie the words "objective reporting": it is an effort to know and communicate knowledge about events, persons, and circumstances outside the persons who are gathering and conveying this knowledge, and at least sometimes it is possible to do this so that what journalists think they know does in fact really exist and what they say does in fact really correspond to what they know. This does not contradict the notion that journalists can neither know nor communicate everything about anything. Nor does it even deny the widespread claim that it is impossible for reporters to do this all the time. But if it is possible to do it at all, then it still may be worth striving for.

THE REAL CHALLENGES TO OBJECTIVE REPORTING

Not yet, however, have we reached the real difficulties implicit in the notion of objective reporting. If pressed on the point, nearly all those who question the possibility of objective reporting would admit that there are things that exist outside the individual person, that we can know at least some of those things, and that we can make statements that accurately express what we know about those things. But the complete operation of news gathering and newswriting is not that simple.

In a letter to *Quill*, Charles L. Klotzer (1984, 23) reminds us that "every reporter always knows more than is included in any report." Then he describes half of the additional difficulty: "The writer selects which facts to include and which to delete whether on the basis of irrelevancy or more suspect motives. Such selection is the core of subjectivity . . . and is the working practice of every reporter on every story at any time."

And the other half of the difficulty? In addition to the possibility of subjectivity due to judgments concerning the inclusion of some facts and the exclusion of others, there is also the possibility of subjectivity due to the organization of news stories. Which facts will come first or early in the story and which will come later or last? For more than a century, most newspapers have organized basic news stories according to the principle of the inverted pyramid, in which the most important material is presented first and the other material follows in order of decreasing importance. Thus, as part of the very nature of news gathering and news dissemination, reporters must choose what to include and what to exclude and, of what they choose to include, what will come first and what will come later.

Choices. Choices made by human beings, by persons who have different standards of judgment, different likes and dislikes, different feelings about and reactions to the events that are taking place. Events do not report themselves. Someone chooses which events to report, what to include in those reports, and in what order to present the elements of those reports. As no two persons are exactly alike, neither will their choices be identical. It is not possible, therefore, many maintain, that there can be any uniformity, any lack of bias, any absence of personal influence in this activity.

Is there any way to remove choices from the selection and organization of knowledge? Not, say those who deny the possibility of objective reporting, as long as human beings are doing it. And news reporting, they remind us, is done by people, not by machines.

MAN AND THE MACHINE

We can contrast the work of the news reporter with its choices to the function of some machines that actually do a certain type of reporting. Automobile speedometers report how fast a car is traveling and odometers how far a vehicle has traveled. Grocery store scanners report what items were purchased, how much was charged for each, the total bill owed, the amount submitted, the amount of change, if any, and very often such other items of information as the date, the store at which the transactions took place, and the amount that was deducted if coupons were submitted. We can have no doubt that these are objective reports. The one produced at the grocery store is particularly interesting because it not only normally records a number of purchases but also provides us with a printed record of the purchases, of the "events" that took place. In addition, although a machine is involved, people are also involved.

The sales slip provided to us could be called an objective report for it lacks the qualities sometimes ascribed to subjective reports. Although a sales clerk prepares it, it is not about the clerk; it is about events that are "out there." It does not express the emotions, the likes or dislikes, the preferences, the values of the clerk who produced it. Although persons are involved in the event, the report itself is impersonal.

Positively and more important, the choices about what is to be included in the report and the order in which these items are presented are not in the hands of the clerk. These choices are determined by the program prior to the events themselves. The program can be designed to list the items purchased in the order in which they are placed on the counter or in alphabetical order or from the most expensive to least expensive. The program can be designed to include the time of the purchases, the name of the checker who was handling the purchases, the number of the counter at which the purchases were recorded. All of these and hundreds of other possible choices concerning inclusion and arrangement are made prior to the event itself. If there has been no malfunctioning in this entire operation, nearly all customers willingly accept the entire sales receipt as an objective report of an event: the purchase of items at a grocery store.

Thus, if "objective reporting" is taken to mean a type of news gathering and news presentation that is about a person, event, or situation that is outside the reporter rather than within or about the person who is the reporter and that is presented with choices concerning selection and arrangement unaffected by the preferences of the reporter, then the grocery sales slip is an example of that type of reporting. This statement does not include everything meant by objective reporting, but at least it is a start.

Even at this point, however, we may have merely pushed the source of subjectivity back one step, from the checkout clerk to the programmer. It is the latter who makes the choices, who decides which items and in what order those items shall be chosen for communication. And the programmer, objectors might point out, is subject to all the risks of bias and arbitrariness characteristic of subjectivity.

But that one step between programmer and clerk is important. Only the latter is in actual and direct contact with the event of the day. For the programmer, everything is conditional. *If* a can of salmon is purchased, the programmer decides, it will be listed in such and such a way, at a certain point in the record, with a specified charge. But the actual event may not include the sale of a can of salmon. The programmer is analogous to the grammarian. *If* one is going to write a complete sentence in English, the grammarian tells us, at least a subject and a predicate must be present and they must be in one order if the sentence is declarative and in a different order if the sentence is interrogative. But the grammarian does not produce the event, the written sentence. Only the author does that.

The grocery store sales slip, of course, is not an example of journalism, because, if for no other reason, it is not an example of mass communication. Is there, however, anything similar in journalistic news reporting to the sales slip with its predetermined selection and organization? Indeed there is, and in great quantity, although its existence is largely ignored in discussions of objective reporting.

LOOKING AT THE FINE PRINT

Newspapers publish a great amount of statistical data. These data were customarily printed in small, agate type (about 5.5 points) and were thus referred to as "agate material." Today, the kind and quantity of agate material vary greatly from newspaper to newspaper, of course, but publications that give heavy attention to business and sporting events devote much of their news space to this type of content. It is not unusual for metropolitan papers to devote three, four, or more full pages to reports of yesterday's activity on the stock exchanges, the bond markets, the mutual funds, and the commodities exchanges; and from many inches to many columns of space to box scores, team and individual standings, and many other athletic summaries and ratings.

Some publications also find room for birth notices, marriage license and divorce listings, the names of recent high school and college graduates, persons cited for driving while intoxicated, tables of campaign expenditures reported by political candidates, yesterday's high and low temperatures in cities throughout the country, and much else.

Many editors decide, for instance, that their papers will publish, in alphabetical order, the names of all the stocks traded on the New York Stock Exchange the preceding day and, for each one that was traded, information about the number of shares traded, the highest price, lowest price, and closing price. Once this policy has been determined, the papers continue to provide this information until readers are informed that some different policy will be in force. This information is provided to readers each day after a day in which the New York Stock Exchange was in operation, and the data are presented no matter what the personal, the subjective preferences of all those who are involved. One editor might be distressed, for instance, because the stock of the company that owns his or her paper dropped precipitously the preceding day; he or she might prefer that this information be concealed from the general public. But if objectivity is to prevail, that news will appear and in its predetermined order along with all the other listings.

Some newspapers make it a policy to publish, in a predetermined order, all the persons arrested during the preceding week for driving under the influence of alcohol. If the editor of the paper is one of those who were arrested, objectivity requires that his or her name be included with all of the others. Such publicity might shame the family, make the paper's campaigns in favor of sobriety appear hypocritical, cost the editor his or her job; journalistic objectivity will accept no excuses. The name will appear, and in the order that had been previously determined.

Does this seem to be mindless, fill-in-the-blanks journalism? Well, it is certainly very much like the machine reporting—the operation of an automobile speedometer or a supermarket scanner—referred to earlier. Much of the work, in fact, is or can be done by computers. For instance, in each instance that a stock is sold, the number of shares that change hands and the price realized are entered into a computer; these machines have been programmed to do all the rest.

However, there is a significant difference between the most mechanical of the machine operations and the most machinelike of human operations. Assuming that in neither case is any mechanical breakdown involved, the former—the operations of a speedometer or gas gauge—differs from the latter—the accumulation of information about stocks bought and sold—in this respect: only in the latter can human intentional misrepresentation be possible. In the operation of a speedometer, the information fed to the reporting instrument—the dial—comes itself from other mechanical operations. A person controls the event being reported by controlling the speed at which the automobile is traveling, but the *reports* of the events are, thereafter, totally mechanical. In the stock market example, however, people enter in at two stages: first, they do the buying and selling, thus determining the event: the number of shares traded and the price involved. Second, a person, by entering these data into the computer, also carries out the first step of the reporting. In both, unintended inaccuracies are possible, but the very fact that inaccuracies can exist in both situations prevents inaccuracy from being a clearly differentiating factor.

If all of the equipment is working properly, the speed at which an automobile is traveling—the event—must be reported as it is actually happening. Because no human intervention is involved, no lie is possible. But under the same conditions, the price at which a stock is traded—the event—can be entered by a person as some number different from the true number. Or a person, by deciding not to enter into the computer any reference at all to the stock, can fail to do what the person and the paper promised to do. Either directly or by omission, therefore, the person can choose to lie.

One of the most stringent forms of journalistic objectivity, therefore—the one in which both order and selectivity are predetermined—remains a peculiarly human activity, for falsification is still a possibility.

The criteria used for determining inclusion and organization are, of course, regularly subject to fine tuning. In the 1990s, for example, many business-page editors began to use boldface type to emphasize those New York Stock Exchange issues whose prices, as the *Wall Street Journal* explains, "changed by 5% or more if their previous closing price was $2 or higher." In general, however, these refinements tend to increase the usefulness—or at least the interest value—of this objective reporting.

This strict type of journalistic objectivity is exemplified in still another class of news presentation, that in which the event is verbal and is re-presented in its entirety. Widely employed by mid-nineteenth-century newspapers (Bovée 1986, 251-59), this form of story still appears in those media that consider themselves publications of record. Complete verbatim texts of presidential inaugural addresses, Supreme Court decisions, budget messages, and the like, would be instances of this form of journalistic objectivity. In such material, no portions of the verbal event are omitted, and it is the presenter of the material, not the journalist, who determines the order in which each sentence is to appear.

Have Possibilities been Ignored?

But such agate material and verbatim texts are not what journalism scholars usually have in mind when they discuss the possibility of objective reporting. Instead of looking at the areas where objective reporting might be located, they focus on the types of stories in which it is probably impossible to find it.

Indeed, objective reporting is not likely to exist in the reports of events that involve a great amount of controversy. Political campaigns, economic disputes, foreign and domestic policy disagreements, environmental debates, religious arguments, and similar events lack any consensus either on what particular data should be included or excluded or on the order in which the included items ought to be presented. In addition, those issues often arouse strong feelings not only among the participants in the discussions but also among the journalists covering the events. Furthermore, except for the representation of complete speeches or other texts, the closer the event comes to being broadly unique the smaller the possibility that there would be any predetermined agreement about how it should be covered.

On the other hand, routine weather, auto accident, house fire, metropolitan burglary, obituary stories—the very ones that come closest to the agate material and verbatim texts discussed earlier—are not the examples chosen by those who deny the possibility of objectivity.

Why this happens is not difficult to understand. Routine stories do not win Pulitzer Prizes. They pose little intellectual challenge. Most often, they are handled by neophyte reporters. One story is so much like all the others of the same type that they lack any distinctiveness; they hardly seem worth discussing.

Most of them, in addition, are concerned with what was previously described as personal affairs—rather than public affairs—news. News helps the public make good decisions about what should be done, but personal affairs news assists in the making of personal decisions, decisions that each person can make for himself or herself; personal affairs news does not lead to decisions that require a consensus. Heated controversy, therefore, is less likely to occur.

But personal affairs news *is* a type of news. It can be useful to enormous numbers of people. The media give it large amounts of space and time. More important, the possibility of objective reporting in at least this type of news keeps alive another, much more important, issue: if objective reporting is at least sometimes possible, must we also conclude that it is, therefore, desirable?

"Objective reporting" can be used as a shorthand term to describe a way of gathering news and a manner of conveying news. News gathering can be considered objective when the knowledge is about persons, events, or situations outside the reporter, when that knowledge does correspond to what is really "out there," when it is gathered on the basis of criteria established prior to the time when this particular knowledge is acquired, and when the criteria are made known to and are not rejected by those to whom the knowledge will be communicated. News presentation can be considered objective when the type of knowledge just described is conveyed truthfully and in a manner that is detached, impersonal, and devoid of any additional value judgments. This is possible.

But the mere fact that something is *possible* to do does not, of course, necessarily imply that it is good to do. Perhaps some of those who say objective reporting is impossible really mean that objective reporting leads to such harm that it would be best to abandon it. In other words, for them, what is impossible is not objective reporting but rather the *good use* of objective reporting.

And, indeed, in many situations it is not possible to achieve the totality of objective reporting. Thus, when we consider whether objective reporting is desirable, it would be helpful if we considered possibility and desirability separately. In the situations in which it is not possible to achieve the totality of objective reporting, we can ask whether it is desirable to aim at as much of it as *is* possible.

IS INCOMPLETE OBJECTIVE REPORTING WORTH PURSUING?

One of the great problems of striving for objective reporting when controversial public affairs are involved is that, although reporters themselves may be truthful, unbiased, and impersonal in reporting an event, they may still communicate one or more falsehoods to the readers or listeners. This can happen because the quoted portion of the report contains one or more lies. Many critics leveled this accusation against the late Senator Joseph McCarthy (R.-Wis.) in the early 1950s. Senator McCarthy, they claim, perpetrated many falsehoods that journalists, maintaining their sense of objectivity, dutifully and accurately conveyed to the public. The reporters did not lie; McCarthy, it is claimed, did. The reporters merely extended the source's lies to a much wider public.

In a strong attack on this and some other characteristics of objective reporting, Theodore L. Glasser (1984, 15) says, "Objective reporting virtually precludes responsible reporting, if by responsible reporting we mean a willingness on the part of the reporter to be accountable for what is reported." But journalists are aware that they have two stages of responsibility in reporting a verbal event. One is the responsibility for reporting the event itself accurately, for conveying to readers or listeners the actual words used. The other is the responsibility for the truth of the statements made by those words. Objective reporters do not assume the second responsibility, but they do assume the first. Thus objectivity does not totally preclude responsibility.

Nevertheless, we dare not ignore Glasser's criticism. Indeed, can any good come from those reports that, under the claim of objectivity, communicate lies? If the job of the reporter is to provide knowledge that will help people make good decisions, how can they make good decisions when what they are being told is not true?

Perhaps the best reply was given by John Stuart Mill (1859, ch. 2) in his essay *On Liberty*. Mill reminds us that, sometimes, what journalists consider to be lies may not be lies at all; the speaker may be right and the journalists wrong. Or, Mill adds, even if the statements are lies, there may be some truth mixed in. Or, even if the statements are total lies, the public must know about them so that they can be refuted and so that the liars can be accurately judged for their defects of character.

Mill was assuming, however, that there were both time and opportunity, first, to reveal what truth, if any, was embedded in the quoted statements or, second, to set forth the evidence that would show the people the falseness of those statements. And many public liars know that, in the rush of practical affairs, neither adequate time nor opportunity may be available. Often, the truth never seems to catch up with the falsehoods.

Yes, say the adherents of objective reporting, but at least sometimes we can unveil a falsehood by turning to another source who will speak the truth. We can maintain our own impartiality and detachment by quoting other people "out there." If the Democrats say one thing, we simply turn to the Republicans for a reply. In fact, we don't have to determine who is speaking the truth; we merely set forth the opposing viewpoints and then let the public decide. But this assumption that journalists can provide their publics with the truths they need to know by presenting "both sides" of a disagreement outrages some critics of objective reporting. Narrowing ideological disagreements to only two sides distorts the realities of actual situations. In fact, it tends to elevate the dominant viewpoints and ignore the unconventional ones: presenting only the views of those who favor and those who oppose a balanced budget omits the views of others, for instance, who want a budget surplus. As J. Herbert Altschull (1984, 128) says: The code of objectivity assists power in the capitalist world to maintain social order and to fix limits to departures from ideological orthodoxy. . . . It safeguards the system against the explosive pressure for change. So long as "both sides" are presented, neither side is glorified above the other, and the status quo remains unchallenged. Dissent is permitted, even encouraged, under the code of objectivity, but its limits are proscribed.

Even when the media present more than just the pro and con positions, they often fail to present a truly balanced account of alternatives. For instance, sometimes the supporters of one or a few positions are well organized, well financed, and insistent upon having their viewpoints publicized, whereas others lack one or more of these qualities. In the 1990s, the National Rifle Association was one of the former, while organizations opposed to the private ownership of handguns lacked some of these characteristics. In addition, editors may find it difficult to locate a person who will set forth a particular point of view. Edward W. Conlon, for instance, who has written about the daily grind of a New York City police officer for the *New Yorker*, has done so under a pseudonym. Sometimes, no recognized spokesman exists, as has long been true of the United States prison population. Or people are afraid to step forth and offer themselves as spokespeople, as was long the case for the gay rights community and for victims of sex crimes.

In other instances, speakers for one position—such as Federal Bureau of Investigation or State Department officials—are restrained by the need to preserve confidentiality, whereas opposing speakers are not. In addition, in trials and ethics hearings, the accusers are given the opportunity to present their viewpoints before—sometimes days and weeks before—the defenders can assert their positions. Also, the glib or well educated usually do a better job of communicating their viewpoints than do the halting or uneducated.

It is understandable that, with all this in mind, many people would cry out against the desirability of objective reporting. Ignoring the routine stories in which it can be achieved, they point to the complex public affairs in which total success is impossible and claim that any attempt to cover those stories objectively is only a pretense. For such major and important stories, in fact, objective reporting is not only impossible but even, they say, misleading.

Objective Reporting as a Defense Against Criticism

Gaye Tuchman faces many of these objections with the suggestion that claims of "objective reporting" are merely tactical devices by which journalists ward off criticism. In a highly respected article, she says that "the correct handling of a story, that is, the use of certain procedures discernible to the news consumer, protects the newspaperman from the risks of his trade, including critics" (1972, 661).

Thus, to minimize the penalties imposed by deadlines, libel suits, and superiors' reprimands, the reporters will adopt procedures that they can claim mark their work as "objective." They will set forth conflicting possibilities, pile up facts to support truth claims, use quotation marks to distance themselves from any opinions, and structure stories according to an accepted sequence, such as beginning with the usual formula: who, what, where, when, why, and how.

Tuchman says these procedures do not actually guarantee objectivity. But linking them with a respected professional quality helps journalists compensate for the fact that their special professional knowledge is not respected by news consumers. In doing this, she says, journalists are like members of other occupations who "develop ritualized procedures to protect themselves from blame" (Ibid., 676). Journalists are using a word, "objectivity," as a means of defense.

Although her argument is interesting and deserves the attention it has received, she sets forth objectivity as a defense and not as a possible journalistic goal. Defenses, of course, are intended to be temporary. Once an attack or an evident threat of attack has ceased, there is no longer any need for the defense. On the other hand, if the attack continues unabated and, in fact, even seems to grow larger and more fierce—as the growing accusations of media bias would indicate is taking place—then it is not a good form of defense and ought to be discarded. (This might account for the disappearance of the term "objectivity" in the Society of Professional Journalists' Code of Ethics.) If objective reporting—at least as much of it as is possible—does have any truly positive and journalistically intrinsic value, therefore, we must search elsewhere in order to find it.

Objective Reporting as Part of the Journalistic Mix

Much of the controversy over journalistic objectivity arises from the failure to recognize that there is more to journalism than news reporting. News reporting is so highly esteemed by members of the Fourth Estate that the words "reporter" and "journalist" are often used interchangeably. But news reporting is only one ingredient in the cake. Explanation, evaluation, and persuasion are also part of the mix. To ignore them is, often, to produce a totally inedible concoction.

Indeed, the more complex and controversial the event, the more likely will be the public need for something beyond the presentation of facts alone. As Douglass Cater (1950, 46) said in his detailed analysis of the media's handling of the Senator Joseph McCarthy accusations, "Faced with a phenomenon as complex as McCarthyism, the 'straight' reporter has become a sort of strait—jacket reporter. . . . His initiative is hogtied so that he cannot fulfill his first duty, which is to bring clearer understanding to his reader." Altschull (1984, 128) said criticisms of Senator McCarthy were limited to the editorial pages, and, because few people read the editorial pages, their influence was limited.

But news analysis and news comment stories—by-lined and printed on news pages but separate from the objective news reports—are common. It is not beyond possibility to place editorials, suitably identified, on page 1. For instance, when the *New York Herald Tribune* on October 25, 1951, wanted to convince its readers that Dwight D. Eisenhower should be the Republican candidate for President, it did so with an editorial at the top and center of page 1. On April 11, 1951, the *New York Journal American* devoted two front-page columns to expressing its outrage when President Truman removed General Douglas MacArthur from his Far East commands. And on March 22, 1991, the *Milwaukee Sentinel* began a page 1 editorial with the reminder, "For seven days, the Milwaukee Sentinel has published front-page editorials urging readers to pressure their elected representatives to support a seven-day waiting period for the purchase of a handgun."

In fact, exclusive reliance upon objective reporting has been declining since the 1950s. One reason is the need by the broadcast media to fill time during the nonstop coverage of major events. Instead of repeating again and again the limited available facts, those media turn to experts and partisans for explanations and evaluations of what is going on. This was particularly evident during the early days of the Gulf War. During that period the print media also broke away from the limitations of objectivity and began to add—usually in bylined stories—background and critiques not only of the events but also of those who had control over information about those events.

The people were repeatedly warned that the war news was censored, and they were cautioned to read, watch, and listen with that in mind. Commenting on government restrictions concerning information about military operations in Iraq and Kuwait, for instance, Max Frankel, executive editor of the *New York Times*, was quoted as saying, "We are not getting any information that really fully and properly describes the magnitude.... We don't know how many are participating, how much ordnance is being dropped. It's hard to remember this is a nonstop, massive operation, the likes of which we may not have seen before" (Rosenbaum 1991, 10).

It is significant that this and other similar material (see Lamke 1991, 2) were appearing in the *news* sections of newspapers. It was not restricted, as it had been during the Senator McCarthy period, to comments "buried" on little read editorial pages. In general, it is not objective reporting that prevents journalists from providing us with the knowledge we need to make good decisions. Rather, it is the failure of both journalists and their publics to make good use of *all* the journalistic resources.

THE POSITIVE GOOD OF OBJECTIVE REPORTING

To say that objective reporting is not necessarily counterproductive still leaves unanswered the question: What good, if any, is it? It is true that now, in the coverage of complex public affairs, it is not possible to achieve the totality of objective reporting. At the present time we do not have a publicly accepted set of criteria on the basis of which the selection and organization of facts can be arranged. But what is possible is for reporters to turn their attention to persons, events, or situations outside themselves, to acquire knowledge about them that is accurate, to convey that knowledge truthfully, impersonally, and devoid of any explicit or intentional value judgments. This is not the whole of objective reporting, but it is a good part of it and a goal that is worth striving for. The people are well served if they are provided with information gained in this way. Even in the most controversial events, such bare facts are the material the public needs for active citizenship. As Jorgen Westerstahl (1983, 407) has said:

The requirement of objective news reporting is intimately related to Western democracy and to one of its basic principles, the freedom of opinion . . . citizens need to be informed of what is happening in the world around them. News reporting must be factual and impartial in order to provide a foundation for independent and rational decision making.

It is important to mention that, although it may often be advisable to segregate the objective reporting from other genres of journalism—explanation, evaluation, persuasion—this is not a universal necessity. We can recognize this most easily if we view journalistic work from the perspective of the journalist who sets out to write a piece of persuasion, an editorial, for example. A persuasive editorial explicitly expresses opinions. It is not objective in the sense described here. Nevertheless, that editorial will normally include some content that sets forth the factual situation upon which the writer's opinions are based. That reportorial portion of the editorial can be—and should be—objective reporting. That is, it should have those portions of objective reporting that are possible to incorporate in even the most contentious material. And what is true of the editorial is equally true of all journalism. Magazine articles, in particular, are most likely to be a combination of journalistic forms, as any glance at the *Nation*, the *Atlantic Monthly*, or the *New York Times Magazine* will reveal. In all those instances in which reporting is involved, that reporting should be as objective as is possible.

OBJECTIVE REPORTING AND THE EMOTIONS

It is sometimes said that, in attempting to be as objective as possible, journalists should strive to be dispassionate (Merrill and Lowenstein 1971, 228). Whether it is possible and desirable for objective reporting to be free of feeling, to be free of emotion, depends on the meaning one assigns to these words.

Most helpful is what Aristotle says about the emotions. If one follows the Aristotelian tradition, then no truly human and alert person is ever free of emotions. In the *Rhetoric,* for example, Aristotle defines emotions as "those states which are attended by pain and pleasure, and which, as they change, make a difference in our judgments" (2:1, 1378a). Thus, if a person is not angry, that person is calm, but *both* anger and calmness (one painful and the other pleasant) are emotions. Likewise, if a person is not fearful, that person is confident, both of which are emotions. Every person, he said, must be one or the other. If everyone, including both journalists and their readers, viewers, or listeners, must always be in one or another emotional state, how, then, is it possible to avoid emotions in the presentation of news?

To answer, one must distinguish between the existence of emotions and changes in emotions, and between the data that cause emotions and the persons who present those data. Let us say that a fictitious Mr. Jones is retired and has all of his funds invested in a single company. The dividends he has been receiving from the company's stock are the principal source of his income. For years, the stock market listings have informed him that the company is doing quite well. Thus, today, when he opens his newspaper, he feels confident.

But then he notices that the price of the stock has dropped precipitously, and when he turns to another objective listing, he learns that the company has omitted its usual dividend. His confidence changes to fear. He will probably have to endure painful financial strictures. Were all of the stock market listings prior to this fateful day unemotional? No. His study of the stock market report each previous day had given him a feeling of confidence. If anything, the repeated reassurances he had received from reading the financial pages probably increased his confidence. Moreover, the day's news, which changed his emotion from confidence to fear, did not change his state from an unemotional to an emotional one. All along, he had been in an emotional state, and he now continued to be in an emotional state.

Thus, when we say that an objective news report is unemotional, we cannot mean that it has no effect upon the feelings of readers and listeners. The report is a stimulus that either maintains an existing feeling or changes that feeling to another feeling. It does not move people from a nonemotional to an emotional state. And what applies to the reading and listening public can be said equally about the journalists themselves. They, too, when normal and alert, are never unfeeling machines.

Both journalists and public, however, are sometimes affected in such a way as to bring about a change in the *type* of emotions they are feeling. Painful emotions sometimes motivate evident exterior actions that will liberate people from painful feelings and replace them with pleasant feelings, as when one escapes from a fearful object. The dash to safety replaces painful fear with pleasant confidence. In some other situations, merely the passage of time can bring about a change of feeling, as when a feeling of anger, as days go by, is replaced by a feeling of calm.

What is the cause of these changes in emotion? For the reading, listening, and viewing public, it could be the journalists themselves, as is most evident in television news reporting. In addition to the spoken words, facial expressions and other body language also convey the reporter's feelings to the public. The American television journalists who reported the assassination of John F. Kennedy, for example, found it enormously difficult to control indications of their own feelings, and the feeling of shared grief intensified the sorrow felt by their viewers. But even if the reporters had controlled indications of their own feelings, they would still have affected the emotions of their viewers, this time by holding somewhat in check the degree of their personal feelings.

In most instances, however, instead of the messenger, it is primarily the content of the message that affects the people's emotions, as when, to use our previous example, Mr. Jones receives word that the company on which he has relied for much of his income will no longer pay a dividend. It is also true that reporters can intentionally shape the telling of the message so that the very process of communicating affects the feelings of the public. The use of emotionally loaded words, for instance, shifts matters so that the cause of emotions is neither the content of the message nor the messenger but the very phrasing of the message itself. If a newspaper reporter would say, for instance, that a source "replied with a sneer," the word "sneer" might arouse anger in the readers who admire that source. Thus objective reporters attempt to use emotion-neutral language: they simply write, for instance, that the source "said" something and then quote what was said.

But what if the source did, in fact, reply with a sneer? Then we must rely upon something beyond objective reporting to let the readers know this fact. Objectivity alone does not guarantee that everything that needs to be said is, in fact, said. When we say, therefore, that an objective news report is unemotional we mean that whatever effect it has on the public—and it will have *some* effect—is not due primarily to the reporters but rather to the data outside the reporters that the latter communicate to the public in otherwise emotion-free language. Not everything can be conveyed in such a language, but, as inspection of agate material reveals, it is possible to do so with some types of content. That is enough to establish it as a possible goal for which journalists can strive.

OBJECTIVE REPORTING IS NOT ALWAYS DESIRABLE

Because objective reporting directs the public's attention to persons, events, or situations *outside* the reporter, there will be some situations in which objective reporting is not desirable. This will happen most clearly when the reporter himself or herself is a part of the event being reported. For example, the September 9, 1940, issue of the *Chicago Daily News* carried Helen Kirkpatrick's account of the bombing of London during World War II. It began this way: London still stood this morning, which was the greatest surprise to me as I cycled home in the light of early dawn after the most frightening night I have ever spent. But not all of London was still there, and some of the things I saw this morning would scare the wits out of anyone.

This account violates several of the characteristics of objective reporting. It is partly about the writer instead of being totally concerned with events outside the writer. It is expressed in the first person, and it sets forth the writer's feelings and judgments about the event. But this subjective report provides useful knowledge about the consequences of warfare, knowledge that objective reporting would not have been able to convey.

Similar characteristics can be found in the story by United Press reporter Russell Jones that was published on November 15, 1956, about the Hungarian rebellion: Life as the only American correspondent left in shattered Budapest is sometimes frightening, sometimes amusing. But mostly it is a continuous feeling of inadequacy both as an American and as a reporter who helplessly watched the murder of a people.

For the first time since I was a boy I wept. I saw a former British soldier break down completely. The situation was worse than the Warsaw uprising into which he was parachuted in 1944. At other times, what the public most deserves is not objective reporting but rather temporary or partial silence. For example, when one party in a dispute launches a criticism against a second party, the entire story can sometimes (not always, of course) be delayed until the journalist has obtained a reply from the latter. Lou Cannon of the *Washington Post* suggests that this is what Daniel Schorr, then of CBS News, might have done when, in July 1975, Air Force Colonel L. Fletcher Prouty told Schorr that Alexander Butterfield had been a CIA spy in the White House. Butterfield could not be reached immediately for a reply because he was on the West

Coast looking for work. Schorr did not wait; he put the story on the air immediately. He gave the competitiveness of his network with NBC as his reason for not delaying the broadcast of Prouty's remarks (Cannon 1977, 47-50). But rarely is the public served (in fact, the public is usually not even aware of, and thus not impressed) by the game of "me first." *By itself* objective reporting is not always fair. It may need to be supplemented by other journalistic genres. But it should not be made even less fair than it has to be.

OBJECTIVE REPORTING RECONSIDERED

Critics who claim that objectivity is impossible because no reporter can know the whole truth about any person, event, or situation are partly correct. No reporter is omniscient. And, of all that is knowable, reporters never attempt to know everything but are selective in the knowledge they attempt to obtain. If they are good news gatherers, they make their selections on the basis of what they judge will be most useful for the public to know when making practical decisions. And, just as they do not attempt to know everything, normally they also do not communicate everything they do know, and for the same reason: some of it is not useful knowledge for the public.

Those who say that objective reporting is possible are also partly right—if they mean that there are some things about a person, event, or situation that reporters can truly know. They can know that a certain senator said, "I am a candidate for the presidency of the United States," and can honestly and accurately report that statement—and much else that they know.

Even in the selection and organization of what they choose to know and of what they choose to communicate, reporters can be objective journalists if we mean by this that they establish *prior to* the events that they cover the criteria on which they base their observations and communications.

Let's consider, for example, the sports reporters who will communicate to readers the information normally included in the box scores for a basketball game. From experience they have learned what the readers want to know and thus, among all the possible bits of knowledge, the specific pieces that they should choose to include: the names of all the players for both teams who actually participated in the game, the number of field goals attempted by each player, the number of field goals made, the number of free throws attempted, the number made, and so on. Although these journalists have feelings, desires, and biases, this format helps them set aside those subjective elements as they go about carrying out an objective investigation. No matter how much they like a certain player, his name will not be included if he did not play in the game. And if the format dictates that the players will be listed in the order in which they are announced to the crowd, then the organization of this material is also determined. Even if a reporter has a favorite player and would like to list him first, the objective journalist will not do so if that player is not the first one whose name was announced.

In doing this, reporters can be objective in the same sense that scientists and other objective data gatherers and communicators are objective. Before conducting any experiments, a biologist, for example, will choose a number of options that he or she knows from experience will be accepted by his or her peers: that measurements will be made according to the International (metric) System rather than the U.S. Customary System; that a certain number and type of class intervals will be employed; that a certain degree of accuracy will be used in measuring continuous variables; that a certain level of significance will be acceptable; that the report will be written in English or in some other chosen language, and the like. As the mathematician R. T. Hayslett Jr. (1968, 83) has said about his own field, often thought of as one where great objectivity can be achieved, in all computations "some assumptions need to be made." Likewise, in the choices and organizations predesigned for agate material, journalists can accomplish the same degree of objectivity that most people find acceptable in scientific endeavors.

Even those who say that objectivity is impossible but worth striving for are partly correct. For the coverage of complex and controversial public affairs, total objective reporting is not possible because there are no accepted criteria for the selection and arrangement of material. But objective reporting is a complex process; thus, even when achieving the totality is not possible, it may be possible to achieve some of the elements. Even in the most contentious affairs, reporters can be accurate in their observations and truthful in their statements. They can direct the public's attention to the object of the story rather than to the writer. They can exclude any explicit statements of judgment or advocacy. Thus, even when insuperably difficult, objective reporting—at least that much of it as it is possible to achieve—may be a goal worth pursuing, for objective news underlies nearly all the other types of journalistic writing.

But whether it is achieved completely or only partially, objective news is not always fair. For example, agate material may show that a quarterback on a professional football team completed only three of the eighteen passes he threw. But if seven of those passes went right into the hands of intended receivers but were dropped, the agate material, though accurate, does not give a fair account of his ability.

And even where fairness is not involved, readers often need more than completely objective material. On November 16, 1996, for instance, many papers reported in their stock market listings that, on the previous day, International Business Machines stock advanced $8.125 to close at $145, a nine-year high. Why this leap in price? The agate material did not give investors the answer. They had to turn elsewhere, perhaps to interpretive reporters, who pointed out that, on the same day, Merrill Lynch & Co. announced that it was raising its target price for the stock from $150 to $195. In general, therefore, journalistic objective reporting can be both possible and desirable. But, by itself, it is not the paragon of all journalism.

8

Journalism Sourcing

In journalism, a source is a person, publication, or other record or document that gives information. Examples of sources include official records, publications or broadcasts, officials in government or business, organizations or corporations, witnesses of crime, accidents or other events, and people involved with or affected by a news event or issue. According to Shoemaker (1996) and McQuail (1994) there are a multitude of factors that tend to condition the acceptance of sources as bona fide by investigative journalists. Reporters are expected to develop and cultivate sources.

This applies especially if they regularly cover a specific topic, known as a "beat". However, beat reporters must be cautious of becoming too close to their sources. Reporters often, but not always, give greater leeway to sources with little experience. For example, sometimes a person will say they don't want to talk, and then proceed to talk. If that person is not a public figure, reporters are less likely to use that information. Journalists are also encouraged to be skeptical without being cynical ("If your mother says she loves you, check it out."). As a rule of thumb, but especially when reporting on controversy, reporters are expected to use multiple sources. Outside journalism, sources are sometimes known as a "news source".

Using Confidential Information

Off-the-record material is often valuable and reporters may be eager to use it, so sources wishing to ensure the confidentiality of certain information are generally advised to discuss the "terms of use" before actually disclosing the information, if possible. Some journalists and news organizations have policies against accepting information "off the record" because they believe it interferes with their ability to report truthfully, or because they suspect it may be intended to mislead them or the public.

Even if they cannot report certain information directly, journalists can use "off the record" information to uncover related facts, or to find other sources that *are* willing to speak on the record. This is especially useful in investigative reporting. Information about a surprise event or breaking news, whether on or off the record, is known as a "tip-off". Information that leads to the uncovering of more interesting information is called a "lead"

Anonymous Sources

The identity of anonymous sources is sometimes revealed to senior editors or a news organization's lawyers, who would be considered bound by the same confidentiality. (Lawyers are generally protected from subpoena in these cases by attorney/client privilege.) Legal staff may need to give counsel about whether it is advisable to publish certain information, or about court proceedings that may attempt to learn confidential information. Senior editors are in the loop to prevent reporters from fabricating non-existent, anonymous sources, and to provide a second opinion about how to use the information obtained, how or how not to identify sources, and whether other options should be pursued.

The use of anonymous sources has been a controversial subject for many years. Some news outlets insist that anonymous sources are required to get certain information while others hold strict prohibitions against the use of unnamed sources at all times. News outlets are often embarrassed by a report from an anonymous source that turns out to be wrong. For instance, much of the O.J. Simpson reporting from unnamed sources was later deemed inaccurate. Newsweek retracted a story about a Qur'an being flushed down a toilet that led to riots in the Middle East. The Qur'an desecration controversy of 2005 was based upon one unnamed military source. The L.A. Times retracted an article that implicated Sean "Diddy" Combs in the beating of Tupac Shakur. The original article was based on documents and a large assortment of unnamed sources. When reporting on the original story, the Associated Press noted that "none of the sources was named."

After the embarrassment, a news organization will often "clamp down" on the guidelines for using unnamed sources, but those guidelines are often forgotten after the scandal dies down. One study found that large newspapers' use of anonymous sources dropped dramatically between 2003 and 2004. The Project for Excellence in Journalism, a research group found use of anonymous sources dropped from 29 percent of all articles in 2003 to just 7 percent in 2004.

Not on Tape

Whether in a formal, sit-down interview setting or an impromptu meeting on the street, some sources request that all or part of the encounter not be captured in an audio or video recording ("tape"), but continue speaking to the reporter. As long as the interview is not confidential, the reporter may report the information given by the source, even repeating direct quotes (perhaps scribbled on a notepad or recalled from memory). This often shows up in broadcasts as "John Brown declined to be interviewed on camera, but said..." or simply "a spokesman said....

Some interview subjects are simply uncomfortable being recorded. Some are afraid that they will be inarticulate and make fools of themselves when the interview is broadcast. Others might be uncooperative or distrust the motives or competence of the journalist, and wish to prevent them from being able to broadcast an unflattering soundbite or part of the interview out of context. Professional public relations officers know that having the reporter repeat their words, rather than being on the air themselves, will blunt the impact of their words. The audience need not see or hear them being uncomfortable (if they have unpleasant news), and not being on air also allows them to be anonymous or identified only by title.

Attribution

In journalism Attribution is the identification of the source of reported information. Journalists' ethical codes normally address the issue of attribution, which is sensitive because in the course of their work journalists may receive information from sources who wish to remain anonymous. In investigative journalism important news stories often depend on such information. For example, the Watergate scandal that lead to the downfall of U.S. President Richard Nixon was in part exposed by information revealed by an anonymous source ("Deep Throat") to investigative reporters Bob Woodward and Carl Bernstein.

Ethics

Divulging the identity of a confidential source is frowned upon by groups representing journalists in many democracies. In some jurisdictions journalists can be compelled by law to identify their sources, and journalists can and have been jailed for upholding this principle. There are several reasons to protect confidential sources:

- In some cases serious harm might befall the source if their identity is uncovered.
- The willingness of other potential sources to share information with reporters may be eroded if confidential sources are identified.
- The public perception of journalistic integrity is damaged when assurances about confidentiality are breached.
- The so-called "chilling effect," which serves to dissuade sources in the future from stepping forward with

unknown information for fear of reprimand or retaliation.

Speaking Terms

There are several categories of "speaking terms" (agreements concerning attribution) that cover information conveyed in conversations with journalists. In the UK the following conventions are generally accepted:

- *"On-the-record"*: all that is said can be quoted and attributed.
- *"Unattributable"*: what is said can be reported but not attributed.
- *"Off-the-record"*: the information is provided to inform a decision or provide a confidential explanation, not for publication.

However, confusion over the precise meaning of "unattributable" and "off-the-record" has led to more detailed formulations:

- *"Chatham House Rules"*: so called after Chatham House (the Royal Institute of International Affairs) which first introduced the rule in 1927, now in widespread use:
  - o *"When a meeting, or part thereof, is held under the Chatham House Rule, participants are free to use the information received, but neither the identity nor the affiliation of the speakes, nor that of any other participant, may be revealed."*
- "Lobby Terms": in the UK accredited journalists are allowed in to the otherwise restricted Members' Lobby on the basis that information received there is never attributed and events there are not reported. "Lobby terms" are agreed to extend this arrangement to cover discussions that take place elsewhere.
- "Not for attribution" (as described by the Canadian Association of Journalists). The comments may be quoted directly, but the source may only be identified in general terms (e.g., "a government insider"). In

practice such general descriptions may be agreed with the interviewee.

- "On background" (Canadian Association of Journalists). The thrust of the briefing may be reported (and the source characterized in general terms as above) but direct quotes may not be used.
- "Deep background" This term is used in the U.S., though not consistently. Most journalists would understand "deep background" to mean that the information may not be included in the article but is used by the journalist to enhance his or her view of the subject matter, or to act as a guide to other leads or sources. Most deep background information is confirmed elsewhere before being reported.

Neologisms

Double Super Secret Background

Double Super Secret Background is a neologism, often used humorously, referring to the journalistic concept of keeping a background source secret. The phrase, coined by *Time Magazine* reporter Matthew Cooper, gained notoriety in July 2005 during the Plame affair. The phrase originally appeared in an e-mail of July 11, 2003 from Cooper to his *Time* bureau chief, referring to a conversation with Karl Rove. In compliance with a court order, the magazine released Mr. Cooper's notes, thus breaking the anonymity of Mr. Rove.

Cooper stated the phrase was "a play on a reference to the film Animal House, in which John Belushi's wild Delta House fraternity is placed on Double Secret Probation." The relationship of journalists to their sources comprises one of the most critical—yet perplexing—areas of reporting. Without sources, there would be no stories. The better the source, the better the story. And yet, for a variety of reasons, sources often get the reporter into hot water or at least make the job tougher. Sometimes sources are not candid; often they are not accurate. Sometimes they are unwilling to talk, and often they request confidentiality. Sometimes they are only too willing to talk-which may say something about their motivation in divulging the information. If so, the reporter must weigh the axe that the source is grinding vs. the possible edge that the information gives. Objectivity, 1980s style, mandates that questionable information be verified through second sources. This then leads the reporter to someone else, who may present the same—or different—problems.

Then there is the special type of source: the public relations person. This individual is *paid* to be a liaison between the journalist and the source that journalist really wants. She or he is also paid to make sources look good and to coach them on how to wrest control of the interview away from the journalist and tackle only the questions that they want to answer. Or, the PR person may simply be a professional leaker of information—a phenomenon seen routinely in Washington, D.C. This person may, in fact, be leaking valid information. But she or he is doing it for ulterior motives, and is using the media to achieve that end. The journalist must then decide whether to be used for someone's private purposes while going about the task of informing the public.

Given these complications, it is not surprising that the journalist's relationship to sources has drawn the attention of numerous researchers during the 1980s. Among the specific areas analyzed by these researchers have been the following:

- How news sources and channels influence television's agenda-setting process
- The diversity of sources used by newspapers and television
- Finding the credible scientific source
- How scientists perceive the accuracy of science news
- Anonymous attribution in network news
- How editors reacted to Janet Cooke's Pulitzer Prize hoax
- The public relations person as mediator between reporter and source
- How sources perceive the accuracy of news magazines
- How and why news magazines use anonymous sources

- The types of sources used most often in medical stories
- The relationship between source identification in stories and the accessibility to those sources

THE DIVERSITY OF SOURCES

How diverse (or representative) are the sources that reporters use for their daily array of new stories? If we assume (1) that sources wield a good deal of power (in that stories emanate from them), (2) that there is a limit to the firsthand knowledge of any source, and (3) that what sources dc know is generally confined to their peer group, then it is important for the journalist to have sources representing as many different demographic groups as possible: rich, poor; Black, White, Asian and Hispanic; male, female; management, worker; married, single; and so on.

Some observers, like John Merrill of Louisiana State University, argue that pluralism among both sources and journalists is the real test of whether a newspaper will have diversity in its news pages. Merrill feels that this type of pluralism is much more important than what he calls "unit pluralism" or a large number of media outlets. After all, a city could have two daily newspapers that still hire only white, middle-class reporters. Such a city would have less pluralism in its news than a city with one newspaper that hires reporters from diverse backgrounds.

So, how much diversity—or pluralism—is there in the ranks of journalistic sources? A quartet of researchers—Jane Delano Brown, Carl R. Bybee, Stanley T. Wearden and Dulcie Murdock Straughan—looked at this issue as they performed a content analysis on newspaper stories during 1979 and 1980. They reported, "Newspapers relinquish control of news to routine channels with male government executives as typical sources." The researchers noted that, while diversity does imply representativeness, it does not always have to imply a broad range of sources. In other words, there can be much diversity among a few sources if they represent different demographics.The researchers studied two different types of publications—large national newspapers (the *New York Times* and the *Washington Post*) and four North Carolina dailies—to see what, if any, differences in source diversity emerged at each type. In all, some 846 front-page stories using a total of 5,248 sources were analyzed. Among the more interesting findings were these:

1. The two national dailies averaged more sources per staff-written story (7.6 sources) than did the North Carolina dailies (5.6 sources) and the wire-service stories (5.4 sources). The most sources used in any national daily story was 26.
2. Some 31 percent of all sources in front-page stories were affiliated with the federal government, while more than 50 percent were affiliated with some level of government.
3. Twenty-five percent were affiliated with private, non-governmental groups.
4. Four percent were U.S. citizens not affiliated with any of 13 different institutions in the United States.
5. Eleven percent were other U.S. citizens whom the researchers could not classify, and 10 percent were foreign citizens.
6. Stories from the national dailies and wire-service stories were quite similar in source affiliation.
7. Stories in local newspapers differed greatly across the board. There were fewer federal government sources, and more state and local government sources. There were also more non-governmental sources. This led the researchers to conclude that, "on the whole, stories in local papers seem to best meet the basic expectations of a pluralistic medium."
8. Overall—in all papers studied—there was a heavy reliance on executives, regardless of their affiliation or the origin of the story. Thus, there was a clear indication of dominance by elite sources, or what some would call "official sources."
9. Of the 50 percent of the sources who could be

identified by sex (many were anonymous), only 10 percent were women.

10. More than half of the front-page stories appearing in the two national papers and 64 percent of the wire stories relied heavily on routine channels (press conferences, news releases, official proceedings), as opposed to informal (leaks and briefings) or enterprise (reporter initiative) channels. This led the analysts to state, that, "when newspapers use routine channels, they allow the source more control over their news product than when enterprise channels are used."
11. More than half of the sources in the national papers and wire stories were veiled (unidentified by name). However, less than 40 percent of the sources in the local dailies were so veiled.

In conclusion, the researchers noted, "By the simplest of criteria... newspapers have failed to live up to the expectations of the media in a pluralistic democracy." Perhaps this is one area that should be researched more, to see if other large dailies and other local dailies around the country exhibit the same lack of diversity in sources. If so, editors would be wise to encourage reporters in reaching out to sources with more representative backgrounds. In 1987, researcher Dan Berkowitz sampled television newscasts and compared his findings with the Brown et al. study. Berkowitz concluded, "Routine sources build the television news agenda." He was working with the following hypotheses:

1. Television news uses more governmental officials than other kinds of sources.
2. Local and network television newscasts have more stories originating through routine channels than through informal or enterprise channels.
3. Network television uses more news from routine channels than local TV does.
4. Television news uses more executives than spokespeople or workers.
5. Television uses more routine-channel stories than newspapers do.

Through his analysis of a large number of television newscasts, Berkowitz confirmed all but the third hypothesis above. For instance, he found about half of all sources in the sampled newscasts to be government officials, and about three-fourths of those stories originated through routine channels. Berkowitz also discovered that television stories averaged fewer sources per story than did the newspapers that Brown and his associates had studied. Local newscasts averaged 1.87 sources per story, while network newscasts averaged 2.93—compared to the 5.6 and 7.6 averages that the previous study had found for local and national dailies, respectively.

If the media are so fond of using government officials as spokespeople, then whom do the media consider the best among such sources? This was the focus of a 1985 article entitled *"Search for the Statehouse Spokesman: Coverage of the Governor and Lawmakers,"* by Frederick Fico. In his content analysis of 11 Michigan dailies, Fico found that statehouse reporters focused more on the governor than on lawmakers, and spotlighted representatives more than senators. The governor received more attribution in 45 percent of the stories, while legislators were quoted in only 17 percent. The remaining sources came from bureaucratic and nongovernmental arenas.

Fico also looked at the motivations that statehouse reporters in Michigan and Indiana give for selecting their sources. Specifically, the study looked at the concerns that reporters perceive in their editors and at the role models to which reporters subscribe. In other words, Fico wanted to know how much influence the reporter's perception of the editor's expectations was having on the choice of sources, as opposed to the reporter's own expectations. To attack this question, Fico examined data from Indiana and Michigan statehouse reporters in 1982 and 1983. The findings suggest that perceived editorial concern can be important in influencing the number and type of sources on whom reporters rely—but so can reporters' self-concepts.

In Indiana, for instance, the more the reporters perceived an editorial concern for stories stressing such things as interpretation and audience understanding, the more they relied on a diversity of sources. But in Michigan, the more the reporters perceived an editorial concern for such things, the less they seemed to rely at all on the sources measured.

In neither state was the perceived editorial concern for newsroom mechanics correlated with sources chosen, once the reporters' experience and time devoted to beat were controlled. As far as role models are concerned, the more the Indiana statehouse reporters subscribed to a self-concept as the people's representative, the more they relied on a number of different interview sources. But that role was associated with using only a few print sources in Michigan. Instead, the more the Michigan statehouse reporters subscribed to a *translator* role, the more they relied on a number of print and interview sources.

It is interesting that reporters allow these concerns and self-concepts to influence their selection of sources. Most people would assume that reporters make the choice solely on the basis of source expertise in regard to the topic addressed. Yet there seems to be a bowing here to *perceived expertise,* and a belief that the sources should reflect a certain editorial role model—both of which act also as criteria for the selection of news sources.

THE CONFIDENTIAL SOURCE

Probably no other area has caused journalists and their media more headaches—professionally, legally and ethically—in recent years than has the source's request for confidentiality. It poses a problem professionally in that, when a source is named, the reader has some way to judge the believability of her or his statement. Anonymity robs the reader of that credibility criterion. By the way, it also robs the editor of the chance to judge the veracity of a story before it goes into print or on the air. That is extremely important, as the infamous Janet Cooke case pointed out.

In that 1980 situation at the *Washington Post,* reporter Cooke fabricated an 8-year-old heroin addict, who then became the subject of a story called *"Jimmy's World."* The newspaper printed the story, it received a Pulitzer Prize, and then the paper found out that there was no Jimmy. In its most embarrassing moment ever, the *Washington Post* returned the prize and faced nationwide criticism for allowing the story to be printed in the first place. If the editors had insisted on knowing who the source was, the story would never have gone into print. Confidentiality poses a problem ethically in that it allows sources more latitude to distort—or lie—because they know that they are not going to be identified. Finally, and possibly most threatening, confidentiality poses a legal problem. If a news operation does not identify its source in a story that leads to a criminal trial, the reporter or editor may go to jail for contempt of court. And if the case is a civil suit, the anonymity could cause a judge to issue an order instructing the jury to assume that there is no source at all.

This possibility was graphically detailed in a Columbia University media seminar entitled *"Business and the Media: Anatomy of a Libel Case,"* which was moderated by well-known Harvard law professor Arthur Miller in the mid-190s. Nevertheless, many journalists—and some judges—feel that the reporter cannot do a decent job of exposing wrongdoing without granting confidentiality to sources. This is especially true in Washington, and it is true of investigative reporting at every level. In a 1987 published study, researchers Mbark A. Algraawi and Hugh M. Culbertson looked at the relationship between attribution specificity and accessibility to news sources. They focused on coverage of two international airline tragedies, and concluded that the press in a more controlled society has less freedom to identify sources than the press in a freer society. They worked from the following hypotheses:

1. In coverage of the Libyan airliner incident, a higher percentage of paragraphs citing Israeli sources than of those citing Arab sources provided the names of one or more news sources.
2. In coverage of the Korean airliner incident, a higher percentage of paragraphs citing U.S. and South Korean sources than of those citing Soviet sources provided the names of one or more news sources.

3. In coverage of the Libyan tragedy, a higher percentage of paragraphs with veiled attribution to Israeli sources than of those to Arab sources quoted specific individuals or identified non-media organizations.
4. In coverage of the Korean tragedy, a higher percentage of paragraphs with veiled attribution to U.S. and South Korean sources than of those to Soviet sources quoted specific individuals or identified non-media organizations.

To test these hypotheses, the researchers performed a content analysis on stories of the two tragedies that appeared in the *London Times*, the *New York Times* and the *Washington Post*. Results of this analysis supported the second, third and fourth hypotheses, but not the first. The researchers found that 68 percent of the paragraphs citing U.S. and South Korean sources provided the names of one or more news sources, while only 59 percent of the paragraphs citing Soviet sources carried such names. Algraawi and Culbertson therefore concluded that access restrictions imposed by controlled societies could indeed reduce the number of identified sources, when contrasted with countries that emphasize press freedom. An earlier study on anonymous sources was carried out by K. Tim Wulfemeyer, who looked at how and why confidential sources are used by *Time* and *Newsweek* magazines. Wulfemeyer found that "overall, 80 percent of national and international stories in *Time* and *Newsweek* contain anonymous attribution." Performing a content analysis on 388 stories in the two publications, the researcher also discovered the following:

1. *Newsweek* quoted more anonymous sources than *Time* in both national and international stories.
2. The most frequently quoted source was some type of official, and "high-status officials" were quoted anonymously most often.

Wulfemeyer, along with Lori L. McFadden, also looked at anonymous attribution in network news in a 1986 published study. Among other things, they found that more than half of the stories appearing on network newscasts featured anonymous attribution. In the prelude to their report, the researchers observe that anonymous attribution has been linked to a general credibility problem being experienced by the media today; some critics see the practice as a type of "quick-fix journalism." Wulfemeyer and McFadden also note that, within the industry itself, one study has shown 60 percent of journalists as disapproving of anonymous attribution. Ironically, however, other studies show that readers are not terribly troubled by the practice.

As it is, some 33 percent of newspaper stories and from 70 to 85 percent of news magazine stories use anonymous attribution—while 30 percent of Washington interviews are off the record, and half of the administration related stories on the network news carry anonymous attribution. All three TV networks allow the use of anonymous attribution, but they also caution against its overuse and abuse. Indeed, all say that it should be used by reporters as a last resort. Among the rules that the networks have laid down are:

1. NBC tells its reporters to verify information received in confidentiality.
2. CBS and NBC caution reporters that they should grant anonymity only to highly reliable and credible sources.
3. CBS also says that the story must be really newsworthy in order to warrant the grant of anonymity.
4. ABC tells its reporters that they must find opposing views to those expressed by confidential sources.
5. All three networks warn reporters to provide necessary information on the source's motivation for providing the news.
6. ABC and CBS say that reporters should be prepared to divulge information-and possibly the names of their sources—to news executives.

Specifically, Wulfemeyer and McFadden were looking at the percentage of network news stories that involve anonymous attribution, the frequency with which unnamed sources are quoted, the types of stories that contain the most anonymous attribution, and the ways in which unnamed sources are described. To study the situation, they analyzed two weeks' worth of network newscasts in 1982, paying special attention to the attributions used. From the collected data, they compiled the following summary:

1. Fifty-five percent of the 416 examined stories had at least one anonymous quote.
2. In all, 484 anonymous quotes were used in the 227 stories that had anonymous sources.
3. Anonymous attribution appeared in 54 percent of national stories and 56 percent of international stories.
4. The percentage of stories with anonymous attribution remained fairly constant across all subject categories.
5. Seventy-one percent of reporter packages used anonymous attribution—compared to 39 percent of voice-over stories, 32 percent of readers, and 22 percent of voice-over/soundbites.
6. The types of anonymous sources varied, too. "Neutral sources" (the researchers' term) were used most often; then, "experts"; and then, "highstatus sources."
7. The most common word used to describe the anonymous source was "official" (used 64 times); then, "sources," "experts" and "aides." Several other descriptions appeared with much less frequency.
8. Adjectives were used with 41 percent (183) of the 450 anonymous source descriptors. Two-thirds of the time, one adjective was used—such as "administration officials," "union leaders" and so on.
9. Sixty percent of the time, the adjectives linked the source to government organizations or represe-ntatives.
10. In addition, some 240 interview subjects were not verbally identified in the newscasts, although they were not considered anonymous sources because their names appeared on the screen.

In their concluding thoughts regarding anonymous attribution, Wulfemeyer and McFadden assert that the real issue is not whether the source is quoted or not, but whether the information is true. As they suggest, if the networks would provide more public information about the standards that their reporters follow with confidential sources, then the public might have more reason to believe what these unnamed sources say. Another study, conducted by Larry L. Burriss, looked at all types of attribution in network radio news and found significant differences among six networks in the attributions used in their news stories. Burriss performed a content analysis of radio newscasts from ABC, CBS, NBC, NPR, the Mutual Broadcasting and Satellite News networks from October 1985 to October 1986. In all, he studied 861 stories and found 845 examples of attribution. A total of 55 different descriptions were used to describe sources, and 365 (42 percent) of the stories carried no attribution at all. Of the 496 stories using attribution, 90 percent used full attribution. Many other sources were veiled by referring to their organization or country (for example, "Israel announced today..."), their expertise, their status as a subordinate or aide, their position of pro or con on an issue, or their association with a group or person.

Of the six radio networks, Burriss found the Satellite News Network most likely to attribute (72 percent of its stories carried attribution), while the Mutual Broadcasting System was least likely (only 47 percent of its stories had identified sources). In between came CBS (68 percent of the stories attributed), NPR (56 percent attributed), NBC (53 percent attributed), and ABC (50 percent attributed). Burriss was also curious about the word used to describe confidential sources, both in network radio newscasts and in newspapers. He found a striking similarity in the rank ordering of different anonymous-source code words. For instance, both the radio and the newspaper stories used "official" more than any other description; and both followed that usage in frequency with "spokesman"; and then, "source." However, Burriss noted that radio networks seem to rely more on organizational attribution (Chrysler said today...") than people attribution ("A spokesman in Lee Iacocca's office announced...") That—said Burriss—makes it even harder for readers to judge the validity of the statement or assertion that the anonymous source makes.

Do reporters use anonymous sources more in the 1980s than they did in the 1970s? In 1985, Byron St. Dizier found the general answer to that question to be no. His study among the reporters at Florida's largest dailies in 1974 and again in 1984 yielded the following comparative summary:

1. Only 12 percent of the reporters surveyed in 1984 said that they used information from an unnamed source weekly, whereas one-third of the reporters surveyed in 1974 acknowledged doing so.
2. Only 23 percent of the reporters in 1984 would be seriously hampered without unnamed sources, while 56 percent in 1974 would be.
3. Seventy-three percent of the reporters in 1984 would consult with an editor before using an unnamed source, while only 51 percent in 1974 would.
4. Although there appeared to be fewer reporters willing to use unnamed sources in 1984, those reporters seemed more dedicated to keeping the names confidential than the reporters of 1974. Only 36 percent of the reporters in 1984 said that they would reveal such sources' identities under certain circumstances, while half of the reporters questioned in 1974 said that they would.
5. Also, fewer reporters in 1984 were opposed to shield laws than in 1974. Only 37 percent of the latter-day reporters opposed any form of shield legislation, while 54 percent of the reporters questioned in 1974 opposed it.

In interpreting these results, two things should be kept in mind. First, the 1974 survey came during the height of the Watergate controversy and just after the close of the Vietnam War. Both of these circumstances necessitated a heavy use of anonymous sources. Second, the Janet Cooke case at the *Washington Post* led editors across the country to tighten the screws on when and how anonymous sources could be used by reporters. St. Dizier's second survey followed that incident by three years. Without a doubt, one of the landmarks in the evolution of anonymous attribution was the Janet Cooke case. With the public disclosure in 1981 that Cooke's Pulitzer Prize-winning story had been a hoax came a change in the way many news executives handled confidential sources. A 1982 study examined that reaction, and reported: "Most editors thought the *Post* was negligent in handling the story of 'Jimmy' and said their newspapers reviewed the use of anonymous sources after the disclosure." Some 107 managing editors responded to this 1982 survey on the hoax. Among its findings were:

1. Almost 90 percent of the editors faulted the *Post* editors for not verifying Cooke's information.
2. Almost three-fourths of those editors, however, admitted that such a story could also get past them.
3. Sixteen percent would publish a story based on an anonymous source if the reporter said that his or her life would be endangered if the source's name were divulged.
4. Three-fourths of the editors said that the press overuses the technique of anonymous attribution.
5. Almost two-thirds said that anonymity leads to distorting and hyperbolic statements on the part of sources.
6. More than 90 percent of the editors intended to look closer at anonymous sources as a result of the Cooke case.
7. Six out of ten editors had personally encountered a Cooke-type situation on their own papers.
8. About two-thirds said that they would now be checking applicants' backgrounds more closely before hiring them as reporters.
9. Only half of the editors had always or usually checked applicants' backgrounds before the disclosure of the Cooke hoax.
10. Eight out of ten editors said that newspapers were more responsible in 1982 than they had been in 1972.

So, researchers spent a lot of time during the 1980s studying the confidential source and its use by the news media. In 1988, Bob M. Gassaway reiterated the basic question: "Are secret sources in the news media really necessary?" Gassaway interviewed 15 people who told him that they had been used in the past as confidential sources for news stories. Most of them had been disseminating information this way for years, feeling it a good way to let the public know what is going on. Interestingly, most of these sources said that, if a reporter does come up against the need to identify the source, that journalist should return to the source and ask her or him to reconsider their prior agreement of confidentiality.

Gassaway also found that, even though these sources had turned over information to reporters following agreements of confidentiality, twothirds of them had provided the information to expose something or to help out the reporter. Gassaway continued, Two findings from this study suggest reporters may be able to drive a harder bargain than they are aware of in persuading confidential sources to go public and provide information on an attributable basis for news stories. First, sources interviewed indicated they derive some satisfaction from giving information to reporters (and, presumably, seeing it used in the news media). Second, only two of 15 respondents said reporters should make whatever sacrifices are necessary to protect sources' anonymity. This interpretation... is in keeping with the professional opinion of newspaper editors who estimated in one study that "about 56 percent of the unnamed sources quoted in America would agree to be quoted by name if reporters insisted."

While not a research study, a recent example of how one newspaper now handles its anonymous-source policy is of interest here. In 1988, the *Twin Cities* (Minn.) *Star-Tribune* lost a case involving a man who was identified in a news story even though the reporter had assured him of anonymity. In that case, the campaign aide for a candidate in a 1982 state race in Minnesota leaked negative information to the press, concerning an opponent. When the editors at the *Star-Tribune* overruled the reporter's promise of anonymity and identified the aide, the latter lost his job, sued the paper, and won. Following that action, the newspaper laid out guidelines for granting confidentiality to sources and for running stories that contain confidential sources.

These guidelines do not prohibit the use of confidential sources, but they alert reporters to the negative impact of using them. A key requirement is that reporters obtain permission from the editor before granting anonymity in cases considered to be potentially dangerous to the newspaper. One example is when a reporter is made privy to accusations against a candidate in a political campaign.

The guidelines also state that, once the promise of confidentiality has been given, it will be honored by the editors—"even if it should not have been made"—unless there is some compelling reason for disclosure.

The *Star-Tribune* guidelines provide only three such reasons for identifying a source, once confidentiality has been granted:

(1) A discovery that the source lied
(2) A life or death situation
(3) A court order demanding disclosure.

The four-page guidelines also declare that too much reliance on confidential sources can only hike the newspaper's risk of inaccuracy; and that, in turn, can adversely affect the newspaper's credibility in the community.

SOURCES AND STORY ERRORS

One of the challenges—and mandates—of effective reporting is accuracy. As Anthony Lewis of the *New York Times* has pointed out on several occasions, the truth is very elusive and is hard for any reporter to obtain. One of the reasons is that sources are generally reluctant to part with any truth that will portray them in a bad light. Keir, McCombs and Shaw go so far as to warn reporters that the interview is not the best way of obtaining information, because the journalist and the source generally have two different goals. The journalist is after the truth, while the source is trying to look good.

Many critics of the media assume that, if there is an error in the paper, it is because of the reporter's inaccuracy.

However, newspapers like the *Boston Globe* have found that this is not always the case. For instance, in 1982, the *Globe* discovered that only 108 of the 187 errors found that year were reporter errors. Some 36 were editing errors, and 13 were source errors.

In a 1982 report, William A. Tillinghast said that, while many sources are quick to notice inaccuracies in news stories, reporters dispute most of these claims and instead call them differences of opinion between the sources and themselves. The sources argue that about half the stories citing them have at least one error—generally, an omission, wrong emphasis or misquote. Is this true? Not according to most reporters, who dispute about 80 percent of such claims.

Tillinghast mentioned the following specifics:

1. Reporters and sources disagree on error claims dealing with areas of judgment.
2. Less-experienced journalists are the ones most likely to disagree with sources over error claims.
3. Sources attack general news and governmental news—especially at the local level—more often than they attack more narrowly focused stories like those on crime, education, transportation and the courts.

Nevertheless, as Tillinghast noted, reporters do agree with sources two out of ten times that an error was committed. Most reporters cite these reasons, in order, as the major causes of error: insufficient time for backgrounding; insufficient time to gather information; insufficient time to write the story; editors editing too much out of a story; insufficient space to include everything; and misunderstandings between reporters and sources. Editors, on the other hand, cite the following chief causes of error: misunderstandings between reporter and source; inaccurate paraphrasing of the source; carelessness by reporters; insufficient time for reporters to gather the information; insufficient space for details; and contradictory information from other sources. Tillinghast came back in 1983 with another study on sources and errors and found, that "even on factual matters, some sources judge published information in light of their version of what ought to be."

Tillinghast also quoted some phrases that sources deemed incorrect because of word omissions or paraphrasing. For instance, one news story had noted: "said bottle rockets are the major cause of fires in the metropolitan area." But the contacted source said that this should have read "the major cause of *illegal fireworks* fires; not of all fires in the area." Another story said: "city officials are crossing their fingers in hopes they won't have a major fire in the eastern foothills before their water expansion is finished this summer." But the contacted source complained that the reservoirs were to be completed in the fall—not the summer.

On some of the above passages, the reporters agreed with the sources' claims of inaccuracy. In others, the reporters felt that the problem was a difference of opinion. Tillinghast, however, found that the primary objection among the sources had to do with their disappointment concerning the image—or lack of image—conveyed by the article. For instance, a source who is a staunch Republican might be upset if the story turned out to be focused on an unflattering side of Ronald Reagan or George Bush. In one specific case of source dissatisfaction, a published story noted that the city council had postponed a decision allowing Yellow Cab Company to continue operations. As the contacted source complained, however, the story did not mention until the sixth paragraph that the cab company had been in violation of at least one city ordinance. Looking at all this, Tillinghast concluded that many sources start becoming dissatisfied in the interview stages when the reporter brings up unpleasant topics. That dissatisfaction sets the stage for more disagreement with the reporter when the story appears. In some cases—the researcher was suggesting—sources may need to develop a better understanding of the newspaper's role.

Reporter bias is linked to source attribution in some cases, according to Pamela J. Shoemaker who researched the subject early in the 1980s. Performing a secondary analysis on story and source data previously collected, Shoemaker concluded, "Groups journalists perceive as deviant are portrayed more negatively in unattributed statements." Analyzing the data, she noted a relationship between group deviance and the way in which unattributed statements are paraphrased. She found no such relationship for attributed statements. In fact, the more deviant a group seemed to be, the more probable that it would receive negative unattributed nouns and adjectives. For instance, reporters called the Ku Klux Klan and the Nazis "racists," "self-righteous," "frightening," "vehement" and "overweight." The Moral Majority was said to have "dangerous and pervasive plans for censorship." However, the attributed nouns and adjectives were more neutral, such as "group," leaders" and "spokesmen." Shoemaker lists four possible reasons for her findings:

1. Journalists are imposing their own biases in stories.
2. Journalists are redefining the concept of common sense—believing, for example, everyone knows and would agree that the KKK is racist and frightening.
3. The journalist has a need to convey "reality" to the public, and that reality sometimes goes beyond the narrow facts obtained in probing a story. This may include background, facts from other stories, or any information that the reporter feels is necessary to put the story into its greater context.

   There is some potential danger here, however, as Roger Rosenblatt wrote in a 1984 *Time* magazine essay entitled "Journalism and the Larger Truth." Rosenblatt explained, When journalists hear journalists claim a "larger truth," they really ought to go for their pistols. The *New Yorker*'s Alastair Reid said the holy words last week: "A reporter might take liberties with the factual circumstances to make the larger truth clear." O large, large truth. Apparently Mr. Reid believes that imposing a truth is the same as arriving at one.... But his error is more fundamental still in assuming that large truth is the province of journalism in the first place. The business of journalism is to present facts accurately.... Those seeking something larger are advised to look elsewhere.

4. Journalists see a need to be tight writers and editors. Tight editing often calls for eliminating words not seen as essential to the copy.

If there is one news medium that sources credit with a great deal of accuracy, it seems to be the news magazine—that is, if the findings of one mid-decade study are true. Larry L. Burris looked at the accuracy of news magazines as perceived by news sources, and found: "The only inaccuracy reported by respondents was that some quotes had been taken out of context. More than 90 percent of the stories were considered accurate."

Interviewing 63 people who had been used as sources for stories in *Time* and *Newsweek*, Burriss could find none who claimed to be misquoted, and only about 18 percent felt that their quote had been taken out of context. Still, only 8 percent of the latter felt that the printed quote was actually inaccurate. Burriss looked for a connection between the length of quote and its perceived accuracy. He found that shorter quotes—averaging 11 words each—were more likely to be seen as inaccurate, while longer ones—averaging 29 words—were generally perceived as being accurate. This could be because shorter quotes may be perceived as lacking needed information. And—as Tillinghast had noted earlier—omissions were one of the chief causes of inaccuracy, according to the sources queried by Burriss.

SCIENTIFIC AND MEDICAL SOURCES

One of the news categories that has grown in popularity over the years is the area of "sci-tech" news, which includes stories dealing with scientific, technical and medical breakthroughs. Numerous large daily newspapers, like the *Boston Globe*, publish regular sci-tech sections. All three television networks have medical and science reporters, and most local television stations feature a medical segment on their late-afternoon newscasts. The trick is for reporters (who may or may not be scientists or physicians themselves) to put some extremely technical material into lay terms. That is not always easy; and often enough, accuracy is lost in the translation itself. Several studies have tried to analyze what scientists feel about the reporting of science and medical news, and often the responses give the media low marks.

One such study was reported in 1985 by Barbara Moore and Michael Singletary. They had looked at science sources' perceptions regarding the accuracy of network television news. In their article the researchers concluded, "Inadequate air time and omission of detail are the most common objections by sources to science coverage on network news." The researchers had identified a large sample of scientific stories and mailed them to the news sources identified in the copy. These sources were asked to comment on the accuracy of the stories, and return the results to the researchers. Among the findings were the following:

1. Fewer than half (48.5 percent) of the scientists said that the stories were completely accurate.
2. Just over one-third (34.3 percent) considered the stories to be generally accurate.
3. The most common source complaint was inadequate air time devoted to explaining the story.
4. About 35 percent said that essential details were deleted from the story.
5. Many of the scientists thought that the coverage was too sensationalized by the reporter.

So, if these perceptions are taken to be sound, the news media should look for ways of ensuring better accuracy in science news. Some are trying to do this by hiring specialists in the sciences, but most are endeavoring to apply the same standards of accuracy to science stories that they apply to other news. Many even go beyond these standards and require reporters to read back technical information to the source before publishing the story. One problem is that, as many journalism educators point out, it is difficult to find college journalism students who will even take a course in science reporting. Generally, the reason cited for this is that journalism students feel more comfortable in the verbal world of the humanities than in the quantitative world of the sciences.

Therefore, science reporting is not a popular subject in most journalism schools, and there is a dearth of journalism graduates who want into the field. How are scientists as mass media sources? Do they avoid the press and cloister themselves in their laboratories? Or do they seek out the press—chasing after popularity and fame for their institutions? Researcher Sharon Dunwoody headed two projects that zeroed in on these questions during the 1980s. The first, published in 1982, was a co-effort with Byron T. Scott. The two researchers presented the following findings:

1. The notion that the average scientist has no experience with the media is invalid.
2. Three-fourths of the surveyed scientists said that they welcome media contact, while only 11 percent see it as a necessary evil.
3. Fifteen percent of the scientists had themselves initiated media contacts.
4. Almost one-third had written at least one story or publicity release about their own research.
5. Scientists feel that magazines do a better job, by far, than newspapers or television in covering the science.

This last finding is not surprising, given the fact that science magazines and journals are highly specialized publications. They can attract more specialists in the respective sciences and, due to their less frequent publication schedule than newspapers or television, they can devote more time and space to each story published. Dunwoody, along with Michael Ryan, conducted a more detailed study in mid-decade. This study suggested that part of the problem in credibility lies in the way journalists select their scientific sources. Among their findings, the researchers discovered that "in selecting scientists as sources, journalists do not always take into account the scientists' areas of expertise." Dunwoody and Ryan note in their preface that—while reporters do feel that a credible scientific source must be one who is communicative, accessible and honest—the notion of credibility is too often left undefined. Is credibility more of an assumption on the reporter's part than an actual judgment based on the scientist's area of expertise? The research suggests yes. In their study, Dunwoody and Ryan worked from the following hypotheses:

1. The number of years spent as a researcher will relate positively to the amount of journalistic contact devoted to topics tangential or unrelated to a scientist's research.
2. Research productivity will be negatively related to the amount of journalistic contact devoted to topics tangential or unrelated to a scientist's research.
3. Social/behavioral scientists discuss topics unrelated or tangential to their research more often than do physical/biological scientists.
4. The greater the percentage of journalistic contacts devoted to tangential and unrelated areas, the more positively will the scientist evaluate the role of popularization within the scientific culture.
5. The greater the percentage of journalistic contacts devoted to tangential and unrelated areas, the greater will be the percentage of journalistic contacts initiated by the scientist.

To test these hypotheses, the researchers surveyed a random sample of 456 scientists. Of 287 respondents, 187 said that they had encountered at least one journalist in the previous year. Of these 187 scientists, 153 estimated the percentage of their contact that had focused on tangential and unrelated areas. Dunwoody and Ryan analyzed the comments of these scientists. Among their findings are the following:

1. The first hypothesis above was rejected. In fact, the opposite proved true: Inexperienced researchers were more likely to discuss areas tangential or unrelated to their specialty.
2. The second hypothesis was supported: The more a researcher discussed areas outside her or his specialty, the less productive in research was the scientist likely to be.
3. The third hypothesis was rejected, although some difference was noted: Fortysix percent of social/

behavioral scientists discussed topics outside their specialty, while only 39 percent of physical/biological scientists did so.

4. The fourth hypothesis was also rejected: There was no relationship found between a researcher's media contact and belief in popular science.
5. The fifth hypothesis was supported: The willingness of a scientist to go public may be related to a willingness to initiate contacts with the media.

Considering these findings, Dunwoody and Ryan suggested that source-based criteria do not adequately predict the selection of scientific sources by the media. In fact, reporters ask one out of three scientists to discuss something outside her or his area of specialization. Therefore, journalists often do not consider the scientist's specialty as they choose sources for their science news.Another study looked specifically at news sources in medical stories. Guido H. Stempel III and Hugh M. Culbertson analyzed Ohio's 11 largest dailies. As they began their study, the researchers assumed that they would find three things:

1. Physicians would be mentioned most often as sources.
2. Physicians would be quoted and would serve as authors of byline columns, as well.
3. Physicians would be quoted often in any given medical article, compared with sources from other occupational categories.

To test these assumptions, Stempel and Culbertson analyzed more than 2,100 medical news articles, editorials, and signed columns from January to March of 1982. Among their findings were the following:

1. Physicians are—by far—the most prominent, frequent sources of health-care news. They were quoted in 42 percent of all the medical news stories, giving them a 3:1 lead over other health-care professionals like therapists, psychologists and nurses.
2. Only physicians were quoted or served as authors in

substantially more items than they appeared in as objects of coverage.

3. Physicians were seen as more salient sources than medical administrative personnel. Overall, the former were cited more than other sources in 72 percent of all stories.
4. Administrators, however, had reasonable levels of dominance in stories dealing with self-help, medical expenses, insurance, and miscellaneous topics.
5. Administrators focused more on system concerns, while physicians focused on specific medical problems.

Therefore—the researchers concluded—physicians exceed medical administrators in both prominence and dominance in medical news stories. Sharon Dunwoody and Michael Ryan conducted yet another study focusing on scientist-journalist contacts in which they looked at the role of the public information person as mediator. From their findings they concluded, "Scientists prefer direct contact with journalists and believe the public information office plays only a minor role in disseminating findings."

As Dunwoody and Ryan discovered, however, many scientists do have positive feelings about public information officers, and most agree that they can act as good mediators sometimes. But a large number of scientists see them as a hindrance in certain situations, and prefer-overwhelmingly—direct contact with the media. In addition, scientists in private industry and government use public information officers more than university-employed scientists, possibly because there is a greater desire by business and government to control the message that gets published or aired.

THE PUBLIC RELATIONS PRACTITIONER AS A SOURCE

One who is paid to be an official source is a PR person—or a public relations practitioner, as the profession calls this individual. Most historians maintain that public relations became a legitimate part of business and government during

World War I and after. It was then that the government of the United States had mounted its most massive effort to date toward unifying public opinion about an issue. That issue was the Wilson administration's belief in U.S. involvement in the war.

The famed journalist and political philosopher Walter Lippmann wrote much about the manipulation of public opinion—stating that it requires the insertion of a "pseudo-environment" between man and reality. As Lippmann noted, The only feeling that anyone can have about an event he has not experienced is the feeling aroused by his mental image of that event.... It is the insertion between man and his environment of a pseudo-environment. To that pseudoenvironment his behavior is a response. But, because it is behavior, the consequences... operate... in the real environment where action eventuates.

It is this pseudo-environment that, often, public relations practitioners are called upon to create. Lippmann warned of the high stakes involved when governments do this because, as in the U.S. entry into World War I, it can send nations spinning headlong into war over a possibly distorted set of beliefs about one another. Seeing the success of that World War I public-relations effort, business and the rest of government wasted no time in establishing public relations or public information departments to liaison with the public through the media. Edward L. Bernays was a guiding light in those early years of public relations. He and his colleagues laid down most of the principles that have steered the profession through the 20th century.

Many of these public relations efforts have been beneficial to society by stirring the conscience of various publics and by helping businesses to create legitimate images of themselves—combatting the distorted ones that may have arisen. It is no scoop to say, however, that a good deal of doubt and suspicion characterizes the relationship of the media with the public relations practitioner. In a 1984 Columbia University seminar on media and society, television journalist Morley Safer discounted the value of researching a company's press releases on its own officials.

Giving a hypothetical scenario in which PR executive Herbert Schmertz starts providing safe handouts just as the reporter is beginning to probe the background of a company official who has been nominated for secretary of defense, Safer quipped, "You start by not reading the Schmertz papers.... I know what's in the Schmertz papers.... I've probably met Schmertz before." One of the most recently published studies on the antagonism between journalism and public relations emerged in 1988. In it, Michael Ryan and David Martinson write, "Practitioners acknowledge that journalists often view public relations negatively, and they accept some of the blame for those negative views." Ryan and Martinson queried 200 public relations people and found the following attitudes to be prevalent.

1. Practitioners say that journalists' negative experiences with individual public relations people cause about 90 percent of the antagonism between the two camps.
2. Three out of four practitioners say that journalists consider their work to be more important than the practitioners', and that also causes some antagonism.

9

On Being a Mass Media Writer

Media writers are critically tuned conduits of information. Information is their stock in trade, but it is information of a verifiable kind, not hearsay, not fiction. Unlike fiction writers, who are free to write from the depths of their imagination, journalists are expected to write from a bank of information checked and re-checked through a series of valid sources in the real world. Without substantiated information, they have nothing to communicate.

To build that bank of information, professional media writers read all types of print materials. They are practiced at absorbing information with a discriminating mind. They observe people, events, and situations. They listen to speeches, comments, and testimonies. They read fine literature as well as general materials. The latter may include books, newspapers, magazines, press releases, newsletters, manuals, government documents, business reports, professional journals, and the like. All these are composed by people who want the reader to accept what they have written. Because media writers bring so much of their background reading to their writing, they first take account of their own biases before determining whether the information they hear or see is accurate, a sham, biased, or controversial. These writers are, therefore, astute judges of information.

Applying certain critical skills, they have learned how to separate the counterfeit from the genuine. For example, one conservationist claims uncontrolled forest fires minimize new growth. Another claim some fires allowed to run their natural course maximize new and diverse growth. Two witnesses give conflicting accounts of the same event. Checks on statements

made by sources or witnesses fail to square with the record. Information in different records concerning the same matter proves contradictory. In the last analysis, it is the writer who must decide what information is valid and how to write about it. That holds true for all areas of the media, whether the written work is produced for a 12-inch news article, a full-length magazine piece, a 20-second radio or TV spot, a 60-minute video, a press release, or a full-page advertisement. The accuracy and merit of information communicated is the professional writer's greatest concern. Of course, a writer may choose to accept received information without question. But then that is the writer who is a passive thinker and an unwitting participant in surface appearances and the claims of others. In addition, the produced copy is more than likely to prove meaningless, inaccurate, incomplete, perhaps even libelous. There is an alternative choice. The writer can adopt the professional practice of methodical and critical behavior.

To act methodically, experienced media writers rely on a systematic strategy. To think critically, they raise relevant questions to evaluate what they observe and what others write or say. They have lerned controlled methods of getting answers and thinking critically to produce reliable copy that is creatively written for a mass audience. The professional media writer is, therefore, an active thinker and a critical conduit of information received and communicated.

When confronted with information requiring a decision, the intellectual independence and self-confidence that accrues from practicing disciplined thinking is rewarding, particularly when that thinking manifests itself in writing. Because critical discipline fosters intellectual freedom, many writers discover that controlled thinking stimulates ideas for creative treatment of what is essentially objective data. Today's sophisticated public expects objective information not fiction from media writers, but they also expect media writers to engage their interest. Your aim is to produce creative copy that is grounded in objective data. However, one's imagination need not recede into cold storage. Imagination has a role in mass media writing, but that role comes into play only after a great deal of objective data has been accumulated, evaluated, and digested.

On the Issue of Objectivity

The aim of media professionals is to be objective. That is, they aim to present the facts without bias. Print and broadcast writers are obliged to de-bias themselves and to present accurate information or face litigation. These days public relations and advertising writers must do as much or face angry consumers and clients.

Because media writers deal with complex social matters and people with varying viewpoints, they avoid making snap decisions. They know employers, clients, media consumers, and writers tend to gravitate toward causes and explanations consistent with personal views, and that individual preferences and decisions often reflect tenaciously held values and motives. The forces on human perception and behavior are so complex, scholars of mass media communication are unable to agree on definitions for *objectivity, fact, truth*. And an approved standard against which media writers can measure objective evidence is still awaiting discovery.

In the physical sciences, researchers answer questions about the world with greater confidence. They measure things: the speed of light, the depth of ocean waters, the age of an unearthed relic. Human behavior is less dependable. Media writers know objectivity is often beyond their grasp, but they also try to get as close to it as possible.

For this reason, professional writers try to be cognizant of motives and values and critically weigh the evidence received. They start with their own biases. They acknowledge them, recognize there is more than one side to any issue, realize even reasonable people will disagree on any matter, and try to determine why they disagree. The ability to recognize one's own biases, raise relevant questions, identify and organize the most substantial evidence from various sides, and still present objective copy creatively requires skill and practice. It is a methodical and critical skill professionals struggle to perfect because mass media audiences demand it.

The Importance of Audience

Before writers undertake any media project, they ask: *Who cares or is interested in this?* The answer identifies the audience and indicates whether the subject matter will serve the interests and needs of that audience. Once the audience is known, the writer tries to anticipate the questions the audience will want answered because what the writer needs to know about the subject of a media project is usually what the audience needs to know as well. To identify your audience and its needs, ask these basic questions:

- *Who cares or is interested in this problem* (issue or question)?
- *Why do they need or want to know about it?*
- *What does my audience need or want to know about this problem?*
- *What do I need or want to know about it?*

Other self-inquiries throughout this book will help you write for an audience instead of writing writing, which means writing to satisfy your ego instead of fulfilling the expectations of media consumers.

Media Voices and Variations

Audiences expect media writers to speak in a voice appropriate to the purpose of the message and the medium. For example, the purpose of the news and magazine writer is to inform without fabrication, error, or bias because their audiences expect accurate, complete, and relevant information.

Public relations (PR) audiences, however, know the purpose of PR is to promote the image of a company, its personnel, its product. Like news readers, PR audiences expect accurate information, but they also know that the PR writer discloses only what the company chooses to disclose. Because the purpose of PR work is to persuade, emphasis is placed on information that portrays the company in a favorable light. Unfavorable information is usually put on hold. However, in recent years, the trend in PR is to tell it like it is when a crisis strikes and to explain what the company is doing, or at least planning to do, to correct a bad situation.

The purpose of advertising, like PR, is to persuade. Here, too, the consumer audience expects accurate information about an advertised product, but like PR audiences, they do not expect an impartial appeal. Consumers realize ads are designed to play on buyers' emotions. They will accept varieties of and varying degrees of honest hyperbole, comedy, and fantasy depending on personal preference or tolerance.

Professional media writers understand these differences in voice, but still rely on verified data to write in whatever creative scope their medium allows. In short, all writers in media have patrons — current, temporary, or prospective — whose attention they must capture, inform, and in some cases convince. However, PR and advertising writers are usually far more selective about information relayed than news and magazine writers. Still, all must be very sure about the information they do relay, or at least indicate its tentative or questionable nature.

Practice is Important

Systematic and critical thinking habits do not happen over night. You learn the skills of professional writers by practicing them, not by being told what to do. It is much like learning how to get a tennis ball over the net or how to play the piano. It takes practice. Acquiring the skills of experienced writers is not easy, but the reward of insight into management of a media assignment is the gratifying outcome.

Refer frequently to the examples and models in this book. They illustrate how the strategy and critical self-inquiries work as a unit to produce a media product worthy of publication.

Apply the strategy and self-inquiries next time you undertake a writing assignment.

Concerning Vocabulary and Sentence Structure

One way to build your vocabulary and become familiar with good sentence structure is to read the work of good writers. Professional media writers have large vocabularies because they read. They are competent writers because they experience good literature. When they are not reading materials related to their writing assignments, they read nonfiction as well as fiction, the classics, stage plays and, yes, even poetry. Reading good literature, more than listening, develops vocabulary and sensitivity to readable copy because seeing the copy imprints images of easily read and clearly understood sentences on the mind.

This is where you will also find some "do's" about sentence structure and criteria for evaluating your written work. In addition, keep some reliable references on grammar, punctuation, and sentence structure within reach. English is a fluid language and exceptions to its rules are numerous and confusing. It is best to refer to more than one reference because not every reference answers all problems, nor do these references always agree. The ultimate test is whether the choices you have made promote understanding of the message.

The habit of systematic procedure and critical thinking helps you recognize weaknesses in the written and spoken word and draws your attention to flaws in your own copy. Because good writing is essentially good thinking.

The Dynamics of Mass Media Writing

In both recursive and linear strategies each step is completed before movement to the next step can occur. In both strategies frequent returns to one or more completed steps are possible to accommodate modifications as new information is obtained. However, a recursive strategy, rather than a linear one, applies more directly to mass media writing, because a recursive model indicates not only accruing data and turning back in the opposite direction, it also suggests continuation. That is, the media assignment rarely ends with one story, one press release, one ad. There is always another angle, another focus, another episode to write about on the same problem or issue.

About the Time Crunch

A frustrating factor in mass media work is time allowed for completion of an assignment. Although no step in the strategy should be circumvented, deadlines and assignment complexity determine the depth of attention given to any one step.

Short deadlines necessarily limit the time spent at certain stages of the strategy and the whole process is, therefore, greatly compressed. Stages in the strategy meld together as one function as they are performed mentally and on the run. The functions become more obvious to the eye on long deadline assignments because extended deadlines permit depth attention to the parts and often permit elaborately drawn plans and data organizations instead of mental or simplified ones. The whole process is, in comparison, expanded. Compressed or expanded, on the run or at the office, each of the functions and mental processes follow a natural sequence.

CRITICAL AREAS OF MEDIA WRITING

When the first edition of *Media Writing-was* conceptualized in the mid-1990s, industry predictions were that media were coming together in "convergence," spurred by the increasingly interrelated technologies of computer, telephone, and TV. Specialization by media, it was said, was on its way out. Print and broadcast journalists and public relations practitioners would not be merely reporters and writers but would increasingly be in the information-processing business, requiring overlapping skills. America Online president Steve Case was quoted in *Broadcasting* magazine as noting that media companies were positioning themselves to take advantage of a synergy of print and video and interactive technologies and, even before the AOL-Time Warner merger, that future media companies would be those that successfully combined the three. Those optimistic predictions were slightly off, of course. The full impact of convergence has been battered by the collapse of the dot.coms and the subsequent decline in stock values across media properties.

On the other hand, hundreds of newspapers have introduced an online presence, many with real-time streaming audio and video. The *Chicago Tribune* and WGN radio and television have a convergent news operation, as does the *Tampa Tribune* and a local TV station. The *Philadelphia Inquirer,* the *Philadelphia Daily News,* three regional newspapers, a local television outlet and 50 radio stations have teamed up in an interactive Web site. The pattern is replicated in many other markets around the country, where broadcast and print reporters prepare copy for each other's medium. Additionally, many corporations and nonprofit organizations are using computer technology to provide newsworthy information directly to their publics.

Instead of being merely writers and reporters, print and broadcast journalists and public relations practitioners increasingly find themselves in the business of information-processing and dissemination. Tomorrow's newswriters will need to be able to write a piece of newspaper copy designed to be read and then converted to a broadcast script that can be heard or with visuals that can be seen. Internet writing requires a mix of print and broadcast writing skills, as well as graphic talents to make Web-based news services interesting to read. Public relations practitioners will need the skills to produce news releases in print and broadcast versions for external media, as information for internal organizational media, or for the organization's Web site.

Although traditional daily and weekly newspaper, radio and television jobs are still available, competition for them has increased. Newspaper readership percentages have been on a downward spiral for years and, although online newspapers are attracting readers, the number of daily newspapers continues to decline. Most local radio stations have abandoned news, and audiences for TV news continue to fragment.

Career options in this new media environment, however, have expanded dramatically for those with interchangeable writing skills. Today's media writers can begin careers in a variety of magazine genres and newsletters. The Internet is providing expanded opportunities. Traditional agency and corporate public relations has expanded to nonprofit organizations, and advertising continues to be the economic backbone supporting the media. Predictions are that in less than 20 years, media writers will be independent contractors, coming together as part of specialized teams, working on a specific project, then leaving to start another. Today's media freelancer is already working in this way.

Media Writingis designed for those who will venture into this new multimedia environment. Although the subject matter is still divided into print, broadcast, and public relations sections—because each writing form has a distinct style—the textbook pulls these three elements together so that at the end of a semester or term you will have a grasp of the basic principles of media writing.

We not only explain the "hows" of media writing but also the "whys" by discussing the theoretical aspects of communication; examining legal and ethical issues; and analyzing what makes news and how it is written and reported, how radio and TV stations operate, and the role of the public relations practitioner in today's media environment. With concentrated effort on your part, you'll possess the skills to go on to more specialized writing courses.

Media Writing seeks to develop professional attitudes and skills that reporters, broadcasters, and public relations professionals need. One objective of the book is to provide beginning newswriting students with a primer that fosters development of the talents needed for a summer job or internship at a small daily or weekly newspaper, at a small- or medium-market radio or TV station, or in public relations.

MEDIA WRITING STYLE

Like all writing, media writing requires discipline because it's hard work. It's also fun and rewarding. A newspaper reporter goes out and covers the news, then comes back and writes a story with his or her byline under the headline. With a constant 24-hours-a-day/ 7-days-a-week deadline, Internet reporters face the same challenge that wire-service reporters did a half-century ago.

TV correspondents report from the scene with their name superimposed on the screen, and radio journalists often have the challenge of working on even tighter deadlines. Public relations practitioners interact with their journalist counterparts to help in reporting the news, then similarly do interviews and research news stories for use in either internal publications or external news releases. Whichever field you choose, it's a great way to make a living!

The professions are very competitive, however: For every job for which you'll be trying, at least 15 other equally or more talented people want the same position. You have to be good to make it! As a prospective communication professional, you need to develop curiosity about the world around you, a broad knowledge base, creativity, attention to detail, and respect for accuracy, objectivity and fairness. You also have to possess solid writing skills and a passion for words, and you must know the correct use of the language. Communicators are "wordsmiths," people who respect language and have learned its usage. Only when you have developed these skills will you be able to effectively interpret the world to other people. *Media Writing* is designed to help you build the necessary foundation to do just that.

On the surface, defining news is a simple task. News is an account of what is happening around us. It may involve current events, new initiatives or ongoing projects or issues. But a newspaper does not only print news of the day. It also prints background analysis, opinions, and human interest stories. The reporter chooses stories from the flood of information and events happening in the world and in their community.

Stories are normally selected because of their importance, emotion, impact, timeliness and interest.

IDENTIFY THE KIND OF A STORY

Hard News (+/- 600 words): This is how journalists refer to news of the day. It is a chronicle of current events/ incidents and is the most common news style on the front page of your typical newspaper. It starts with a summary lead. What happened? Where? When? To/ by whom? Why? (The journalist's 5 W's). It must be kept brief and simple, because the purpose of the rest of the story will be to elaborate on this lead. Keep the writing clean and uncluttered. Most important, give the readers the information they need. If the federal government announced a new major youth initiative yesterday, that's today's hard news.

Soft News (+/-600 words): This is a term for all the news that isn't time-sensitive. Soft news includes profiles of people, programs or organizations. As we discussed earlier, the "lead" is more literary. Most of YPP's news content is soft news.

Feature (+/-1500 words): A news feature takes one step back from the headlines. It explores an issue. News features are less time-sensitive than hard news but no less newsworthy. They can be an effective way to write about complex issues too large for the terse style of a hard news item. Street kids are a perfect example. The stories of their individual lives are full of complexities which can be reflected in a longer piece. Features are journalism's shopping center. They're full of interesting people, ideas, color, lights, action and energy. Storytelling at its height! A good feature is about the people in your community and their struggles, victories and defeats. A feature takes a certain angle (i.e. Black youth returning to church) and explores it by interviewing the people involved and drawing conclusions from that information. The writer takes an important issue of the day and explains it to the reader through comments from people involved in the story.

Hint: Remember to "balance" your story. Present the opinions of people on both sides of an issue and let the readers make their own decision on who to believe. No personal opinions are allowed. The quotes from the people you interview make up the story. You are the narrator.

Editorial: The editorial expresses an opinion. The editorial page of the newspaper lets the writer comment on issues in the news. All editorials are personal but the topics must still be relevant to the reader. Young People's Press publishes two types of editorials:

Youthbeat (+/- 700 words): Youthbeat's are YPP's editorial bread and butter. It's your story, from your point of view. Tell it like it is. Youthbeats usually (but not always) combine personal experience(s) with opinion/ analysis. Essentially, you establish your credibility by speaking from experience.

My Word! (+/-600 words): An opinion piece. Short, sweet and to the point. Not as likely to be a personal narrative. Christmas "spirit" bugs you? Say why. Had an encounter with a cop that left you sour? Same deal. Be strong. If you don't like something, don't beat around the bush. This is a space for you to rant and roll with as much emotive power as possible.

Structure for your Article

The structure of a news story (hard & soft news & features) is simple: a lead and the body.

The Lead

One of the most important elements of news writing is the opening paragraph or two of the story. Journalists refer to this as the "lead," and its function is to summarize the story and/or to draw the reader in (depending on whether it is a "hard" or "soft" news story - See below for the difference between these two genres of news stories). In a hard news story, the lead should be a full summary of what is to follow. It should incorporate as many of the 5 "W's" of journalism (who, what, where, when and why) as possible. (e.g. "Homeless youth marched down Yonge St. in downtown Toronto Wednesday afternoon demanding the municipal government provide emergency shelter during the winter months." - Can you identify the 5 W's in this lead?) In a soft news story, the lead should present the subject of the story by allusion. This type of opening is somewhat literary. Like a novelist, the role of the writer is to grab the attention of the reader. (e.g. "Until four years ago, Jason W. slept in alleyways...") Once the reader is drawn in, the 5 "W's" should be incorporated into the body of the story, but not necessarily at the very top.

The Body

The body of the story involves combining the opinions of the people you interview, some factual data, and a narrative which helps the story flow. A word of caution, however. In this style of writing, you are not allowed to "editorialize" (state your own opinion) in any way.

Remember: The role of a reporter is to find out what people are thinking of an issue and to report the opinions of different stakeholders of an issue. These comments make up the bulk of the story. The narrative helps to weave the comments into a coherent whole. Hint: Stick to one particular theme throughout the story. You can put in different details but they all have to relate to the original idea of the piece. (e.g. If your story is about black youth and their relationship with the police you DO NOT want to go into details about the life of any one particular youth).

As a reporter, you are the eyes and ears for the readers. You should try to provide some visual details to bring the story to life (this is difficult if you have conducted only phone interviews, which is why face-to-face is best). You should also try to get a feel for the story. Having a feel means getting some understanding of the emotional background of the piece and the people involved in it. Try to get a sense of the characters involved and why they feel the way they do.

Some Tips for News Writing

Finding story ideas—

- Keep your eyes and ears open; listen to what your friends are talking about.
- Read everything you can get your hands on; get story ideas from other newspapers and magazines.
- Think of a youth angle to a current news story.
- Research a subject that interests you ask yourself what you would like to know more about.
- Talk to people in a specific field to find out what is important to them.

Newsgathering

- Begin collecting articles on your subject.
- Talk to friends and associates about the subject.
- Contact any agencies or associations with interest or professional knowledge in the area.
- Create a list of people you want to interview; cover both sides of the story by interviewing people on both sides of the issue.
- Collect government statistics and reports on the subject get old press releases or reports to use as background.

Interviewing Do's and Don'ts

- Be polite.
- Explain the ground rules of the interview to people unfamiliar with how the media works - this means that you tell them the information they give you can and will be published. If they do not want any part of what they say published, they need to tell you it is "off the record."
- Tape the interview (so if anyone comes back at you, you have the proof of what was said).
- Build a relationship with the person being interviewed.

- Start with easy questions; end with difficult questions.
- Read the body language of the person you're interviewing and if they get defensive, back away from the question you are asking and return later.
- Don't attack the source.
- Keep control of the interview; don't let the subject ramble or stray from the subject.
- On the other hand, don't let your "opinion" of what the story should be colour the interview. Always remember that the person you are talking with knows more about the subject than you do.

Organizing the Information

- Gather your notes, interviews and research into a file.
- Review your notes.
- Look for a common theme.
- Search your notes for good quotes or interesting facts.
- Develop a focus.
- Write the focus of the article down in two or three sentences.

Writing and Editing

- Remember you are the narrator, the story teller.
- Don't be afraid to rewrite.
- Be as clear and concise in the writing as possible.
- Avoid run-on sentences.
- Be direct.
- Tell a good story.
- Tell the reader what you think they want to know.
- Always ask yourself what the story is about.
- Read the story out loud; listen carefully.

10

Communication Theory and News Values

There is much discussion in the academic world of communication as to what actually constitutes communication. Currently, many definitions of communication are used in order to conceptualize the processes by which people navigate and assign meaning. Communication is also understood as the exchanging of understanding. Additionally the biocommunication theory investigates communicative processes within and among non-humans such as bacteria, animals, fungi and plants.

We might say that communication consists of transmitting information from one person to another. In fact, many scholars of communication take this as a working definition, and use Lasswell's maxim, "who says what to whom in what channel with what effect," as a means of circumscribing the field of communication theory.

Other commentators suggest that a ritual process of communication exists, one not artificially divorceable from a particular historical and social context. Communication stands so deeply rooted in human behaviors and the structures of society that scholars have difficulty thinking of it while excluding social or behavioral events. Because communication theory remains a relatively young field of inquiry and integrates itself with other disciplines such as philosophy, psychology, and sociology, one probably cannot yet expect a consensus conceptualization of communication across disciplines.

Currently, there is no paradigm from which communication scholars may work. One of the issues facing scholars is the possibility that establishing a communication metatheory will negate their research and stifle the broad body of knowledge in which communication functions.

In 1934, when federal agents in Chicago shot and killed John Dillinger, then America's most wanted bank robber, the story was reported mainly by newspapers. Radio, which began broadcasting as we know it in 1920, was in its infancy, newsreels were not able to produce and distribute a report to movie theaters until days after a major event, and TV was still only a laboratory experiment. Public relations was primarily about publicity—at times even involved in keeping stories *out* of the press. Weekly general-circulation magazines offered some news, but they mostly carried features, short literary stories and advertisements. Back then, only newspapers and the wire services that provided copy for papers around the country were capable of thoroughly reporting the story. Media writing was defined as newspaper journalism.

Nearly 70 years later, when a string of deadly sniper shootings terrorized Washington, D. C., Virginia and Maryland in late 2002, television transmitted the ongoing drama live to millions of viewers around the country. Radio provided extensive coverage, print reporters wrote reams of copy, and public-information specialists from federal, state and local law enforcement agencies interpreted events, as did legal experts and consultants hired by cable and traditional TV networks. Although the coverage was still identifiable as reporting, the technology, the immediacy it made possible, and a 24-hour/7-days-a-week news cycle dictated a media writing environment far different from what had gone before. Media writing is more than a matter of gathering facts and putting words together. Writers must work within the opportunities and limits provided by the technology, society, communications process, demands of the business, and needs of the audience.

MEDIA WRITING AS MASS COMMUNICATION

Mass communication is a powerful force in modern society. Radio, television, newspapers, magazines, film, public relations and advertising all shape the way we react to the world around us.

Over the years, various communication theories have been developed about the role of the mass media in society. It can be theorized, for instance, that media writing has changed because of the immediacy and intensity made possible by today's portable communication technology and the demands of the 24/7 news cycle. Communication theories have implications for the media writer because they attempt to explain what people pay attention to and why, and how messages become lost or distorted despite communicators' best efforts.

The Purpose of Communication

One of the early communication researchers, Harold Lasswell, identified three functions of the mass media: (1) surveillance of the environment, (2) correlation of the parts of society in responding to that environment (explaining to various publics what the news and information being transmitted means to them), and (3) transmission of the cultural heritage from one generation to the next. Another prominent researcher, Wilbur Schramm, said that in order for media messages to be successful, they must be designed and delivered in ways that gain attention, using language commonly understood by communicator and audience, and that the message must arouse needs and present ways to meet them.

Although those propositions were first offered more than 50 years ago, they remain a valid description ofthe task facing today's media writers. A reporter's job is to look around and see what is happening, and then communicate those happenings that he or she deems important to the reading, listening and viewing public. Clarity in presenting the message is extremely important: If the audience doesn't understand what is being communicated, it will turn away from or misinterpret the message.

Communication Challenges

Increasingly, media messages have become part of the babble of background sound and activities. Nowadays it is rare for people to *only* read a newspaper or *only* watch TV or *only have* a conversation. Often they do one or more while engaged in other activities without paying attention to the background the various mass media provide.

In many respects, Canadian communication theorist Marshall McLuhan was right when he said, "The medium is the message," meaning that societies have always been more influenced by the form of communication than by its content. Long before CNN and satellite TV, McLuhan envisioned an electronic "global village" of shared experiences and information, a holistic environment shattering the isolated "linear" bonds that print communication fostered. McLuhan said that society had entered a new age in which our world and surroundings were changing rapidly, especially due to television, which was responsible for "reshaping and restructuring patterns of social interdependence and every aspect of our personal life." This new world of electronic information media involves all of us all at once, McLuhan said. Information pours upon us instantaneously and continuously; as soon as we acquire information, it is rapidly replaced by still newer information. The accuracy of McLuhan's observations 40 years ago about the power of TV has been compounded by the rise of the Internet and the World Wide Web (WWW).

Ironically, with all of the various information resources available today, people often read superficially or listen with only one ear to a TV report. This inattention contributes to what is known as perceptual distortion, the tendency to introduce inaccuracies in perceiving what the writer or announcer said. A cardinal rule of newswriting is that what the communicator sends by way of a message is less important than what the audience receives and perceives. Often, these two are quite different.

One reason why people of different ages, genders, races or religions sometimes receive the same information but take from it different meanings is addressed by the theory of denotative and connotative meanings. Communication research recognizes denotative and connotative meanings of words and symbols, which complicate the communication process. People attach denotative labels (standard, descriptive names) to things, concepts, and ideas but they also put their own connotations (interpretations of meaning or value) on those same things, concepts and ideas based on their experiences, attitudes, opinions and beliefs. For instance, the denotative meaning of a "No Smoking" sign outside your classroom building is that no smoking is permitted inside. Even that simple message has connotations. If a student has trouble making it through a 50-minute class without a cigarette, he or she might feel that "they" are abridging personal rights by prohibiting smoking. A nonsmoker, on the other hand, might interpret the sign as protecting the health of students and faculty.

Another source of message distortion is audience reaction to cognitive dissonance. The theory of cognitive dissonance says that people can tolerate only so much emotional upset and, when information we receive is different from that which we accept or with which we are comfortable, our mind seeks a balance by rejecting or modifying the dissonant information. An example is when a news report is so emotionally jarring that people set up internal psychological defenses to deal with the message.

Finally, two types of communication interference, called noise, are present in the process of message transmission: physical noise and semantic noise. Physical noise is anything that distorts the reception of the message—background sounds that drown out a speaker, static, or similar problems. In theory, it can be corrected. Semantic noise is confusion caused by using words or phrases that the audience cannot understand or might misinterpret. Although semantic noise is harder to deal with, effective media writing can eliminate most of the associated problems.

MEDIA RESEARCH AND THEORY

Media research shows audiences are very interactive. Although many people think TV audiences are composed of mindless "couch potatoes," in fact, only a small proportion of viewers falls into that category. More typical is the "channel surfer," who zips through cable-system offerings—a type of behavior that also shows up in print media use.

Several theories have been developed to explain differences and similarities in media habits. All are directly applicable to media writers because they explain how people receive and distort media messages.

Individual Differences Theory

According to the theory of individual differences, people are unique in the way they approach media messages. Individual demographics and experiences shape audience perceptions of communicators and their transmissions. Therefore, the credibility of sources and the way issues-oriented messages are viewed can change from person to person.

Social Categories Theory

While audiences possess individual traits that determine responses to messages, social categories theory maintains that people who share similar demographic characteristics will respond similarly to a message. Research has shown, for instance, that women interpret a television news report differently than men. Women (a social category) tend to remember feature news and pay attention to visual background detail, while men (another social category) tend to remember factual detail at the expense of the other.

Social Influence

Often, social categories can be particularly strong when they involve members of a close-knit group, even though the group may have a diversified membership. The theory of social influence states that members of a group can construct an artificial reality for themselves, strong enough even to reject appealing mass-media messages or portrayals. Young members of a close-knit religious fellowship who do not drink, for example, will not change their behavior no matter how appealing the beer commercial—with all those suntanned people frolicking on the beach and drinking lots of beer with nary a bathroom in sight—because of the social ostracism that would follow.

Selective Processes

Because so many media voices compete for attention, people's media behaviors are influenced by the so-called selective processes: selective attention or exposure, selective perception, selective retention, and even selective recall. The selective processes theory contends that although exposure to some media messages may be accidental, for the most part audience members choose whether to pay attention. Because it is impossible to read, hear and see everything in our mass-media environment, people selectively expose themselves to messages they feel will be of interest or help them, and perceive them according to their biases. Then, because it is impossible to remember everything, only information that seems important is retained. What is retained, some scholars insist, is subject to the distortion of selective recall. Events or facts are remembered or subconsciously altered in a way that reinforces beliefs and attitudes or staves off cognitive dissonance.

Stereotypes

A filtering process takes place as readers, listeners and viewers interpret facts, statements and events. Audiences rely on stereotypes, the mental images people use as a simplified representation of reality. According to newspaper columnist

Walter Lippmann, who first wrote about stereotypes in 1921, "Whatever we believe to be a true picture, we treat as if it were the environment itself, for the real environment is altogether too big, too complex and too fleeting for direct acquaintance." Gradually, we develop a mental picture of the world that seems true to us, then respond to this pseudo-environment as though it were true. Although stereotypes impede information flow, audiences—as well as news organizations—have long used them in stories about race, gender, age, politics or international affairs.

Wants and Needs Gratification

In explaining basic audience behavior, the theory of wants and needs gratification maintains that an audience will not pay attention to a media message unless the message or the medium fulfills some perceived want or need. According to the theory, all media behavior is based on the expectation of reward. Even collapsing on the couch at the end of the day "just to watch some TV" is a form of the wants and needs theory in operation. So is watching a "slice-and-dice" horror film with friends in order to be part of the group, even though one may not care for that film genre.

Opinion Leaders

Years ago, researchers identified what became known as the two-step flow of communication, in which media messages travel to influential community members known as opinion leaders, who then explain the significance of media messages to those who look to them for guidance. For example, labor leaders are opinion leaders for union members; respected business leaders are opinion leaders for residents of a town. Opinion leaders also may be influential people in medicine, education or the clergy. This theory has since been expanded to a multi-step flow of mediated communication, with multiple opinion leaders providing various levels of influence and interpretation in a dynamic process in which mutual influence takes place between receiver and sources. Individuals may bypass opinion leaders entirely, creating their own interpretation of events and ideas relayed by the media. Thus, instead of creating messages for a relatively homogeneous audience, today's media writers must consider a diverse audience, with each member having distinct interests and insisting that individual demands be met.

Narcotizing Dysfunction

Members of audiences sometimes remain unmoved by media messages. For example, although the amount of political information and number of advertisements have increased, political participation continues to decline. Research has identified a phenomenon known as the narcotizing dysfunction, which is often seen among people who pay close attention to news and public affairs issues without acting on that knowledge. Those well-informed people choose not to vote or take part in community government because overexposure to the issues has created burnout or confusion. According to the narcotizing dysfunction theory, audience members perceive media messages as confusing and contradictory, so they do not make decisions, even though they are relatively well informed.

Cultivation

Media research has identified that many people's values and worldview are related to their media exposure. For heavy viewers of news, public affairs and talk shows, those programs become their version of reality and topics discussed on the programs become important. Likewise, someone who views violent TV programs may cultivate that view of the environment as reality—"the city is a dangerous place"—or similar stereotypes. Cultivation theory explains this by saying that mass media, especially television, "cultivate" a perception of reality. Thus people who consume the mass media extensively share those views more than mild or moderate media users. Local news broadcasts are particularly important in cultivating certain perceptions of reality.

Spiral of Silence

Not everyone adopts the values and worldview expressed by the mass media. The spiral of silence theory says that fear of isolation or separation from those around them prevents people from expressing their opinions when they are in the minority. As more people with out-of-the-mainstream views withdraw from public debate, the majority appears stronger. Because the media combine to present a common view of the world and imply that it is accepted by most people, those who disagree with the media's perception often remain silent for fear of being considered out of step. Minority views are expressed, however, when legitimized by the media.

The spiral of silence theory also explains the hostility many people feel toward the news media. People who do not agree with the thrust or bias of a news report may believe they are in the minority or powerless to effect change. If so, they may internalize their resentment rather than speak out.

Implications for Media Writers

What does all this theory mean for the practical media writer? It is a reminder that communication is not simple and carries no guarantee of success. What the media most commonly do is reinforce opinions, attitudes and beliefs, and maintain the status quo. For the most part, the audience will reject or ignore messages that run counter to already-held opinions, attitudes and beliefs, even if they are carried by the powerful media.

Some attitude modification is possible through the mass media, an effect often seen when public opinion polls record a decline in "undecided" respondents in favor of one position or another. The mass media also can provide powerful educational mechanisms in the diffusion of new ideas or the creation of new attitudes in novel or changing circumstances.

The challenge to the media writer is to write and report stories in a way that avoids creating cognitive dissonance and slips through the selective process filters to be retained because the stories appeal to some want or need felt by members of the audience. Such writing is not always easy.

The Media Business

Like many other businesses—and journalism, broadcast news and public relations are businesses, make no mistake about that—the field has its maxims and sayings. One of them is attributed to Wilbur Storey, editor of the *Chicago Times* during the late 19th century, who said the role of the newspaper was "to print the news and raise hell." His contemporary, Charles A. Dana of the *New York Sun,* said newspapering consisted of buying newsprint at two cents a pound and selling it for 10 cents a pound. About 80 years after Storey and Dana, broadcast journalist Edward R. Murrow told his colleagues that television was a mixture of information, entertainment, and sales and that when the three were gathered together under one tent, the dust never settled.

Public relations began with communication efforts of organizations to generate positive public opinion. Edward Bernays, one of the original thinkers in the field, broke new ground in the early 1920s when he helped create what was to become the public relations profession. He defined public relations as the process of "crystallizing public opinion," which involved the "engineering of consent" based on Thomas Jefferson's principle that in a democratic society, everything depends on the consent of the public.

All these quotes reflect a tension that remains in the communication business to this day. The organizational structure, management and newsroom operations reflect the at times conflicting dynamics of serving the public and making money. Although all three media formats share news values and the need for solid writing skills, they differ in their treatment of the news message. Print can go in depth on non-visual stories that broadcasting would never cover. Broadcasters are interested in sound bites and visuals that may not lend themselves to print treatment. Editorial decisions are dictated by both the medium and the economic necessity of drawing and keeping an audience.

Roles within the Media

As a beginning journalist, broadcaster or public relations practitioner, you will find realities far different from the idealistic concepts lectured about in colleges and universities.

To print or broadcast the news, the businesses that run newspapers, radio and television have to make money; public relations practitioners also must be sensitive to the well-being of their businesses or organizations when they deal with reporters.

Gatekeeping. Communication theory recognizes people called gatekeepers, those who open and shut the gates of communication, thereby determining what an audience sees, hears and reads. Individual newspaper beat reporters and editors are gatekeepers; they decide which stories will be covered, whether the coverage appears in print, and, if so, how it is reported. Radio and television news directors, assignment editors, program producers, and field reporters perform a similar gatekeeping function, as do those who determine a radio station's playlist for the week or a TV station's late-movie offerings. Newsletter gatekeepers include the editor and contributors. Public relations practitioners are also gatekeepers, controlling the flow of information from their organizations as well as access to their sources.

As the information environment has become more complex, the number of gatekeepers has soared. Their decisions are generally based upon news values, with some attention both to what will be effective in the competition for audiences and how the information will affect the person or organization controlling that information.

Agenda Setting. An important element of the news professional's job is agenda setting. The agenda-setting theory holds that the mass media determine what is important by starting newscasts with a particular story or printing it on page one. When news gatekeepers no longer consider an item to be of importance, they allow it to slip off the public agenda. Although agenda-setting theory concedes the primacy of the media's role in determining which events are important, it concludes that media outlets only tell audiences what to think about, not what to think. A related theory, the issue attention cycle, says that the news media and public ignore a serious problem for years, then for some reason they suddenly notice it, declare it a crisis, and concoct a solution. When they realize the problem will be costly and not easily fixed, they grow angry, then bored, and finally resume ignoring the problem.

Status Conferral. This theory says that, because of their influential nature, the mass media confer status and legitimacy on people, organizations and ideas. Thus, if a person appears on TV as an expert on an issue, that appearance enhances his or her reputation. After all, if people were not important, according to the theory, they wouldn't appear on television, because TV doesn't have time for unimportant issues, ideas or people. The status-conferral theory implies that reporters need to be careful in covering news about groups. When choosing sources to quote, it is necessary to ensure that the source or organization is indeed legitimate and representative.

Specialization. Traditionally, the mass media have provided a sense of broader community, reflecting who and what Americans are as people, while also influencing social trends and traditions. In recent years, however, newspapers and news reports have become as fractionalized as the audiences they serve. Reporters are often assigned specialized beats beyond the traditional ones of police, courts and city or county government. Sports, business, the environment, entertainment, lifestyles and religion are staples of what is denned as news, and many newspapers have created special-interest pages catering to seniors, youth or ethnic groups within a community.

Theories of the Press

The way in which news is covered in American society reflects two important press theories: libertarianism and social responsibility. Historically, when printing by movable type developed in the latter half of the 15th century, governments sought to control this new and expanding form of communication. Printers were licensed and expected to support and advance the cause of the government. Criticism of the political system or those in power was not tolerated. The press was regulated by government guidelines, restrictive press laws and censorship.

Libertarianism. Although the authoritarian system still exists under some repressive governments, authoritarian press theory gave way in the 18th and 19th centuries in the United States and parts of Western Europe to a libertarian concept, based on the philosophy of rationalism and natural rights. Libertarianism relies on a "marketplace of ideas," in which anyone with a viewpoint has the right to publish it without prior government approval. Although the purpose of the press is to inform, entertain, and sell goods, its primary responsibilities are to help discover truth, be a "watchdog" for society and provide a check on government.

Crucial to the American media system is the First Amendment to the Constitution, a logical extension of libertarian theory, which says, "Congress shall make no law... abridging the freedom of speech, or of the press." Because of the First Amendment, the mass media are permitted a wide latitude in what they can report and relatively narrow constraints are placed on what is actionable in court. There have been restrictions, of course, on the press throughout U. S. history: Abolitionist newspapers were barred from the Southern mails during the 1830s, President Lincoln briefly shut down two Northern newspapers critical of his Civil War policies, and sedition acts were passed during World War I. Some press coverage was restricted during World War II, and information flow has been tightened as part of the war on terrorism since September 11, 2001. For the most part, however, any action related to content has come after publication.

Social Responsibility. While libertarianism says that anyone with the economic means to be heard is entitled to a voice in the marketplace of ideas, by the early 20th century access to the marketplace was being choked off by increased costs. Not everyone who wanted to could afford to start or own a newspaper. Libertarianism thus began to break down. To counter this negative impact caused by market forces, the concept of social responsibility developed in the 1940s and 1950s. Social responsibility promoted the proposition that because all voices could no longer be represented in the marketplace of ideas, the media had a responsibility to ensure that all viewpoints were expressed and that conflict was elevated to a plane of discussion. If the media did not voluntarily assume this role, the theory said, it might be necessary for some governmental or other agency to see that they did so.

The notion of social responsibility reached its high point in the 1960s as an activist Federal Communications Commission (FCC) threatened and cajoled the radio and television industry in an attempt to elevate American broadcast standards and the U. S. Supreme Court began to pay more attention to media issues.

Broadcast Regulation

Since the earliest days of radio, government has exercised limited intervention through regulation and court decisions based upon the doctrine of scarcity, which considers the physical limits to the amount of space available on the electromagnetic spectrum for broadcasting. According to this doctrine, the airwaves belong to the people and broadcast station owners are merely temporary custodians of the frequencies licensed to them. Under the terms of the 1934 Communications Act, broadcasters are expected to operate in the "public interest, convenience and necessity"—a broad standard open to interpretation, but one that reflects the fact that the FCC cannot censor programming.

There is little regulation of print media because, in theory, anyone can start a newspaper, newsletter or magazine. Radio and TV stations, however, do not enjoy the same First Amendment rights as their print counterparts. The Communications Act prohibits profanity and obscenity, and gives political candidates equal-time access to broadcast stations. There was a seldom-used right of rebuttal against personal attack and, for nearly 40 years, broadcasters had to abide by provisions of a Fairness Doctrine that encouraged them to undertake a balanced examination of controversial issues of public importance. The FCC allowed the Fairness Doctrine to lapse in the deregulatory climate of the 1980s, its rationale being that growth of the multiplicity of voices in the marketplace made it unnecessary for the government to mandate "fairness." The FCC also took the position that the Fairness Doctrine unnecessarily restricted the journalistic freedom of broadcasters and actually inhibited airing controversial issues of importance or presenting unorthodox or unpopular viewpoints.

What makes news?

Charles Dana, editor of the *New York Sun* during the late 19th century, is credited with the axiom, "If man bites dog, that's news." News is an outstanding deviation from the norm, something that doesn't ordinarily happen. Another definition applies the theory of wants and needs gratification, saying that news is a combination of what audiences need to know and want to know. However news is defined, whether it involves "hard" breaking news or "soft" feature stories, it has certain characteristics, known as the criteria of news value, or the news pegs on which the story is "hung. " They include timeliness, proximity to the audience, prominence of those involved, consequence, conflict, suspense, human interest, novelty, and progress. The more characteristics present in an event, the more it is newsworthy.

Timeliness

By any standard, especially in this era of instantaneous satellite communication and today's 24/7 news cycle, timeliness—or immediacy—is the most important criterion of news value. News is change, something that has just occurred; what happened a few days ago is history. Few events of major significance can be defined as news if they fail to meet the standard of timeliness. However, an event that occurred some time ago can still meet the timeliness standard if the news of it was just revealed. When in doubt about how to lead a story, go for timeliness: Tell what is happening *now.*

Proximity

We are all interested in what is going on around us; therefore, proximity is an important news element. Proximity means giving the local angle, telling about an event near the readers, listeners or viewers, and explaining how closely it touches their lives. Harry Tammen and Fred Bonfils, editors of the *Denver* Post in the early 20th century, said that the news value of a dogfight on the street in front of their newspaper office was worth two European archduke assassinations. Local news is also important because people like to see their names in print for the positive things they do or say.

Prominence

"Names make news." When it comes to prominent people, whether the president of the United States or a famous movie or rock star, virtually anything he or she does or says is newsworthy. If a prominent person missteps, his or her transgression merits page one. If an average person does the same thing, it might not make the news at all.

Consequence

The more people affected, generally the greater is the news value. Proposed changes in Social Security benefits might not be newsworthy in many regions of the country, but in Florida and Arizona—states with a large percentage of retired people—that story will have consequence. Newswriters, editors, and producers need to understand local demographics and know what is important to their audience.

Conflict

Whether or not we like it, conflict is a universal news value, the most common examples being sporting events, political contests, wars and revolutions. Whether it's team against team, nation against nation, or men and women against the natural elements, conflict sells newspapers and draws broadcast audiences.

Suspense

Related to conflict is the news peg of suspense. Following an explosion in a coal mine, hours or days may go by while rescue workers look for survivors or bring out additional bodies. A search for an escaped convict, the tracking of a kidnapper, the journey of a damaged aircraft attempting to land—all are examples of suspense stories in which audiences have an interest.

Human Interest

People like to read about other people, which is why much of the news lends itself to feature treatment that emphasizes human nature. Features are often characterized by their human-interest elements: the creation of emotional responses such as happiness, sadness, anger, sympathy, hate, love, envy or humor.

Novelty

An unusual or strange aspect will help lift a story out of the ordinary. If an ordinary man jumps out of an ordinary airplane with an ordinary parachute and makes an ordinary landing, the event has no news value. But if the man has only one leg, his jump is newsworthy, just as it is if the parachute fails to open but he lands safely. In public relations, writers look for an unusual element because it might determine whether or not the media use the story.

Progress

The most upbeat news and feature stories are often about people accomplishing goals and making their communities better places in which to live or work. Progress stories that involve local business and industry improving life for their community or customers are naturals for public relations and are the staple of small- and medium-market television and smaller newspapers.

CHANGING DEFINITIONS OF NEWS

In the view of many members of the public, the media seem to use yet another definition: "If it's good news, that's bad news; if it's bad news, that's good news!" Part of the public's hostility toward the news media arises from the sense that journalists glorify social misfits and ignore the accomplishments of average people who lead ordinary lives and stay out of trouble. Whether audiences really want to know some of what today passes for "news" is open to question.

For instance, an argument was made after *Wall Street Journal* reporter Daniel Pearl was killed by Pakistani terrorists in early 2002 that the public had a right to see the graphic, gory videotape shot by his captors. The video was put online and some TV stations even used portions. If you become a news reporter, you will see many things that the public doesn't need or wouldn't want to see. Your job is not to titillate the audience or appeal to their base instincts while pursuing ratings points or circulation numbers. The job at times involves discretion about what not to show or say.

Ironically, despite so much information in the traditional marketplace of ideas, polls show that the public is increasingly dissatisfied with the quality of news and information. To counter this perception, newspapers are becoming more readeroriented to retain their share of a fragmenting audience. Broadcast reporters are finding the competition even more intense. News is becoming more featurized and user-oriented—more of what people appear to want, rather than what the newspaper editor or broadcast-news director thinks they need.

A study conducted by the Project for Excellence in Journalism, which measured changes in news content during a 20-year period, seems to bear out this observation. In 1977, more than half of all stories (52%) were basically straight news accounts of what had happened. By 1997, that figure had fallen to less than one in three stories (32%), with stories tending to have a more mediated or thematic approach. The emphasis was on people, human interest and "news you can use." The study also found a new emphasis on scandal, the bizarre, and fear about the future. In 1977, stories with a traditional news emphasis dominated stories with a feature or scandal by a two-to- one margin. By 1997, that order was essentially reversed. Stories about government and foreign affairs dropped, but the number of stories about celebrities, entertainment and celebrity crime tripled.

Network newscasts, the study found, moved toward consumer and health news. Like other media, the greatest shift in emphasis was toward coverage of scandal, followed by human interest and quality of life stories, and there was a substantial decline in straight news stories or in-depth analyses or updates. Prime time network news magazines, which have replaced documentaries on network television, have all but abandoned traditional topics such as government, social welfare, education, and economics in favor of celebrities, sensational crime, lifestyles and news-you can-use. News magazines once concentrated on the coverage of ideas. The study found that only eight percent of the stories concern the combined areas of education, economics, foreign affairs, the military, national security, politics or social welfare issues. Instead, celebrity profiles and crime were the most popular categories of stories, followed closely by stories about consumer news, health and medicine, and law and justice.

The print news magazines *Time* and *Newsweek* have seen broad shifts in emphasis, the most notable being a decline in coverage of ideas. In 1977, nearly one in five cover stories concerned policies or ideas; by 1987, the number had fallen to one in 20 covers, where it remains. *Time* and *Newsweek* most often have cover stories in the area of consumer and health news and celebrity entertainment, and even serious topics are often presented through a Hollywood prism. In 1977, political or international figures represented nearly one in three of all *Time* and *Newsweek* covers. By 1997, that number had fallen by more than 60 percent to one in 10 covers. Covers that sold the story with celebrities, a sexy man or woman, or an image story about sex, doubled between 1977 and 1997.

Front page newspaper trends during the same 20-year period saw shifts in emphasis similar to network TV, although not to the same extent because newspaper front pages remained oriented primarily around traditional news categories.

PUBLIC PERCEPTIONS OF NEWSPEOPLE

People in the communication professions must deal with the expectations of their reading, viewing and listening publics. If polls are any indication, most people don't like what "The Media" tell them, and regard reporters to be at about the same level as politicians and used-car dealers. Critics say that journalists engage in unseemly behavior and reflect a pack or herd mentality. Some journalists are perceived as seeking a celebrity status for themselves while covering the famous or infamous.

They are said to be arrogant, abrasive and cynical, an out-of-touch elite not necessarily knowledgeable about what they report. There also is a lingering suspicion that journalists bring their own political or social agenda into news reports. That accusation, by the way, maybe inherent in the role of reporter. Kansas editor William Allen White said nearly a hundred years ago that journalism should "comfort the afflicted and afflict the comfortable."

When people turn on the TV, they see the problems of the world, live and in color. No wonder people don't like journalists! Nobody likes the bearers of bad news. Critics of journalism claim that it is superficial and unduly negative, values appearance over substance, appeals to emotion and celebrity worship, and has moved increasingly to being a forum for conflict rather than conciliation. Critics also say that journalism sets the political agenda instead of allowing the campaign dynamic to play itself out, hinders solutions to social problems, and pays inordinate attention to society's misfits and dysfunctional people.

What is new and troubling is that those attitudes have turned into measurable numbers. A national survey conducted for the Center for Media and Public Affairs found that a substantial number of respondents said they perceived journalists to be arrogant and cynical, and 52 percent believed that the news media abuse the First Amendment guarantees of freedom of the press. A survey by the Freedom Forum's First Amendment Center found that 51 percent of the respondents think the press in America has too much freedom;

one in five said that newspapers shouldn't be allowed to publish without governmental approval.

Keep in mind, however, that journalists, broadcasters, and public relations people are describing reality; they don't cause bad things to happen. Ours is a world of political scandals, drive-by shootings, volcanoes, earthquakes, international bullies and terrorism, famine, disease, violence, and a myriad of other problems that crowd out good news. Nevertheless, the media report a fair amount of upbeat news, although at times some searching is necessary. In particular, public relations practitioners help journalists and broadcasters report on the positive side of life: medical breakthroughs, scientific advances, social accomplishments and personal achievements. Beyond the world of the newsroom, special interest publications and programs focus on self-improvement, education and wholesome entertainment.

As social institutions and technology become more complex, the media increasingly rely on public relations practitioners to provide information that individual reporters or news organizations lack the capability or expertise to gather. Public relations professionals have meshed their standards with those of the news media to effectively convey organizational messages, and they use similar principles to enhance communication within their organizations.

NEWSPEOPLE'S PERCEPTIONS OF THE NEWS

News professionals are not immune to being influenced by what they do. The theory of acculturation suggests that news reporters adopt the attitudes and behaviors of those they cover. Police reporters, for instance, may be stronger supporters of law and order than many police officers. Political reporters may take on the views of people about whom they report, which is why the networks periodically shift White House, State Department and Pentagon correspondents to different beats. In those examples, newspeople have become socialized into accepting the values of their environment—often without their conscious knowledge—and they pass those values on to the audience.

Reporters Look at Their Profession

Journalists seem to agree with criticism by the public about their profession and the quality of their work. In a 1999 study by the Pew Research Center for the People and the Press, media executives, editors, producers and reporters conceded that reporting has become sloppy, with numerous factual errors, and that the lines have blurred between commentary and reporting and between entertainment and news. Many said the press drives controversies, especially in the way it covers the personal and ethical behavior of political figures. Lack of credibility was cited as the most important problem facing journalism today; loss of public trust was given as the reason for declining news audiences.

Journalists complain that business pressure is hurting the quality of news coverage. To reach wider audiences and sell more advertising to make more profit—the ultimate measure of the "bottom line" to stockholders—the media increasingly sensationalize stories. This trend leads to an erosion of confidence by the public, which

A Question of Balance

Your job in the communication business will be difficult because your "balanced perspective" is going to differ from that of the people you write about or who read, watch and listen to what you write. Cognitive dissonance, the selective processes and the theory of wants and needs gratification conspire to make the media writer's job more difficult. The individual audience member is in control of how the message will be received, and people may not perceive it in ways the writer intended, or like what they read or hear. For years, journalists have adhered to the concepts of objectivity and fairness: All sides of an issue must be presented neutrally for the readers, viewers or listeners to make up their mind. Although media writers continue to strive for fairness and balance, there's no guarantee that our sources or audience will like us in the future any more than they do now.

11

Ethical and Legal Issues in Media Writing

Whether it is the lurid sensationalism of tabloid newspapers at supermarket checkout stands, overdramatized coverage by mainstream television news programs, or slanted reportage passing for "news" on the Internet, it is easy to find much to criticize about American journalism. In recent years, there have been a number of sensational criminal cases and events, and the media have covered them extensively, often to excess. Keep in mind, however, that many of the complaints have been around in different forms even before America was a nation, and today's media critics are saying some of the same things that were said in the past. Sensationalism that panders to the lowest common denominator invariably sells. It always has; it probably always will.

Ironically, one reason for the decline in standards may well be the proliferation of media voices in the traditional marketplace of ideas. The three major television networks found it much easier to be socially responsible 30 years ago when they were essentially splitting the audience three ways. Now, with all the various cable channels added to the mix, the audience is fragmented and everyone is fighting over increasingly smaller pieces of the pie. With the audience divided into identifiable marketbased niches, news programmers find that catering to the lowest common denominator yields the largest share of audience. Part of the shift is due to education and income: better educated, economically well-off people don't watch those programs.

News as Entertainment

Over the years, as was noted in Chapter 1, there has been a shift toward lifestyles, celebrity, entertainment, and celebrity scandal as entertainment at the expense of the more traditional "hard" news stories. Media critic Jeffrey Scheuer says that this is characteristic of what he calls a "sound bite society," one that is flooded with images and slogans, bits of information and abbreviated or symbolic messages— a culture of instant but shallow communication. It is not just a culture of gratification and consumption, but one of immediacy and superficiality, in which the very notion of "news" erodes in a tide of formulaic mass entertainment.

It has created, scheuer said, "a society that thrives on simplicity and disdains complexity." Because the news media are expensive big businesses, reporters and producers increasingly go with sensational aspects of a story to draw readers and viewers and make a profit for their newspapers and broadcast outlets. Let's face it: Not only does sensationalism draw audiences, the stories also are generally exciting to cover and they don't require a lot of preparation, just a live camera at the scene for "reality" TV. But while the sensational is colorful and exciting, it often eclipses "real" news of substance.

The OJ. Simpson case is an illustration. The public was fascinated with the story because the defendant was a well-known, popular football superstar accused of two horrific murders. But, with the exception of discussions about the problem of spousal abuse, some of the major issues—such as the question of unequal justice before the law depending on the size of one's bank account or the color of one's skin—went largely unreported. The same pattern continued with the Kobe Bryant rape case, the Martha Stewart trial, and Michael Jackson.

Overblown coverage resulted from the deaths of Princess Diana and John E Kennedy Jr., President Clinton's indiscretions, the saga of the California congressman and his intern, and the D. C. sniper. This is not to say that the events did not deserve coverage—just not saturation coverage. More important events occurring around the nation and the world were shunted aside because only so much airtime was available on radio and television and only so many column inches in newspapers and magazines.

A Crisis of Confidence

"Instead of distinguishing ourselves from tabloids and from pseudo news programs like 'Hard Copy' or from Web gossip mongers like Matt Drudge, we are starting to resemble them," press critic Tim Rosensteil declared. Part of the problem is the necessity for visuals to feed TV's needs. Because television has been the primary source of information for the past several decades, it sets the agenda for all media. Former *New York Times* managing editor Max Frankel, for instance, expressed his concern about "the murder, mayhem and medicine that passes for news on local television," which, he said, was "pushing all journalism into trashy territory." Many critics argue that the dividing line between entertainment and reality has blurred and merged, adversely affecting the quality of news and information we receive. Consider these statistics from a report by the Pew Research Center for the People and the Press:

- The number of Americans who say they enjoy the news continues to decline. In 1995, 54 percent said they enjoyed keeping up with the news a lot. That number fell to 50 percent in 1998 and to 45 percent in 2000.
- More than six in 10 people now watch television news with their remote control in hand. Overall, news consumption remains largely event-driven. Slightly less than half of the public actually follows national

news on a regular basis; fully 50 percent tune in only for significant or interesting events.

- Fully 64 percent of Americans say they only follow international events closely when something interesting or important is happening; just 33 percent pay close attention most of the time.
- A substantial portion, 28 percent of the respondents, said they preferred news that focuses on their own concerns and interests rather than general news information. This group is less educated, male and young.
- Crime, health, sports, community news and religion are followed most closely by Americans. News about political figures and Washington events continues to rank low on the public's list of news stories.

Influence of the Bottom Line

One aspect of sensationalism is checkbook journalism, the practice of paying for stories that people formerly gave freely out of a desire for publicity or to share information. The payment of standard talent fees is not considered unethical, nor is a network program's picking up the expenses of a guest whose appearance will enhance the show. What is troubling is a person selling his or her story to the highest bidder or arranging with several tabloid-TV programs to air sleaze and gossip, especially if those people are witnesses in a trial or legal proceeding. This type of coverage detracts from important happenings and constricts the voices present in the media's marketplace of ideas. If a publication or program can outspend everyone else, soon it will be the only voice left—or else everyone will imitate what it does. How is the public good served by having only one voice or one message?

To some journalists, there has been an unmistakable intrusion of commercial interests into newsroom decisions. In a 2000 study of 300 journalists, four in 10 said they had avoided newsworthy stories or softened the tone to benefit the interests of their news organizations. Majorities in print, especially broadcast media, admitted that newsworthy stories were often or sometimes avoided because they were regarded as too complicated for the average person or because of a lack of audience appeal. More than a third said news that would hurt the interests of a news organization often or sometimes goes unreported. Slightly fewer said the same about stories that could adversely affect advertisers.

Local reporters said they faced more pressure than did major market journalists. Half the investigative reporters in the sample said newsworthy stories were often or sometimes ignored because they conflicted with a news organization's economic interests, and six in 10 said they believed corporate owners exert at least a fair amount of influence on which stories to cover.

Recent corporate mergers in the mass communication industry raise concerns that reporters will be confronted by what has been called journalistic incest when covering their corporate parent and its related holdings. How independent can a broadcast or print journalist be when working on a story detrimental to corporate interests? If nothing else, such reportage will lead viewers and readers to secondguess news judgments, suspect hidden agendas, or raise questions about journalistic credibility.

Robert McChesney of the University of Illinois, who has studied the impact of media consolidation, states the problem more bluntly: "The preponderance of U. S. mass communication is controlled by less than two dozen enormous profitmaximizing corporations, which receive much of their income from advertising placed largely by other corporations." One result is that newsroom managers increasingly find their pay, and even their job survival, tied to profits and meeting shareholder expectations. This results, says media critic Jeffrey Scheuer, "in a lack of diversity, self-censorship, and other troubling conflicts and compromises between news values and commercial interests."

At times, the print and broadcasting media speak with one voice, when all of them—the *New York Times*, *Washington Post*, and TV networks—cover the same story the same way. This phenomenon is known as herd or pack journalism, in which other media outlets adopt the agenda set by the leaders. Smaller papers, bureaus, and broadcasters have trouble avoiding this practice. What reporter would tell his or her editor that the *New York Times* or the networks are following the wrong trail and that the editor's paper or station should do something different? Increasingly, reporters seem to be covering more sensational trivia at the expense of important news; however, when those stories draw readers and viewers, news producers are hard-pressed to argue that other things should take precedence.

Public relations, too, has been accused of being overly concerned with image or "spin control," even charged at times with downright misrepresentation. Thus, for seemingly good reasons, politicians and a large segment of the public are angry at "The Media." That anger is unfortunate because most of those who work diligently in print, broadcasting and public relations have high personal and ethical values and take seriously their responsibilities in the information process.

What all this means to those aspiring to careers in print, broadcast or online journalism or public relations is that economic realities are constraints that must be faced on a daily basis. The challenge is to provide meaningful news and information for audiences despite those pressures.

ROLE OF THE NEWS MEDIA

Consider the role of the print or broadcast reporter, who often has the unenviable task of going into a conflict-ridden situation to determine what is and is not true, of identifying the good guys and the bad guys. When making such judgment calls, a reporter is likely to alienate at least half the participants. If the news story says the majority of those involved are wrong, or if the reported facts leave that impression, then the reporter has made almost everyone angry. That's when the charges begin to fly about media bias.

For example, photographs and headlines can cause problems because of their juxtaposition with other stories or because they have been altered in some manner, especially with new video and computer technology. Tampering with a photograph can cause a crisis of public confidence, even if a lawsuit does not result—consider the furor a few years ago when Time magazine darkened the features of OJ. Simpson on its cover when he was first arrested. Even the prestigious *National Geographic* opened itself to criticism when it moved one of Egypt's Great Pyramids to create better photo composition on its cover.

Journalists, of course, are not perfect; they do make mistakes and can be biased. However, most mistakes are inadvertent, not deliberate. Often, people being covered cause part of the problem: If they don't tell reporters something that they should know, then the story is incomplete, like a jigsaw puzzle put together without all the pieces. Sometimes people lie to reporters or at least give the truth a good deal of elasticity. Other times, people are honest, but their honesty reflects bigotry or hostility that shows up in the news report. When it does, the public frequently concludes that reporters are distorting the truth. Also, it's human nature to view it as distortion when reporters criticize someone or something we approve of but to call it hard-hitting, interpretative reporting when we agree with a reporter's perspective. Actually, a greater danger may be that reporters become co-opted by the people they cover, a process called acculturation, denned in Chapter 1 as the tendency of reporters to identify with and take on the belief system of those they cover.

An Ideal Media Role

Although reporters should maintain the traditional "watchdog" role with news sources, reporters and sources should be respectful rather than argumentative adversaries. A novice reporter would be well advised to presume good will and openness on the part of those being covered, unless the news source has acted differently. Too many reporters approach all news sources with a level of distrust perhaps appropriate for politicians and industrial polluters but inappropriate for people in less combative environments.

This philosophy of "reporter as attack dog" makes its way into local news reporting as well, generating a lot of unnecessary hostility between news sources and inexperienced reporters who are following a stereotype.

Professional Ethics

The major professional communication organizations each have their own code of ethical standards. Newspaper organizations were among the first, with the Canons of Journalism adopted by the American Society of Newspaper Editors in 1923, in part as a response to the tabloid excesses of the Jazz Journalism era of the 1920s. Today, the Society of Professional Journalists Code of Ethics reflects similar highminded sentiments. The preamble says that the duty of journalists is to serve the truth and that agencies of mass communication are carriers of public discussion and information, responsible for distributing news and enlightened opinion to serve the general welfare. Journalists, the code says, must be free of obligation to any interest other than the public's right to know the truth. News reports must be objective, free of opinion or bias, and represent all sides of an issue. Journalists are to show respect for the dignity, privacy, rights and well-being of people encountered in the course of gathering and presenting the news.

Similar sentiments and language appear in the Code of Broadcast News Ethics of the Radio-Television News Directors Association. It says that the responsibility of broadcast journalists is to gather and report information of importance and interest accurately, honestly and impartially. Sensationalism is to be rejected and listeners and viewers are not to be misled or deceived. Broadcast reporters are to avoid conflict of interest, respect the right to a fair trial, and be concerned about the dignity, privacy and well-being of people with whom they interact.

The vast majority of public relations professionals, like print and broadcast journalists, have high ethical standards reflecting a commitment to truth, accuracy and a concern for the public well-being. Many public relations practitioners are members of professional organizations such as the Public Relations Society of America (PRSA) or the International

Association of Business Communicators (IABC). These organizations have codes of ethics dealing specifically with matters relating to news and journalism. The PRSA code, for example, calls for public relations practitioners to serve the public interest, exemplify high standards of honesty and integrity, deal fairly with the public, adhere to the highest standards of accuracy and truth, not knowingly disseminate false or misleading information, and act promptly to correct erroneous communications. IABC members pledge to practice honest, candid and timely communication, foster the free flow of essential information in accordance with the public interest, disseminate accurate information, and promptly correct any erroneous communication.

The code of the Canadian Public Relations Society similarly binds members to the highest standards of honesty, accuracy and truth, and requires members to avoid disseminating false or misleading information. The code of the International Public Relations Association pledges the following: A member shall conduct his or her professional activities with respect to the public interest and for the dignity of the individual. A member shall not engage in practice that tends to corrupt the integrity of channels of public communication, or intentionally disseminate false or misleading information. A member shall at all times seek to give a faithful representation of the organization that he or she serves.

It is commonly understood that many public relations practitioners are advocates for someone or something. Most difficulties arise when those they represent stray from truth or objectivity. Then, it is up to the public relations professional to deal with the consequences. At times, often due to privacy statutes, the spokesperson is constrained by specific directions *not* to provide certain information, even when reporters can clearly see that he or she knows the answers to their questions. Under those conditions, everyone appears tainted.

Despite the challenges, you should enter the communication business with high ethical standards and stick to them. Yes, ethical decisions sometimes are not obvious and clear-cut, and trade-offs must be made. However, if you get into a situation where you are constantly asked to compromise your values of fairness and objectivity, find work someplace else. To go against your own ethical standards takes an emotional toll; it's not worth destroying the best in you.

Legal Pitfalls

The remainder of this section provides an overview of legal challenges facing journalists, broadcasters and public relations practitioners. To deepen your understanding of the law and the difficulties that reporters face, consider taking a law and ethics course, even if it's not a requirement of your communication program. If you are already working in the field and have no previous exposure to media law, make it a point to enroll in a law course at a nearby college or university or at least acquire a good communication law textbook and become familiar with its provisions.

Reporters and broadcasters do not have a greater legal right of access to news events than other members of the public. Although courts have struck down some rules barring or limiting access of reporters, the U. S. Supreme Court ruled in 1999 that law enforcement officers who invite journalists to go with them on raids violate the Fourth Amendment right to privacy of those being raided. Media representatives are permitted at the scene of breaking news events, but journalists can be arrested for refusing the order of police or fire officials to leave the scene of accidents, fires or disasters. There is even less latitude regarding reporters' access to what are termed "quasi-public" facilities such as military bases and nuclear power plants.

The Supreme Court has ruled that the First Amendment does not protect news *gathering to* the same degree it guarantees the *publication* of most truthful, lawfully acquired information. The public does not have a right to information, the court has ruled, and the public's right to know can be balanced against at-times conflicting social needs. Generally, the media may record or take photographs of what is seen, said, and heard in public and semipublic places, but harassment or overzealous surveillance is not permitted.

Libel and Defamation

Reporters get into the most legal trouble over libel, defined as a false, defamatory (damaging to one's reputation) statement published or broadcast to a third party that holds someone up to public hatred, contempt or ridicule and, in the case of a business, causes monetary damages. What makes matters difficult is that each state is free to enact its own libel statutes, subject to First Amendment constraints. Because each state's laws differ, media writers need to be familiar with the nuances of libel law where they work.

Defamation involves a fault (negligence or recklessness of some type), and compensation for defamation is based on the amount of harm a jury determines was done. Libel was traditionally defined as printed defamation and slander as spoken defamation, but the courts have held broadcasters subject to libel law even though the defamatory material was spoken.

During World War II, a popular slogan warned shipyard workers, Loose lips sink ships. This message was an appeal to be careful and avoid talking with strangers, who might be spies, about shipyard work or the movements of ships. Reporters should have their own version of this adage: "Sloppy reporting causes libel suits." It is easy to slip and make a mistake that will cost your organization thousands of dollars, and possibly ruin your career as well.

The Chilling Effect of Libel Suits

The cost of libel suits has gone up tremendously in the past 20 years. Damages being sought are often in the millions of dollars, even against small- to mediumsized newspapers and broadcast outlets. The cost of libel insurance has steadily increased, and the cost of defending against a libel suit can run into the hundreds of thousands of dollars. The fact that more than two thirds of libel verdicts against news organizations are reversed on appeal is of small consolation.

The threat of libel action can exert what has been called a chilling effect on news coverage, as reporters become more cautious about what is printed and broadcast because they or their news organizations are fearful of big-money lawsuits. ABC News, for example, retracted a 1995 report saying tobacco companies "spiked" cigarettes with nicotine after Philip Morris and R. J. Reynolds Co. filed a $10 billion lawsuit against the network. In its settlement with the cigarette companies, ABC apologized twice in prime time and paid the plaintiffs' legal expenses, estimated at $15 million to $17 million.

In another case involving ABC, the network was ordered to pay the Food Lion supermarket chain $5.5 million in punitive damages after two reporters with concealed cameras produced an expose accusing several of the chain's stores of selling tainted meat and poultry. The facts of the story were not at issue. Instead, the jury awarded damages based upon the reporting methods, having determined that the network committed fraud, trespass and breach of loyalty—in part for the way in which the two producers misrepresented themselves to get jobs as clerks at the food chain. Even though a U. S. district court judge reduced the punitive damage award to $315,000 and an appeals court cut the amount to only $2, the case tied up the network in years of costly litigation.

One can only speculate about how many of the recent corporate scandals were suspected by national media long before they burst into public view but weren't reported because tips and hunches wouldn't be enough to satisfy a libel jury. It seems reasonable to assume that the threat posed by big-money lawsuits has deterred smaller market broadcast outlets and newspapers from pursuing undercover investigative pieces and controversial news stories that cannot be completely verified, or from doing stories about actions that can be interpreted in various ways.

For example, a newspaper in Minnesota lost a libel judgment filed by a public works supervisor who, the paper said, ordered a city work crew to pave a road where he owned the only house. A lawyer for the state newspaper association warned that the decision "will eliminate a large chunk of people from scrutiny by the press, and that chunk of people are middle-level government officials, many of whom wield great power over us and have authority to spend tons of money. "

The chilling effect means that the public does not get the news and information it should have. Instead, the fear of being sued, or of not being backed by news organizations when stories are questionable, has effectively pulled the teeth from the media watchdog.

Allegations in News Stories

"The news stories that generate the most claims of injury to reputation," the Associated Press says in its libel primer, "result from publication of charges of crime, immorality, incompetence or inefficiency." Although truth is generally an absolute defense against a libel suit and those bringing the action are obligated to prove falsity, the Associated Press warns that there is no substitute for accuracy. There might be legal challenges even when statements made by someone else have been accurately reported. Court verdicts have gone to plaintiffs (those bringing the suit) .

Public and Private Figures

Courts have always made a distinction between public and private figures. A public figure is either a person of widespread fame or notoriety, with celebrity or special prominence in society, or a public official, elected to public office or appointed to a position and responsible for public policy. Public figures generally have far less recourse to the libel courts than do private citizens, especially if the contested material reflects upon the performance of their official duties. Even personal lives and activities have traditionally been given less protection if those individuals have willingly put themselves in the public spotlight.

A private figure, in contrast, is someone who is neither a famous person nor a public official. In libel suits, private figures are held to an easier standard, having to prove only that the reporter failed to act with reasonable care in determining whether a story was true or false. The process of defining who is a private figure is still evolving and presents a gray area in communication law. The law recognizes limited or vortex public figures, people who are public figures only in matters of public controversy in which they voluntarily participate. They must prove actual malice only in situations involving their voluntary participation; they are treated as private persons in other matters.

An example is the previously mentioned Minnesota case of the public official who ordered a city work crew to pave a road where he owned the only house. Although a subsequent city investigation called the improvements "highly unusual" and said the official's action "created the appearance of impropriety," a jury said the news stories and related editorials were "provably false" and ruled that the official was a private figure, thus making possible the awarding of damages.

Fair Comment

The media often comment about matters of public importance or interest, especially in reviews of public performances or those who offer their services to the public. The courts have traditionally permitted fair comment as long as factual material is truthful and opinions are stated without malice or prospect of gain. Determining "truth" is often difficult, however; reviewers generally mix fact and opinion. Lawsuits may result, for instance, if an unfair negative review forced the premature closing of a play or if the loss of business following a bad write-up forces a restaurant to close. In theory, those who present themselves to the public implicitly agree to accept public comment (a role traditionally given to the media), but because some have sued anyway, media writers should exercise caution.

Most libel cases involve newspapers or broadcast media, but news releases and other public relations vehicles are not immune from charges of defamation. For the public relations practitioner, the same law applies, although the application may be somewhat different. Public relations and advertising professionals sometimes face problems with what is known as misappropriation: taking what belongs to someone else and using it unfairly for monetary gain. An example is the use, without permission, of look-alikes or sound-alikes of famous people or celebrities. Public relations practitioners should probably be more concerned about copyright violations and trademark infringements than traditional libel- and privacy-law problems because they are not as likely to run into the same type of situations as are news reporters.

Privacy

One complaint of readers and viewers is that the media violate personal privacy, whether with exposes of politicians' sexual peccadilloes from years before or intrusions on the space of celebrities and private individuals. An American Society of Newspaper Editors survey found that more than half of the respondents said that the press has no right to invade the privacy of politicians. The public places a high value on protecting the privacy of people in situations that journalists consider "news." In fact, many people believe that journalists are willing to hurt people just to publish a story.

The Supreme Court has interpreted the Constitution as offering privacy protection to private citizens, and lawsuits in this area focus on the issue of whether a person has been singled out for attention without his or her consent. State laws vary but, in general, they protect people from being exposed against their will to the glare of publicity. The media are prevented from revealing private facts about people, especially when the information is personal and not of legitimate public concern. Protection extends to a person's finances, sexuality and health, unless it can be shown that such information is newsworthy.

There can be controversy even in the case of public figures, such as when *USA Today* revealed a fewyears ago that popular tennis star Arthur Ashe had AIDS. One of the most sensitive issues in publication is the identification of sex-crime victims, still considered confidential information in some states or jurisdictions. Other problem areas concern the debate over whether information should be published about convicted sex offenders being released from prison into a community, and whether television should broadcast pictures of "deadbeat dads" or men who have been arrested for soliciting prostitutes. Faced with invasion-of-privacy charges, the media can defend themselves by showing that either the person gave consent or the information is newsworthy and thus belongs in the public domain. Explicit consent refers to signed or taped releases. The courts presume implicit consent when it is apparent that a person willingly exposed himself or herself to publicity, such as by posing for a photograph or participating in a public rally. The courts generally consider on-the-spot news reporting as being in the public domain, although follow-up reporting is not necessarily exempt.

Like reporters, public relations practitioners are concerned with privacy issues. They also face problems in preparing material for internal media and in providing information to external news media. Such was the case of the public relations director for a company under investigation for mismanaging a government contract. Allegation had been made by a "whistle-blower," a former company employee, who told the district attorney that the company had handled the contract illegally. The public relations director could not point out that the former employee may have had a grievance against the company or that he had made similar allegations against a prior employer. By law, the director could only verify the accuser's name, job title and dates of employment. She was criticized by reporters and fellow employees for sitting on information about the case—which, of course, she was, because the law prevented her from doing anything else.

Accusations of Wrongdoing

If a potentially libelous statement is published or broadcast, and the statement is drawn to the attention of the reporter by a person who believes he or she has been libeled, the reporter should *never try* to solve the problem alone. The reporter should not admit guilt but rather take the matter to the editor or news director. (The worst your boss can do is fire you!) Often, people who have been libeled merely want to clear their name. In that case, the reporter and editor, generally in concert with the attorney for the paper or station, can work out a compromise to resolve.

Free Press-Fair Trial

Among its implicit provisions, the First Amendment to the Constitution protects a journalist's right to report news about criminal cases. The Sixth Amendment provides a defendant's right to a speedy, fair and impartial public trial. Often, the two amendments have collided. Which is better for society: to have full disclosure through reporting, even though it may taint prospective jurors, or to limit the scope of criminal justice proceedings to better ensure that an innocent person is not wrongly convicted?

Media involvement in sensational murder trials is not new in the United States. One hundred years ago, Lizzie Borden of Fall River, Mass., was acquitted in the hatchet murder of her father and stepmother, in part because of a sympathetic climate generated by maudlin and sentimental newspaper stories about her. New York City tabloid newspaper coverage of the lurid details of the turn-of-the-century trial of Harry Thaw, who killed famed architect Stanford White, his wife's former lover—prompted President Theodore Roosevelt to ask for censorship, and Canada made it a crime to print accounts of the Thaw trial. The *New York Daily News caused* controversy in the 1920s—and broke circulation-sales records—when it published a full front-page picture of convicted murderer Ruth Snyder receiving a fatal jolt of current in the Sing Sing Prison electric chair. The trial of Bruno Hauptmann, accused in the kidnapping and murder of the infant son of aviation hero Charles Lindbergh, became a media circus in the mid-1930s. Photographers were so unruly that the American Bar Association later enacted Canon 35 of its Code of Standards, effectively keeping cameras out of courtrooms for the next 30 years.

Cameras in the Courtroom

In the 1960s, two cases seemed to portend that cameras would stay out of courtrooms. One of the most sensational murder trials before the O. J. Simpson case was that of Sam Sheppard in 1954. He told police a "bushy haired intruder," not he, had killed his pregnant wife. Local newspapers jumped on the story with sensational pretrial publicity, and one editorial demanded that police "stop stalling" and charge Sheppard with the murder. During the trial, which drew national attention and coverage, the judge exercised little control over the disruptive media in the courtroom. After Sheppard had served 11 years in prison, the Supreme Court reversed his conviction on grounds that he did not receive a fair trial because of prejudicial publicity and a circus-like atmosphere. The case was retried and Sheppard was acquitted, but he died shortly thereafter.

The Supreme Court also reversed the fraud conviction of Texas grain dealer Billie Sol Estes, a case made noteworthy because he was a protege of then-Vice President Lyndon Johnson. The court said that the mere presence of television cameras in the courtroom during pretrial motions and his trial violated his Sixth Amendment rights. The court's ruling caused state courts, which had begun to permit television coverage, to rethink their position. Many terminated TV access to courtrooms, especially in sensational cases, to avoid a reversal based on the *Estes* decision.

In the late 1970s, the Supreme Court ruled in a Florida case that the Constitution does not prohibit states from experimenting with cameras in courts, as long as the defendant's right to a fair trial is not affected. Cameras eventually came into courtrooms in most states, although cameras are not permitted in federal courts. Some jurisdictions restrict televised trial coverage; others allow it with the permission of the judge or defendants.

The executive director of the Reporters Committee for Freedom of the Press, Jane Kirtley, made the following strong appeal for cameras in the courtroom after the O. J. Simpson case: A camera in the courtroom is the logical extension of the First Amendment right of the media, the public's surrogate, to attend a criminal trial. It provides a more accurate version of court proceedings than a third-person account can ever hope to do. A fixed, silent camera in the courtroom commits no excesses, but instead neutralizes inaccurate and sensational reports based on out-of-court interviews. It doesn't intimidate witnesses or jurors, but helps keep them alert and mindful of their sacred mission. Nor does a camera cause flamboyant behavior on the part of lawyers, judges or witnesses. It simply records and exposes it to public scrutiny when it occurs.

The New Hampshire Supreme Court recently ruled that cameras in the courtroom should be the state standard. "The use of cameras by the electronic media is merely an extension of the reporting function of the more traditional arms of the press," the decision declared. Judges should limit electronic media coverage only if there is a "substantial likelihood" of harmful consequences, and only when no other practical alternative is available. The ruling came after the judge in a murder case said the defendant's right to a fair trial would be infringed by cameras. After the defendant pleaded guilty, the *Boston Globe,* a television station and the New Hampshire Association of Broadcasters challenged the ban.

There is always a question about whether publicity prevents a fair trial. None of the convictions of the Watergate defendants was overturned in the 1970s, even though their actions were the subject of massive publicity during congressional hearings on the matter. The conviction of newspaper heiress Patty Hearst on bank robbery charges in a case that drew national and, at times, sympathetic media coverage, was not overturned, nor were cases with other celebrated defendants. In fact, experience has shown that a defendant can be acquitted by an unsequestered jury despite massive unfavorable media attention to the case.

Taking no chances, attorneys in the D. C. sniper case asked that cameras be excluded from the trial in Virginia. Prosecution and defense attorneys argued against live television coverage, saying that it would potentially affect how witnesses testified and their conduct in court, and could potentially taint jurors in other jurisdictions where the accused face charges. The judge ruled that electronic coverage could intimidate witnesses, affect testimony, cause counsel to behave differently, and make it difficult for jurors to follow the court's instructions.

Judges and the Media

Although judges have the authority to control the behavior of the press within the courtroom—the judge in the O. J. Simpson case once ordered two reporters expelled for continually talking—courts generally cannot prohibit news media from publishing any details they legally uncover about a case. In an effort to restrict the spread of information about pretrial motions—generally concerning evidence, a defendant's mental condition or whether to try a juvenile offender as an adult— judges have sought to close proceedings to the public. The Supreme Court ruled, however, that courts can be closed for only the most compelling of reasons, after alternatives have been considered, and only for as long as necessary.

In a series of decisions, the Supreme Court upheld the right of the news media— a segment of the public—to attend trials and judicial proceedings. To minimize the possibility of prejudicial publicity, trial judges can restrict court officers and law enforcement personnel from making out-of-court statements to the news media about a case (called a gag order by reporters) or direct that only limited information may given to the media. News media can also be prohibited from interviewing jurors about deliberations after the trial has concluded.

Voluntary Press-Bar Guidelines

Over the years, the U. S. Justice Department, the American Bar Association and various press-bar advisory panels have issued guidelines about information that reporters should not use in stories. Journalists are asked to restrict reports about confessions, prior criminal records, results of tests conducted during investigations, rumor or hearsay about a defendant's habits or lifestyle, speculation about potential witnesses, evidence or testimony, speculation by officials, and any sensational or inflammatory statements. The rationale is that unsubstantiated allegations often surface but are never introduced in court as evidence—as happened before the O. J. Simpson case went to trial in 1995 and during the Oklahoma

City federal building bombing case. If the news media report those allegations, it is argued, potential jurors may find them difficult to disregard, even if the allegations are not introduced during the trial.

The effectiveness of these and similar guidelines is debatable, of course. With the proliferation of media channels in recent years, not to mention the impact of the Internet on news dissemination, it is increasingly difficult for mainstream media to avoid publishing some of the same material as the sensationalist tabloids or questionable online sources. In the O. J. Simpson case, for instance, the *New York Times* and TV networks were printing and airing some of the tabloid allegations, whether or not their truth could be verified. The economics of the media marketplace (discussed previously in this chapter) increasingly dictates that media outlets will go with sensational aspects of a case to draw audiences. Such sensationalism is not conducive to following guidelines to ensure a fair trial.

Some would argue that the only way to ensure a fair and speedy trial is to exclude television cameras, as a South Carolina judge did in the 1995 trial of Susan Smith, accused of murder in the drowning death of her two small sons. Although the case had sensational elements, her trial lasted only several weeks. Simpson's legal struggle in the criminal case went on for more than a year.

Police and the Media

Law officers, as well as defense and prosecuting attorneys, continue to use the news media to present their cases to the public, despite judicial admonitions to the contrary. Believing they have cracked an important case, police may attempt to manipulate public opinion to pressure prosecutors into moving for an indictment or to reassure a jittery public, as happened once the D. C.-area snipers were reported captured. In fact, it was revealed in the sniper case that law enforcement officers were attempting to communicate with the perpetrators through the news media. Accused conspirators in the September 11,2001, terrorist attacks were subjected to prejudicial publicity, as occurred when others charged with terrorist activity were taken into custody.

The criminal justice system is sometimes part of an elaborate ritual, and unless a news reporter is aware of the dynamics involved, justice may not be served. Defense attorneys will attempt to create doubt about evidence or witnesses or make a bid for sympathy for the defendant. Prosecuting attorneys try to create pressure for high bail or maximum charges. A new form of prejudicial publicity takes advantage of television's need for visuals in covering the arrest on fraud charges of CEOs of nowbankrupt companies. Instead of permitting those charged to quietly turn themselves in, the usual practice, federal officers staged early morning raids, quickly hustling the handcuffed accused past a throng of news reporters. This staged event, called a "perp walk" ("perp" is the abbreviation for *perpetrator),* is usually reserved for more heinous criminal defendants. In this case, however, the government wanted to send a signal that it was going to be tough on corporate crime in order to restore confidence in the nation's business system. Another objective was to stop the slide in the stock market. In one case, the tactic worked. On the day the top executives of cable giant Adelphia were arrested and paraded before news cameras, the stock market jumped nearly 500 points!

On the other hand, in many jurisdictions, police, courts and media have agreed on voluntary cooperative measures to reduce conflict and minimize harmful pretrial publicity. Most working reporters would say that police generally arrest the right person for a crime and innocent people are seldom convicted. But there *are* cases when the wrong person is picked up or found guilty. However infrequent those cases might be, reporters need to remember that under the American justice system, the accused is considered innocent until proven guilty in a court of law.

Reporters should write stories with a presumption of innocence and should never allow themselves to identify with police, prosecution or defense. Journalists should report the news with as little sensationalism and speculation as possible.

They should treat the defendant impartially and the victim, or the family of a victim, with consideration, making every effort to avoid "victimizing the victim" by unnecessary, intrusive or insensitive coverage.

ACCESS TO INFORMATION

Although reporters try to stay out of the criminal justice process, sometimes they are dragged into legal proceedings because of interviews they conducted, videotapes they made, or photographs they shot. The U. S. Supreme Court ruled that judges can order reporters to turn over notes or names of sources in criminal proceedings. This ruling collides head on with journalists' perceptions of themselves as professionals who are duty-bound not to share such information. Reporters argue that they are not agents of law enforcement and that their ability to report news about crime and corruption often depends on promises of confidentiality.

The Reporters Committee for Freedom of the Press, in an effort to deal with the problem, has released a detailed compendium of reporter's privilege in every state and federal circuit to help journalists quash subpoenas for their work product and testimony. The guide, compiled by lawyers who handle subpoena cases in their jurisdictions, contains summaries of the law and practical advice on fighting subpoenas through trial and appellate courts. The Reporters Committee said that it developed the project because of the number of subpoenas served on journalists nationwide.

Jeopardy of source confidentiality was one of the side issues in the $10 billion libel suit filed by Philip Morris against ABC. The cigarette company subpoenaed the expense reports of the story's producer and reporter, including specifics such as pick-up and drop-off points for taxi rides, in an effort to retrace the journalists' steps and reveal primary sources for the story. Such tactics mean that reporters need to exercise more care and that would-be whistleblowers, not only those in the tobacco industry, will be more cautious about giving out damaging information about organizations—even if such information *ought to* be in the public domain.

In an unusual twist, a Minnesota public relations consultant was awarded $200,000 from newspapers in St. Paul and Minneapolis after his name was published, even though reporters had pledged confidentiality. The consultant gave reporters negative information about an opposing candidate. Editors overruled the reporters and said the public was entitled to know from where the ll th-hour information had come. The consultant was fired and he sued. The case, which went through several reversals, was decided by the Supreme Court, which said that the First Amendment gives no protection to journalists who reveal the names of sources who were promised confidentiality.

Reporters and Their Sources

Law enforcement officials contend that journalists have a civic duty to cooperate with the courts and provide evidence against criminal suspects. After several reporters were jailed for contempt of court in the eamher materials, which maybe subpoenaed as evidence. Generally, reporters' rights groups encourage newspeople to be familiar with the provisions of their state's shield laws and how they are interpreted by the courts before relying too much on the laws to avoid facing unexpected penalties. There is no federal shield law, although the attorney general has adopted guidelines designed to limit the use of subpoenas served on journalists.

The Supreme Court, in the *Stanford Daily* case in 1971, upheld the use of search warrants by law enforcement authorities to make unannounced searches of newsrooms for journalists' notes and photographs. The search warrant was not used widely, but predictable excesses in some jurisdictions led to modification of the policy. The Privacy Protection Act of 1980 restricts the use of warrants to exceptional circumstances to seize information in the possession of public communicators. State and federal statutes encourage the use of subpoenas rather than search warrants.

Several years ago, police in Kansas City, Mo., confiscated a videotape for use in a murder case. The videotape, which a local station had purchased from a tourist, showed a man dragging a woman into an apartment house, recorded the sound of a gunshot, then showed the same man coming out of the building. The station aired the tape on its 6 o'clock news program, and police conducted a knock-and-enter search of the newsroom later that evening. Although station employees offered to give the officers a copy of portions of the tape aired by the station and the name of the person from whom the tape was purchased, police confiscated the original 14-minute tape, saying the evidence was crucial in order to charge the man. A Missouri federal court later ruled that police had violated the Privacy Protection Act and ordered them to pay the station $1,000, the maximum penalty.

The problem continues, however. A legal newspaper in Los Angeles recently sued the district attorney for violation of the Privacy Protection Act after a warrant was served during a corruption investigation. The newsroom was searched for three hours by armed investigators after employees were ordered out of the building. The warrant called for seizure of records showing the identity of a customer who had placed legal advertisements. The complaint asks for a declaration that the search violated the privacy act, and seeks damages for trespass, interference with business, and civil rights violations.

Access to Records and Documents

All states and the federal government have adopted statutes mandating access to many government documents. While some lower courts seal records, official court documents have long been open for inspection and copying by the public and the news media, although the Supreme Court has not specifically declared a constitutional right to inspect or copy materials.

RIGHT TO INFORMATION ACT

The Right to Information Act 2005 is a law enacted by the Parliament of India giving citizens of India access to records of the Central Government and State Governments. The Act applies to all States and Union Territories of India, except the State of Jammu and Kashmir - which is covered under a State-level law. Under the provisions of the Act, any citizen (including the citizens within J&K) may request information from a "public authority" (a body of Government or "instrumentality of State") which is required to reply expeditiously or within thirty days. The Act also requires every public authority to computerise their records for wide dissemination and to proactively publish certain categories of information so that the citizens need minimum recourse to request for information formally.

This law was passed by Parliament on 15 June 2005 and came fully into force on 13 October 2005. Information disclosure in India was hitherto restricted by the Official Secrets Act 1923 and various other special laws, which the new RTI Act now relaxes. Disclosure of Government Information in India is governed by a law enacted during the British rule over large parts of what is now India, the Official Secrets Act of 1889 which was amended in 1923.This law secures information related to security of the State, sovereignty of the country and friendly relations with foreign states, and contains provisions which prohibit disclosure of non-classified information. Civil Service conduct rules and the Indian Evidence Act impose further restrictions on government officials' powers to disclose information to the public. In 1975, the Supreme Court delivered a landmark judgement on the citizen's Right to Know.

State-level Laws

The RTI Laws were first successfully enacted by the state governments — Tamil Nadu (1997), Goa (1997), Rajasthan (2000), Karnataka (2000), Delhi (2001), Maharashtra (2002), Madhya Pradesh (2003), Assam (2002) and Jammu and Kashmir (2004). The Maharashtra and Delhi State level enactments are considered to have been the most widely used. The Delhi and J&K Right to Information Acts are still in force, and the latter was amended in 2008 to incorporate features of the (Central) Right to Information Act, 2005.

Freedom of Information Act

Passage of a national level law, however, proved to be a difficult task. Given the experience of state governments in passing practicable legislation, the Central Government appointed a working group under H. D. Shourie and assigned it the task of drafting legislation. The Shourie draft, in an extremely diluted form, was the basis for the Freedom of Information Bill, 2000 which eventually became law under the Freedom of Information Act, 2002. This Act was severely criticised for permitting too many exemptions, not only under the standard grounds of national security and sovereignty, but also for requests that would involve "disproportionate diversion of the resources of a public authority". There was no upper limit on the charges that could be levied. There were no penalties for not complying with a request for information. The FoI Act, consequently, never came into effective force.

Enactment

The doomed FoI Act led to sustained pressure for a better National RTI enactment. The first draft of the Right to Information Bill was presented to Parliament on 22 December 2004. After intense debate, more than a hundred amendments to the draft Bill were made between December 2004 and 15 June 2005, when the bill finally passed. The Act came fully into effect on 13 October 2005.

Scope

The Act covers the whole of India except Jammu and Kashmir. It is applicable to all constitutional authorities, including the executive, legislature and judiciary; any institution or body established or constituted by an act of Parliament or a state legislature. It is also defined in the Act that bodies or authorities established or constituted by order or notification of appropriate government including bodies "owned, controlled or substantially financed" by government, or non-Government organizations "substantially financed, directly or indirectly by funds" provided by the government are also covered in the Act's ambit.

Private bodies are not within the Act's ambit directly. However, information that can be accessed under any other law in force by a public authority can also be requested for.

In a landmark decision of 30-Nov-2006 ('Saibajit Roy versus DERC') the Central Information Commission also reaffirmed that privatised public utility companies continue to be within the RTI Act- their privatisation notwithstanding. The Act also explicitly overrides the Official Secrets Act and other laws in force on 15-June-2005 to the extent of any inconsistency.

Information

The Act specifies that citizens have a right to:

- Request any information (as defined).
- Take copies of documents.
- Inspect documents, works and records.
- Take certified samples of materials of work.
- Obtain information in form of printouts, diskettes, floppies, tapes, video cassettes or in any other electronic mode or through printouts.

Process

Under the Act, all authorities covered must appoint their Public Information Officer (PIO). Any person may submit a request to the PIO for information in writing. It is the PIO's obligation to provide information to citizens of India who request information under the Act. If the request pertains to another public authority (in whole or part) it is the PIO's responsibility to transfer/forward the concerned portions of the request to a PIO of the other within 5 days. In addition, every public authority is required to designate Assistant Public Information Officers (APIOs) to receive RTI requests and appeals for forwarding to the PIOs of their public authority. The citizen making the request is not obliged to disclose any information except his name and contact particulars. The Act specifies time limits for replying to the request.

- If the request has been made to the PIO, the reply is to be given within 30 days of receipt.
- If the request has been made to an APIO, the reply is to be given within 35 days of receipt.

- If the PIO transfers the request to another public authority (better concerned with the information requested), the time allowed to reply is 30 days but computed from the day after it is received by the PIO of the transferee authority.
- Information concerning corruption and Human Rights violations by scheduled Security agencies (those listed in the Second Schedule to the Act) is to be provided within 45 days but with the prior approval of the Central Information Commission.
- However, if life or liberty of any person is involved, the PIO is expected to reply within 48 hours.

Since the information is to be paid for, the reply of the PIO is necessarily limited to either denying the request (in whole or part) and/or providing a computation of "further fees". The time between the reply of the PIO and the time taken to deposit the further fees for information is excluded from the time allowed.

If information is not provided within this period, it is treated as deemed refusal. Refusal with or without reasons may be ground for appeal or complaint. Further, information not provided in the times prescribed is to be provided free of charge.

For Central Departments as of 2006, there is a fee of Rs. 10 for filing the request, Rs. 2 per page of information and Rs. 5 for each hour of inspection after the first hour. If the applicant is a Below Poverty Card holder, then no fee shall apply. Such BPL Card holders have to provide a copy of their BPL card along with their application to the Public Authority. States Government and High Courts fix their own rules.

7(3) Controversy

There is a raging controversy whether sub-section 7(3) of the Act permits the PIO to demand unprescribed "further fees" from the applicants "representing the cost of providing the information". A full Bench of the Central Information Commission is likely to hear the matter in the second week of December 2008.

Information Defined

In terms of the section 2(f) of the Act, information has been defined as any material in any form including records, documents, memos, e-mails, opinions, advices, press releases, circulars, orders, logbooks, contracts, reports, papers, samples, models, data material held in any electronic form and information relating to any private body which can be accessed by a public authority under any other law for the time being in force.

Right to Information

Under the Act (section 2 (j), right to information includes the right to:

- Inspect works, documents, records.
- Take notes, extracts or certified copies of documents or records.
- Take certified samples of material.
- Obtain information in form of printouts, diskettes, floppies, tapes, video cassettes or in any other electronic mode or through printouts.

What is Not Open to Disclosure?

The following is exempt from disclosure [S.8)]

- Information, disclosure of which would prejudicially affect the sovereignty and integrity of India, the security, strategic, scientific or economic interests of the State, relation with foreign State or lead to incitement of an offence;
- Information which has been expressly forbidden to be published by any court of law or tribunal or the disclosure of which may constitute contempt of court;
- Information, the disclosure of which would cause a breach of privilege of Parliament or the State Legislature;
- Information including commercial confidence, trade secrets or intellectual property, the disclosure of which would harm the competitive position of a third party, unless the competent authority is satisfied that larger

public interest warrants the disclosure of such information;

- Information available to a person in his fiduciary relationship, unless the competent authority is satisfied that the larger public interest warrants the disclosure of such information;
- Information received in confidence from foreign Government;
- Information, the disclosure of which would endanger the life or physical safety of any person or identify the source of information or assistance given in confidence for law enforcement or security purposes;
- Information which would impede the process of investigation or apprehension or prosecution of offenders;
- Cabinet papers including records of deliberations of the Council of Ministers, Secretaries and other officers;
- Information which relates to personal information the disclosure of which has no relationship to any public activity or interest, or which would cause unwarranted invasion of the privacy of the individual (but it is also provided that the information which cannot be denied to the Parliament or a State Legislature shall not be denied by this exemption);
- Notwithstanding any of the exemptions listed above, a public authority may allow access to information, if public interest in disclosure outweighs the harm to the protected interests. (NB: This provision is qualified by the proviso to sub-section 11(1) of the Act which exempts disclosure of "trade or commercial secrets protected by law" under this clause when read along with 8(1)(d)))

Partial Disclosure

Section 10 of the Act allows those parts of the record which are not exempt from disclosure and which can reasonably be severed from parts containing exempt information to be provided.

Exclusions

Central Intelligence and Security agencies specified in the Second Schedule like IB, RAW, Directorate of Revenue Intelligence, Central Economic Intelligence Bureau, Directorate of Enforcement, Narcotics Control Bureau, Aviation Research Centre, Special Frontier Force, BSF, CRPF, ITBP, CISF, NSG, Assam Rifles, Special Service Bureau, Special Branch (CID), Andaman and Nicobar, The Crime Branch-CID-CB, Dadra and Nagar Haveli and Special Branch, Lakshadweep Police. Agencies specified by the State Governments through a Notification will also be excluded. The exclusion, however, is not absolute and these organizations have an obligation to provide information pertaining to allegations of corruption and human rights violations. Further, information relating to allegations of human rights violation could be given but only with the approval of the Central or State Information Commission

Role of the Government

Section 26 of the Act enjoins the central government, as also the state governments of the Republic of India (excluding J&K), to initiate necessary steps to:

- Develop educational programmes for the public especially disadvantaged communities on RTI.
- Encourage Public Authorities to participate in the development and organization of such programmes.
- Promote timely dissemination of accurate information to the public.
- Compile and disseminate a User Guide for the public in the respective official language.
- Publish names, designation postal addresses and contact details of PIOs and other information such as notices regarding fees to be paid, remedies available in law if request is rejected etc.

Power to Make Rules

- The Central Government, State Governments and the Competent Authorities as defined in S.2(e) are vested with powers to make rules to carry out the provisions of the Right to Information Act, 2005. (S.27 & S.28)

Who has the Power to Deal with the Difficulties While Implementing this Act?

- If any difficulty arises in giving effect to the provisions in the Act, the Central Government may, by Order published in the Official Gazette, make provisions necessary/expedient for removing the difficulty. (S.30)

Effects

In the first year of National RTI, 42,876 (not yet official) applications for information were filed to Central (ie.Federal) public authorities. Of these 878 were disputed at the final appellate stage - the Central Information Commission at New Delhi. A few of these decisions have thereafter been mired in further legal controversy in the various High Courts of India. The first stay order against a final appellate decision of the Central Information Commission was granted on 3.May.2006 by the High Court of Delhi in WP(C)6833-35/2006 cited as "NDPL & Ors. versus Central Information Commission & Ors". The Government of India's purported intention in 2006 to amend the RTI Act was postponed after public disquiet.

12

THE PRASAR BHARTI BROADCASTING CORPORATION OF INDIA ACT, 1990

CHAPTER I

PRELIMINARY

1. Short title, extent and commencement.
   (1) This Act may be called the Prasar Bharati (Broadcasting Corporation of India) Act, 1990
   (2) It extends to the whole of India.
   (3) It shall come into force on such date as the Central Government may, by notification, appoint.
2. Definitions.

   In this Act, unless the context otherwise requires:

   a. "Akashvani" means the offices, stations and other establishments, by whatever name called, which, immediately before the appointed day, formed part of or were under the Director-General, All India Radio of the Union Ministry of Information and Broadcasting;

b. "Appointed day" means the date appointed under section 3;

c. "Broadcasting" means the dissemination of any form of communication like signs, signals, writing, pictures, images and sounds of all kinds by transmission of electro-magnetic waves through space or through cables intended to be received by the general public either directly or indirectly through the medium of relay stations and all its grammatical variations and cognate expression shall be construed accordingly;

d. "Board" means the Prasar Bharati Board;

e. "Broadcasting Council" means the Council established under section 14;

f. "Chairman" means the Chairman of the Corporation appointed under section 4;

g. "Corporation" means the Prasar Bharati (Broadcasting Corporation of India) established under section 3;

h. "Doordarshan" means the offices, kendras and other establishments, by whatever name called, which, immediately before the appointed day, formed part of or were under the Directorate-General, Doordarshan of the Union Ministry of Information and Broadcasting;

i. "Elected Member" means a Member elected under section 3;

j. "Executive Member" means the Executive Member appointed under section 4;

k. "Kendra" means any telecasting centre with studios or transmitters or both and includes a relay station;

l. "Member" means a Member of the Board;

m. "Member (Finance)" means the Member (Finance) appointed under section 4;

n. "Member (Personnel)" means the Member (Personnel) appointed under section 4;

o. "Nominated Member" means the Member nominated

by the Union Ministry of Information and Broadcasting under section 3;

p. "Non-lapsable Fund" means the Fund created from the commercial revenues of Akashvani and Doordarshan to meet expenditure on certain schemes;

q. "Notification" means a notificaion published in the official Gazette;

r. "Part-time Member" means a Part-time Member of the Board appointed under section 4, but does not include an ex-officio Member, the Nominated Member or an elected Member;

s. "Prescribed" means prescribed by rules made under this Act;

t. "Recruitment Board" means a board established under sub-section (I) of section 10;

u. "Regulations" means regulations made by the Corporation under this Act;

v. "Station" means any broadcasting station with studios or transmitters or both and includes a relay station;

w. "Whole-time Member" means the Executive Member, Member (Finance) or Member (Personnel);

x. "year" means the financial year.

Chapter II

Prasar Bharati (Broadcasting Corporation of India)

3. Establishment and composition of Corporation.

(1) With effect from such date as the Central Government may by notification appoint in this behalf, there shall be established for the purposes of this Act a Corporation, to be known as the Prasar Bharati (Broadcasting Corporation of India).

(2) The Corporation shall be a body corporate by the name aforesaid, having perpetual succession and a common seal with power to acquire, hold and

dispose of property, both movable and immovable, and tc contract, and shall by the said name sue and be sued.

(3) The headquarters of the Corporation shall be at New Delhi and the Corporation may establish offices, kendras or stations at other places in India and, with the previous approval of the Central Government, outside India.

(4) The general superintendence, direction and management of the affairs of the Corporation shall vest in the Prasar Bharati Board which may exercise all such powers and do all such acts and things as may be exercised or done by the Corporation under this Act.

(5) The Board shall consist of:

(a) A Chairman;

(b) One Executive Member;

(c) One Member (Finance);

(d) One Member (Personnel);

(e) Six Part-time Members;

(f) Director-General (Akashvani), ex-officio;

(g) Director-General (Doordarshan), ex-officio;

(h) one representative of the Union Ministry of Information and Broadcasting, to be nominated by that Ministry; and

(i) Two representatives of the employees of the Corporation, of whom one shall be elected by the engineering staff from amongst themselves and one shall be elected by the other employee from amongst themselves.

(6) The Corporation may appoint such committees as may be necessary for the efficient performance, exercise and discharge of its functions, powers and duties:

Provided that all or a majority of the members of each committee shall be Members and a member of any such committee who is not a Member shall have only the right to attend meetings of the committee and take part in the proceedings thereof, but shall not have the right to vote.

(7) The Corporation may associate with itself, in such manner and for such purposes as may be provided by regulations, any person whose assistance or advice it may need in complying with any of the provisions of this Act and a person so associated shall have the right to take part in the discussions of the Board relevant to the purposes for which he has been associated, but shall not have the right to vote.

(8) No act or proceeding of the Board or of any committee appointed by it under sub-section (6) shall be invalidated merely by reason of——

a. Any vacancy in, or any defect in the constitution of, the Board or such committee; or

b. Any defect in the appointment of a person acting as a Member or a member of such committee; or

c. Any irregularity in the procedure of the Board or such committee not affecting the merits of the case.

4. Appointment of Chairman and other Members.

(1) The Chairman and the other Members, except the ex-officio Members, the Nominated Member and the elected Members shall be appointed by the President of India on the recommendation of a committee consisting of–

a. The Chairman of the Council of States, who shall be the Chairman of the Committee;

b. The Chairman of the Press Council of India established under section 4 of the Press Council Act, 1978; and

c. One nominee of the President of India.

(2) No appointment of a Member shall be invalidated merely by reason of any vacancy in, or any defect

in the constitution of, the committee appointed under sub-section (1).

(3) The Chairman and the Part-time Members shall be persons of eminence in Public life; the Executive Member shall be a person having special knowledge or practical experience in respect of such matters as administration, management, broadcasting, education, literature, culture, arts, music, dramatics or journalism; the Member (Finance) shall be person having special knowledge or practical experience in respect of financial matters and the Member (Personnel) shall be a person having special knowledge or practical experience in respect of personnel management and administration.

(4) The recommendations made by the committee constituted under sub-section (1) shall be binding for the purposes of appointments under this section.

5. Powers and functions of Executive Member.

(1) The Executive Member shall be the Chief Executive of the Corporation and shall, subject to the control and supervision of the Board, exercise such power and discharge such functions of the Board as it may delegate to him.

6. Term of office, conditions of service, etc, of Chairman and other Members.

(1) The Chairman shall be Part-time Member and shall hold office for a term of six years from the date on which he enters upon his office.

(2) The Executive Member, the Member (Finance) and Member (Personnel) shall be Whole-time Members and every such Member shall hold office for a term of six years from the date on which he enters upon his office or until he attains the age of sixty-two years whichever is earlier.

(3) The term of office of Part-time Members shall be six years, but one-third of such Members shall retire on the expiration of every second year.

(4) The term of office of an elected Member shall be two years or till he ceases to be an employee of the Corporation, whichever is earlier.

(5) As soon as may be after the establishment of the Corporation, the President of India may, by order, make such provision as he thinks fit for curtailing the term of office of some of the Part-time Members then appointed in order that one-third of the Members holding office as such Part-time Members shall retire in every second year thereafter.

(6) Where before the expiry of the term of office of a person holding the office of Chairman, or any other Member, a vacancy arises, for any reason whatsoever, such vacancy shall be deemed to be a casual vacancy and the person appointed or elected to fill such vacancy shall hold office for the unexpired period of the term for which his predecessor in office would have held office if such vacancy had not arisen.

(7) The Whole-time Members shall be the employees of the Corporation and as such shall be entitled to such salaries and allowances and shall be subject to such conditions of service in respect of leave, pension (if any), provident fund and other matters as may be prescribed:

Provided that the salaries and allowances and the conditions of service shall not be varied to their disadvantage after their appointment.

(8) The Chairman and Part-time Members shall be entitled to such allowances as may be prescribed.

7. Removal and Suspension of Chairman and Members.

(1) Subject to the provisions of sub-section (3), the Chairman or any other Member, except an ex-officio Member, the Nominated Member and an elected Member shall only be removed from his office by order of the President of India on the ground of misbehaviour after the Supreme Court, on a

reference being made to it by the President, has, on inquiry held in accordance with such procedure as the Supreme Court may by rules provide, reported that the Chairman or such other member, as the case may be, ought, on such ground, be removed.

(2) The President may suspend from office the Chairman or other Member, except an ex-officio Member, the Nominated Member or an elected Member, in respect of whom a reference has been made to the Supreme Court under sub-section (1) until the president has passed orders on receipt of the report of the Superme Court on such reference.

(3) Notwithstanding anything contained in sub-section (1), the President may, by order, remove the Chairman or any Whole-time Member from his office if such Chairman or such Whole-time Member :

(a) Ceases to be a citizen of India; or

(b) Is adjudged an insolvent; or

(c) Engages during his term of office in any paid employment outside the duties of his office; or

(d) Is convicted of any offence involving moral turpitude; or

(e) Is, in the opinion of the President, unfit to continue in office by reason of infirmity of body or mind:

Provided that the President may, by order, remove any part-time Member from his office if he is adjudged an insolvent or is convicted of any offence involving moral turpitude or where he is, in the opinion of the President, unfit to continue in office by reason of infirmity of body or mind.

(4) If the Chairman or any Whole-time Member, except any ex-officio Member, the Nominated Member or any elected Member, is, or becomes in any way concerned or interested in any contract or

agreement made by or on behalf of the Corporation or the Government of India or the Government of a State or, participates in any way in the profit thereof, or in any benefit or emolument arising therefrom than as a member, and in common with other members of an incorporated company, he shall, for the purposes of sub-section (1), be deemed to be guilty of misbehaviour.

(5) If a Part-time Member is, or becomes in any way concerned, or interested in any contract, or agreement made by or on behalf of the Corporation, he shall, for the purposes of sub-section (1), be deemed to be guilty of misbehaviour.

(6) The Chairman or any other Member may resign his office by giving notice thereof in writing to the President of India and on such resignation being accepted, the Chairman or other Member shall be deemed to have vacated his office.

8. Meetings of Board

(1) The Board shall meet at such times and places and shall observe such rules of procedure in regard to the transaction of business at its meetings (including the quorum at meetings) as may be provided by regulations:

Provided that there shall not be less than six meetings every year but three months shall not intervene between one meeting and the next meeting.

(2) A Member shall be deemed to have vacated his office if he absents himself for three consecutive meetings of the Board without the leave of the Chairman.

(3) The Chairman shall preside at the meetings of the Board and if for any reason he is unable to attend any meeting, the Executive Member and in the absence of both, any other Member elected by the Members present at such meeting, shall preside at the meeting.

(4) All questions which come up before any meeting of the Board shall be decided by a majority of the votes of the Members present and voting and, in the event of an equality of votes, the Chairman, or in his absence, the person presiding, shall have and exercise a second or casting vote.

9. Officers and other employees of Corporation.

(1) Subject to such control, restrictions and conditions as may be prescribed, the Corporation may appoint, after consultation with the Recruitment Board, the Director-General (Akashvani), the Director-General (Doordarshan) and such other officers and other employees as may be necessary.

(2) The method of recruitment of such officers and employees and all other matters connected therewith and the conditions of service of such officers and other employees shall be such as may be provided by regulations.

10. Establishment of Recruitment Boards.

(1) The Corporation shall, as soon as may be, after the appointed day and in such manner and subject to such conditions and restrictions as may be prescribed, establish for the purposes of section 9, one or more Recruitment Boards consisting wholly of persons other than the Members, officers and other employees of the Corporation:

Provided that for the purposes of Appointment to the posts carrying scales of pay which are not less than that of a Joint Secretary to the Central Government, the Recruitment Board shall consist of the Chairman, other Members, the ex-officio Members, the Nominated member and the elected Members.

(2) The qualifications and other conditions of service of the members constituting the Recruitment Board and the period for which such members shall hold office, shall be such as may be prescribed.

11. Transfer of service of existing employees to Corporation.

(1) Where the Central Government has ceased to perform any functions which under section 12 are the functions of the Corporation, it shall be lawful for the Central Government to transfer, by order and with effect from such date or dates as may be specified in the order, to the Corporation any of the officers or other employees serving in the Akashvani or Doordarshan and engaged in the performance of those functions:

Provided that no order under this sub-section shall be made in relation to any officer or other employee in the Akashvani or Doordarshan who has, in respect of the proposal of the Central Government to transfer such officer or other employee to the Corporation, intimated within such time as may be specified in this behalf by the Central Government, his intention of not becoming an employee of the Corporation.

(2) The provision of sub-section (1) shall also apply to the members of the Indian Information Service, the Central Secretariat Service or any other service or to persons borne on cadres outside Akashvani and Doordarshan who have been working in Akashvani or Doordarshan immediately before the appointed day:

Provided that where any such member intimates, within the time specified in sub-section

(1) His intention of not becoming an employee of the Corporation but to continue on deputation, he may be allowed to continue on deputation in accordance with such terms and conditions as may be prescribed.

(3) In making an order under sub-section (1), the Central Government shall, as far as may be, take into consideration the functions which the

Akashvani or, as the case may be, Doordarshan has ceased or ceases to perform and the area in which such functions have been or are performed.

(4) An officer or other employee transferred by an order under sub-section (1) shall, on and from the date of transfer, cease to be an employee of the Central Government and become an employee of the Corporation with such designation as the Corporation may determine and shall, subject to the provisions of sub-sections (5) and (6), be governed by such regulations as may be made as respects remuneration and other conditions of service including pension, leave and provident fund and shall continue to be an officer or other employee of the Corporation unless and until his employment is terminated by the Corporation.

(5) Every officer or other employee transferred by an order made under sub-section (1) shall, within six months from the date of transfer, exercise his option, in writing, to be governed –

(a) By the scale of pay applicable to the post held by him in the Akashvani or Doordarshan immediately before the date of transfer or by the scale applicable to the post under the Corporation to which he is transferred;

(b) By the leave, provident fund, retirement of other terminal benefits admissible to employees of the Central Government in accordance with the rules or orders of the Central Government, as amended from time to time, or the leave, provident fund or other terminal benefits admissible to the employees of the Corporation under the regulations, and such option once exercised under this Act shall be final:

Provided that the option exercised under clause (a) by an officer or other employee shall be applicable only in respect of the post under the Corporation to which such officer or other employee is transferred and on appointment to a higher post under the Corporation he shall be eligible only for the scale of pay applicable to such higher post:

Provided further that if immediately before the date of his transfer any such officer or other employee is officiating in a higher post under the Government either in a leave vacancy or any other vacancy of a specified duration, his pay on transfer shall be protected for the unexpired period of such vacancy and thereafter he shall be entitled to the scale of pay applicable to the post under the Government to which he would have reverted or to the scale of pay applicable to the post under the Corporation to which he is transferred, whichever he may opt:

Provided also that when an officer or other employee serving in the Union Ministry of Information and Broadcasting or in any of its attached or subordinate offices is promoted to officiate in a higher post in the Ministry or office subsequent to the transfer to the Corporation of any other officer or employee senior to him in that Ministry or office before such transfer, the officer or other employee who is promoted to officiate in such higher post shall, on transfer to the Corporation, be entitled only to the scale of pay applicable to the post he would have held but for such promotion or the scale of pay applicable to the post under the Corporation to which he is transferred, whichever he may opt.

(6) No officer or other employee transferred by an order made under sub-section (1) or sub-section (2), —

(a) Shall be dismissed or removed by an authority subordinate to that competent to make a similar or equivalent appointment under the Corporation as may be specified in the regulations;

(b) Shall be dismissed or removed or reduced in rank except after an inquiry in which he has been informed of the charges against him and given a reasonable opportunity of being heard in respect of those charges:

Provided that where it is proposed after such inquiry to impose upon him any such penalty, such penalty may be imposed on the basis of evidence adduced during such inquiry and it shall not be necessary to give such person an opportunity of making representation on the proposed penalty:

Provided further that clause (b) shall not apply where an officer or other employee is dismissed or removed or reduced in rank on the ground of conduct which has led to his conviction on a criminal charge.

12. Functions and Powers of Corporation.

(1) Subject to the provisions of this Act, it shall be the primary duty of the Corporation to organise and conduct public broadcasting services to inform, educate and entertain the public and to ensure a balanced development of broadcasting on radio and television.

Explanation — For the removal of doubts, it is hereby declared that the provisions of this section shall be in addition to, and not in derogation, of the provisions of the Indian Telegraph Act, 1885.

(2) The Corporation shall, in the discharge of its functions, be guided by the following objectives, namely:-

(a) Upholding the unity and integrity of the

country and the values enshrined in the Constitution;

(b) Safeguarding the citizen's right to be informed freely, truthfully and objectively on all matters of public interest, national or international, and presenting a fair and balanced flow of information including contrasting views without advocating any opinion or ideology of its own;

(c) Paying special attention to the fields of education and spread of literacy, agriculture, rural development, environment, health and family welfare and science and technology;

(d) Providing adequate coverage to the diverse cultures and languages of the various regions of the country by broadcasting appropriate programmes;

(e) Providing adequate coverage to sports and games so as to encourage healthy competition and the spirit of sportsmanship;

(f) Providing appropriate programmes keeping in view the special needs of the youth;

(g) Informing and stimulating the national consciousness in regard to the status and problems of women and paying special attention to the upliftment of women;

(h) promoting social justice and combating exploitation, inequality and such evils as untouchability and advancing the welfare of the weaker sections of the society;

(i) Safeguarding the rights of the working classes and advancing their welfare;

(j) Serving the rural and weaker sections of the people and those residing in border regions, backward or remote areas;

(k) Providing suitable programmes keeping in view the special needs of the minorities and tribal communities;

(l) Taking special steps to protect the interests of children, the blind, the aged, the handicapped and other vulnerable sections of the people;

(m) Promoting national integration by broadcasting in a manner that facilitates communication in the languages in India; and facilitating the distribution of regional broadcasting services in every State in the languages of that State;

(n) Providing comprehensive broadcast coverage through the choice of appropriate technology and the best utilisation of the broadcast frequencies available and ensuring high quality reception;

(o) Promoting research and development activities in order to ensure that radio and television broadcast technology are constantly updated; and

(p) Expanding broadcasting facilities by establishing additional channels of transmis- sion at various levels.

(3) In particular, and without prejudice to the generality of the foregoing provisions, the Corporation may take such steps as it thinks fit ———

(a) To ensure that broadcasting is conducted as a public service to provide and produce programmes;

h. To establish a system for the gathering of news for radio and television;

i. To negotiate for purchase of, or otherwise acquire, programmes and rights or privileges in respect of sports and other events, films, serials, occasions, meetings, functions or incidents of public interest, for broadcasting and to establish procedures for the allocation of such programmes, rights or privileges to the services;

j. To establish and maintain a library or libraries of radio, television and other materials;

k. To conduct or commission, from time to time, programmes, audience research, market or technical service, which may be released to such persons and in such manner and subject to such terms and conditions as the Corporation may think fit;

l. To provide such other services as may be specified by regulations.

(4) Nothing in sub-sections (2) and (3) shall prevent the Corporation from managing on behalf of the Central Government and in accordance with such terms and conditions as may be specified by that Government the broadcasting of External Services and monitoring of broadcasts made by organisations outside India on the basis of arrangements made for reimbursement of expenses by the Central Government.

(5) For the purposes of ensuring that adequate time is made available for the promotion of the objectives set out in this section, the Central Government shall have the power to determine the maximum limit of broadcast time in respect of the advertisement.

(6) The Corporation shall be subject to no civil liability on the ground merely that it failed to comply with any of the provisions of this section.

(7) The Corporation shall have power to determine and levy fees and other service charges for or in respect of the advertisements and such programmes as may be specified by regulations:
Provided that the fees and other service charges levied and collected under this sub-section shall not exceed such limits as may be determined by the Central Government, from time to time

14. (a) Parliamentary Committee.

(1) There shall be constituted a Committee consisting of twenty-two Members of Parliament, of whom fifteen from the House of the People to be elected

by the Members thereof and seven from the Council of States to be elected by the Members thereof in accordance with the system of proportional representation by means of the single transferable vote, to oversee that the Corporation discharges its functions in accordance with the provision of this Act and, in particular, the objectives set out in section 12 and submit a report thereon to Parliament.

(2) The committee shall function in accordance with such rules as may be made by the Speaker of the House of the People.

14. (b) Establishment of Broadcasting Council, term of office and removal, etc., of members thereof.

(1) There shall be established, by notification, as soon as may be after the appointed day, a Council, to be known as the Broadcasting Council, to receive and consider complaints referred to in section 15 and to advise the Corporation in the discharge of its functions in accordance with the objectives set out in section 12.

(2) The Broadcasting Council shall consist of ———

(i) A President and ten other members to be appointed by the President of India from amongst persons of eminence in public life;

(ii) Four Members of Parliament, of whom two from the House of the People to be nominated by the Speaker thereof and two from the Council of States to be nominated by the Chairman thereof.

(3) The President of the Broadcasting Council shall be a whole-time member and every other member shall be a part-time member and the President or the part-time member shall hold office as such for a term of three years from the date on which he enters upon his office.

(4) The Broadcasting Council may constitute such number of Regional Councils as it may deem

necessary to aid and assist the Council in the discharge of its functions.

(5) The President of the Broadcasting Council shall be entitled to such salary and allowances and shall be subject to such conditions of service in respect of leave, pension (if any), provident fund and other matters as may be prescribed.

Provided that the salary and allowances and the conditions of service shall not be varied to the disadvantage of the President of the Broadcasting Council after his appointment.

(6) The other members of the Broadcasting Council and the members of the Regional Councils constituted under sub-section (4) shall be entitled to such allowances as may be prescribed.

15. Jurisdiction of, and the procedure to be followed by, Broadcasting Council.

(1) The Broadcasting Council shall receive and consider complaints from ——

(i) Any person or group of persons alleging that a certain programme or broadcast or the functioning of the Corporation in specific cases or in general is not in accordance with the objectives for which the Corporation is established;

(ii) Any person (other than officer or employee of the Corporation) claiming himself to have been treated unjustly or unfairly in any manner (including unwarranted invasion of privacy, misrepresentation, distortion or lack of objectivity) in connection with any programme broadcast by the Corporation.

(2) A complaint under sub-section (1) shall be made in such manner and within such period as may be specified by regulations.

(3) The Broadcasting Council shall follow such procedure as it thinks fit for he disposal of complaints received by it.

(4) If the complaint is found to be justified either wholly or in part, the Broadcasting Council shall advise the Executive Member to take appropriate action.

(5) If the Executive Member is unable to accept the recommendation of the Broadcasting Council, he shall place such recommendation before the Board for its decision thereon.

(6) If the Board is also unable to accept the recommendation of the Broadcasting Council, it shall record its reasons therefor and inform the Broadcasting Council accordingly.

(7) Notwithstanding anything contained in sub-section (5) and (6), where the Broadcasting Council deems it appropriate, it may, for reasons to be recorded in writing, require the Corporation to broadcast its recommendations with respect to a complaint in such manner as the Council may deem fit.

CHAPTER III

ASSETS, FINANCES AND ACCOUNTS

16. Transfer of certain assets, liabilities, etc., of Central Government to Corporation. As from the appointed day,——

(a) All property and assets (including the Non-lapsable Fund) which immediately before that day vested in the Central Government for the purpose of Akashvani or Doordarshan or both shall stand transferred to the Corporation on such terms and conditions as may be determined by the Central Government and the book value of all such property and assets shall be treated as the capital provided by the Central Government to the Corporation;

(b) All debts, obligations and liabilities incurred, all contracts entered into and all matters and things engaged to be done by, with or for the Central Government immediately before such day for or in connection with the purposes of Akashvani or Doordarshan or both shall be deemed to have been incurred, entered into and engaged to be done by, with or for the Corporation;

(c) All sums of money due to the Central Government in relation to the Akashvani or Doordarshan or both immediately before such day shall be deemed to be due to the Corporation;

(d) All suits and other legal proceedings instituted or which could have been instituted by or against Central Government immediately before such day for any matter in relation to the Akashvani or Doordarshan or both may be continued or instituted by or against the Corporation.

17. Grants, etc., by Central Government.

For the purposes of enabling the Corporation to discharge its functions efficiently under this Act, the Central Government may, after due appropriation made by Parliament by law in this behalf, pay to the Corporation in each financial year, ——

(i) The proceeds of the broadcast receiver licence fees, if any, as reduced by the collection charges; and

(ii) Such other sums of money as that Government considers necessary, by way of equity, grant-in-aid or loan.

18. Fund of Corporation.

(1) The Corporation shall have its own Fund and all the receipts of the Corporation (including the amounts which stand transferred to the Corporation under section 16) shall be credited to the Fund and all payments by the Corporation shall be made therefrom.

(2) All moneys belonging to the Fund shall be deposited in one or more nationalised banks in such manner as the Corporation may decide.

(3) The Corporation may spend such sums as it thinks fit for performing its functions under this Act and

such sums shall be treated as expenditure payable out of the Fund of the Corporation.

Explanation —— For the purpose of the section, "nationalised bank" means a corresponding new bank specified in the First Schedule to the Banking Companies (Acquisition and Transfer of Undertakings) Act, 1970 or a corresponding new bank specified in the First Schedule to the Banking Companies (Acquisition and Transfer of Undertakings) Act, 1980.

19. Investment of Moneys.

The Corporation may invest its moneys in the securities of the Central Government or any State Government or in such other manner as may be prescribed.

20. Annual Financial Statement of the Corporation.

(1) The Corporation shall prepare, in each financial year, an Annual Financial Statement for the next financial year showing separately ——

(a) The expenditure which is proposed to be met from the internal resources of the Corporation; and

(b) The sums required from the Central Government to meet other expenses, and distinguishing —

(i) Revenue expenditure from other expenditure; and

(ii) Non-plan expenditure from plan expenditure.

(2) The Annual Financial Statement shall be prepared in such form and forwarded at such time to the Central Government for its approval as may be agreed to by that Government and the Corporation.

21. Accounts and Audit of Corporation.

(1) The Corporation shall maintain proper accounts and other relevant records and prepare an annual statement of accounts in such form and in such manner as may be prescribed.

(2) The accounts of the Corporation shall be audited by the Comptroller and Audio-General of India at such intervals as may be specified by him and any expenditure incurred in connection with such audit shall be payable by the Corporation to the Comptroller and Auditor-General.

(3) The Comptroller and Auditor-General and any person appointed by him in connection with the audit of the accounts of the Corporation shall have the same rights and privileges and authority in connection with such audit as the Comptroller and Auditor-General has in connection with the audit of Government accounts and, in particular, shall have the right to demand the production of books, accounts, connected vouchers and other documents and papers and to inspect any of the offices of the Corporation.

(4) The accounts of the Corporation as certified by the comptroller and Auditor-General of India or any other person appointed by him in this behalf together with the audit report thereon shall be forwarded annually to the Central Government and that Government shall cause the same to be laid before each House of Parliament.

22. Corporation not Liable to be Taxed.

Notwithstanding anything contained in the Income-tax Act, 1961, or any other enactment for the time being in force relating to income-tax or any other tax on income, profits or gains, the Corporation shall not be liable to pay any income-tax or any other tax in respect of ———

(a) Any income, profit or gains, accruing or arising out of the Fund of the Corporation or any amount received in that Fund; and

(b) Any income, profits or gains, derived or any amount received, by the Corporation.

Chapter IV

Miscellaneous

23. Power of Central Government to give directions.

    (1) The Central Government may, from time to time as and when occasion arises, issue to the Corporation such directions as it may think necessary in the interests of the sovereignty, unity and integrity of India or the security of the State or preservation of public order requiring it not to make a broadcast on a matter specified in the direction or to make a broadcast on any matter of public importance specified in the direction. (1) The Central Government may, from time to time as and when occasion arises, issue to the Corporation such directions as it may think necessary in the interests of the sovereignty, unity and integrity of India or the security of the State or preservation of public order requiring it not to make a broadcast on a matter specified in the direction or to make a broadcast on any matter of public importance specified in the direction.

    (2) Where the corporation makes a broadcast in pursuance of the direction issued under sub-section (1), the fact that such broadcast has been made in pursuance of such direction may also be announce along with such broadcast, if the Corporation so desires.

    (3) A copy of every direction issued under sub-section (1) shall be laid before each House of Parliament.

24. Power of Central Government to Obtain Information. The Central Government may require the Corporation to furnish such information as that Government may consider necessary.

25. Report to Parliament in certain matters and recommendations as to action against the Board.

    (1) Where the Board persistently makes default in

complying with any directions issued under section 23 or fails to supply the information required under section 24, the Central Government may prepare a report thereof and lay it before each House of Parliament for any recommendation thereof as to any action (including supersession of the Board) which may be taken against the Board.

(2) On the recommendation of the Parliament, the President may by notification supersede the Board for such period not exceeding six month,. as may be specified in the notification:

Provided that before issuing the notification under this sub-section, the President shall give a reasonable opportunity to the Board to show cause as to why it should not be superseded and shall consider the explanations and objections, if any, of the Board.

(3) Upon the publication of the notification under sub-section (2),——

(a) All the Members shall, as from the date supersession, vacate their offices as such;

(b) All the powers, functions and duties which may, by or under the provision of this Act be exercised or discharged by or on behalf of the Board, shall until the Board is reconstituted under this Act, be exercised and discharged by such person or persons as the President may direct.

(4) On the expiration of the period of supersession specified in the notification issued under sub-section (2), the President may reconstitute the Board by fresh appointments, and in such a case any person who had vacated his office under clause (a) of sub-section (3) shall not be disqualified for appointment:

Provided that the President may, at any time before the expiration of the period of supersession, take action under this sub-section.

(5) The Central Government shall cause the notification issued under-sub-section (2) and a full report of the action taken under this section to be laid before each House of Parliament.

26. Office of member not to Disqualify a Member of Parliament.

It is hereby declared that the office of the member of the Broadcasting Council or of the Committee constituted under section 13 shall not disqualify its holder for being chosen as or for being a Member of either House of Parliament.

27. Chairman, Members, etc., to be public servants.

The chairman and every other Member, every officer or other employee of the Corporation and every member of a Committee thereof, the President and every member of the Broadcasting Council or every member of a Regional Council or a Recruitment Board shall be deemed to be a public servant within the meaning of section 21 of the Indian Penal Code.

28. Protection of action taken in good faith.

No suit or other legal proceeding shall lie against the Corporation, the Chairman or any Member or officer or other employee thereof or the President or a member of the Broadcasting Council or a member of a Regional Council or a Recruitment Board for anything which is in good faith done or intended to be done in pursuance of this Act or of any rules or regulations made thereunder.

29. Authentication of Orders and other Instruments of Corporation.

All orders and decisions of the Corporation shall be authenticated by the signature of the Chairman or any other Member authorised by the Corporation in this behalf and all other instruments executed by the corporation shall be authenticated by the signature of the Executive Member or by any officer of the Corporation authorised by him in this behalf.

30. Delegation of Powers

The Corporation may, by general or special order, delegate to the Chairman or any other Member or to any officer of the Corporation, subject to such conditions and limitations, if any, as may be specified therein, such of its powers and duties under this Act as it may deem fit.

31. Annual Report.

(1) The Corporation shall prepare once in every calendar year, in such form and within such times as may be prescribed, an annual report giving a full account of its activities (including the recommendations and suggestions made by the Broadcasting Council and the action taken thereon) during the previous year and copies thereof shall be forwarded to the Central Government and that Government shall cause the same to be laid before each House of Parliament.

(2) The Broadcasting Council shall prepare once in every calendar year, in such form and within such time as may prescribed, an annual report giving a full account of its activities during the previous year and copies thereof shall be forwarded to the Central Government and that Government shall cause the same to be laid before each House of Parliament.

32. Power to make rules.

(1) The Central Government may, by notification, make rules for carrying out the provisions of this Act.

(2) In particular, and without prejudice to generality of the foregoing power, such rules may provide for all or any of the following matters, namely:——

a. The salaries and allowances and conditions of service in respect of leave, pension (if any), provident fund and other matters in relation to the Whole-time Members under sub-section (7) of section 6;

b. the allowances payable to the Chairman and Part-time Members under sub-section (8) of section 6;

c. the control, restrictions and conditions subject to which the Corporation may appoint officers and other employees under subsection (1) of section 9; the manner in which and the conditions and restrictions subject to which a Recruitment Board may be established under sub-section (1) of section 10;

d. the qualification and other conditions of service of the members of a Recruitment Board and their period of office under sub-section (2) of section 10;

e. the terms and conditions in accordance with which the deputation may be regulated under sub-section (2) of section 11;

f. the salary and allowances and conditions of service in respect of leave, pension (if any), provident fund and other matters in relation to the President of the Broadcasting Council under sub-section (5) of section 14;

g. the allowances payable to other members of the Broadcasting Council and the members of the Regional Councils, under sub-section (6) of section 14;

h. the manner in which the Corporation may invest its moneys under section 19;

i. the form and the manner in which the annual statement of accounts shall be prepared under sub-section (1) of section 21;

j. the form in which, and the time within which the Corporation and the Broadcasting Council shall prepare their annual report under section 31;

k. any other matter which is required to be, or may be, prescribed.

33. Power to make regulations.

(1) The Corporation may, by notification, make regulations not inconsistent with this Act and the rules made thereunder for enabling it to perform its functions under this Act.

(2) Without prejudice to the generality of the foregoing power such regulations may provide for all or/any of the following matters, namely ——

a. The manner in which and the purposes for which the Corporation may associate with itself any person under sub-section (7) of section 3;

b. The times and places at which meetings of Board shall be held and, the procedure to be followed thereat, and the quorum necessary for the transaction of the business at a meeting of the Board under sub-section (1) of section 8;

c. the methods of recruitment and conditions of service of officers and other employees of the Corporation under sub-section (2) of section 9;

d. the remuneration and other conditions of service, including pension, leave and provided fund in relation to an officer or other employee of the Corporation under sub-section (4) of section 11;

e. The authority competent to make certain appointments referred to in clause (a) of sub-section (6) of section 11;

f. the services which may be provided by the Corporation under clause (f) of sub-section (3) of section 12;

g. the determination and levy of fees and other service charges in respect of advertisements and other programmes under sub-section (7) of section 12;

h. the manner in which and the period within

which complaints may be made under sub-section (2) of section 15;

i. any other matter in respect of which provision is, in the opinion of the Corporation, necessary for the performance of its functions under this Act:

Provided that the regulations under clause (c) or clause (d) shall be made only with the prior approval of the Central Government.

34. Rules and regulations to be laid before Parliament.

Every rule and every regulation made under this Act shall be laid as soon as may be after it is made, before each House of Parliament, while it is in session for a total period of thirty days which may be comprised in one session or in two or more successive sessions, and if, before the expiry of the session immediately following the session or the successive session aforesaid, both Houses agree in making any modification in the rule or regulation, or both Houses agree that the rule or regulation should not be made, the rule or regulation shall thereafter have effect only in such modified form or be of no effect, as the case may be; so, however, that any such modification or annulment shall be without prejudice to the validity of anything previously done under that rule or regulation.

35. Power to remove difficulties

If any difficulty arises in giving effect to provisions of this Act, the Central Government may, by order, published in the official Gazette, make such provisions, not inconsistent with the provisions of this Act, as it may deem necessary, for the removal of the difficulty:

Provided that no such order shall be made after the expiry of a period of three years from the appointed day.

Bibliography

Abbott, Randy. "A Critical Analysis of the Library-Related Literature Concerning Censorship in Public Libraries and Public School Libraries in the United States During the 1980s." Project for degree of Education Specialist, University of South Florida, December 1987

Associated Press . *Broadcast News Handbook: A Manual of Techniques and Practices*. New York: McGraw-Hill, 2001

Bell, A. and Garrett, P. (eds) . *Approaches to Media Discourse.* Oxford: Blackwell, 1998

Berger, A. A . *Essentials of Mass Communication Theory.* London: Sage, 1995

Branston, G. and Stafford, R .*The Media Studentas Book.* 4th ed. London: Routledge, 2006

Brooks, Brian . *Telling the Story: The Convergence of Print, Broadcast and Online Media.* Boston: Bedford, St. Martin's Press, 2004

Buckingham, D. (ed.) . *Reading Audiences: Young People and the Media.* Manchester: Manchester University Press, 1993

Burress, Lee. *Battle of the Books.* Metuchen, NJ: The Scarecrow Press, 1989

Butler, Judith, "Excitable Speech: A Politics of the Performative", 1997

China criticizes McCain-Dalai Lama meeting". Washington, D.C.: WTOPews.com. July 27, 2008

Curran, J. and Gurevitch, M. (eds) . *Mass Media and Society.* 4th ed. London: Hodder Arnold, 2005

Daft, R.L. & Lengel, R.H .Information richness: a new approach to managerial behavior and organizational design. In: Cummings, L.L. & Staw, B.M. (Eds.), Research in organizational behavior 6, (191-233). Homewood, IL: JAI Press, 1984

Daft, R.L. & Lengel, R.H .Organizational information requirements, media richness and structural design. Management Science 32(5), 554-571, 1986

Daft, R.L., Lengel, R.H., & Trevino, L.K .Message equivocality, media selection, and manager performance: Implications for information systems. MIS Quarterly, 355-366, 1987

DeFleur, Melvin . *Understanding Mass Communication*. New York: Houghton Mifflin Company, 2002

Do journalists have the right to work in Chechnya without accreditation?". Moscow Media Law and Policy Center, March 2000

Dutton, B .*The Media*. London: Longman, 1986

Dyer, R .*Heavenly Bodies: Film Stars and Society*. 2nd ed. London: Routledge, 2004

Eco, U .*Travels in Hyperreality*. London: Picador, 1987

Economist . Videodrome. *Economist*, 7876, 13 August, p. 73, 1994

Foucault, Michel, edited by Lawrence D. Kritzman. *Philosophy, Culture: interviews and other writings 1977–1984* , 1988

Gant, Scott . *We're All Journalists Now: The Transformaiion of the Press and Reshaping of the Law in the Internet Age*. New York: Free Press, 2007

Gauntlett, D .*Media, Gender and Identity: An Introduction*. London: Routledge, 2002

Gauntlett, D .*Moving Experiences: Understanding Television's Influences and Effects*. John Libbey Media, 1995

Gauntlett, D .'Ten Things Wrong With the Media 'Effects' Model. In: Dickinson, R., Harindranath, R. and Linn, O., eds. *Approaches to Audiences: A Reader*. London: Arnold, 1998

Gauntlett, D .*Video Critical: Children, the Environment and Media Power*. Luton : University of Luton Press, 1997

Gauntlett, D. and Annette Hill . *TV Living: Television, Culture and Everyday Life*. London: Routledge, 1999

Gill, R .*Gender and the Media*. Cambridge: Polity, 2007

Grant, B. K. (ed.) . *Film Genre Reader III*. Austin, TX: University of Texas Press, 2003

Hall, S .*Representation: Cultural Representations and Signifying Practice*. London: SAGE/Open University, 1997

Hansen, Terry. *The Missing Times: News media complicity in the UFO cover-up*, 2000

Hendrikson, Leslie. "Library Censorship: ERIC Digest No.

23." ERIC Clearinghouse for Social Studies/Social Science Education, Boulder, Colorado, November 1985

Herman, E. S. and Chomsky, N .*Manufacturing Consent: The Political Economy of the Mass Media*. London: Vintage, 1994

Hermes, J .Media Figures in Identity Construction. In: Alasuutari, P., ed. *Rethinking the Media Audience: The New Agenda*. London: Sage, pp. 69-85, 1999

Hinton, P. R .*Stereotypes, Cognition and Culture*. London: Taylor & Francis, 2000

Hoffman, Frank. "Intellectual Freedom and Censorship." Metuchen, NJ: The Scarecrow Press, 1989

India praises McCain-Dalai Lama meeting". Washington, D.C.: WTOPews.com. July 27, 2008

Indonesia: Police Abuse Endemic in Closed Area of Papua". Human Rights Watch. May 7, Archived from the original on 2007-09-15, 2007

Innis, H .*The Bias of Communication*. Toronto: University of Toronto Press, 1999

Jenkins, H .*Textual Poachers: Television Fans & Participatory Culture*. London: Routledge, 1992

Key, W. B .*Subliminal Seduction: Ad Media's Manipulation of a Not So Innocent America*. Englewood Cliffs, NJ: Prentice-Hall, 1973

Klein, N .*No Logo*. London: Flamingo, 2000

Kress, G. R. and Leeuwen, T .*Reading Images: a Grammar of Visual Design*. London: Routledge, 1996

Landay, Jonathan S. "Radical Islamists no longer welcome in Pakistani tribal areas". McClatchy Washington Bureau. , 2008

Lasn, K .*Culture Jam: How to Reverse America's Suicidal Consumer Bing - and Why We Must*. New York: Quill, 2000

Laughey, D .*Key Themes in Media Theory*. Maidenhead: Open University Press, 2007

Laursen, John Christian . "David Hume and the Danish Debate about Freedom of the Press in the 1770s". *Journal of the History of Ideas* (University of Pennsylvania Press) 59 (1): 167–172, January 1998

Lawrence, J. S. and Jewett, R .*The Myth of the American Superhero.* Cambridge: Wm. B. Eerdmans. Lawrence and Jewett apply Campbell's monomyth to a variety of contemporary texts and situations. A selection of reviews of this book is available here, 2002

Lengel, R.H. & Daft, R.L .The Selection of Communication Media as an Executive Skill. Academy of Management Executive, 2(3), 225-232, 1988

Levinson, P .*The Soft Edge: A Natural History and Future of the Information Revolution.* London: Routledge, 1997

Lewis, L. A .The Adoring Audience: Fan Culture and Popular Media. London: Routledge, 1992

Lippmann, W .*Public Opinion.* New York: Free Press, 1997

Lum, C. M. K .*Perspectives on Culture, Technology And Communication: The Media Ecology Tradition.* Cresskill, New Jersey: Hampton, 2005

Lupton, E. and Miller, A .*Design Writing Research: Writing on Graphic Design.* London: Phaidon, 1996

Lupton, E. and Miller, A .Graphic Design in America. In: *Design Writing Research: Writing on Graphic Design.* London: Phaidon, pp. 168-202. A brief history of graphic design, with useful material on advertising and branding, 1996

Lupton, E. and Miller, A .High and Low: Design in Everyday Life. In: *Design Writing Research: Writing on Graphic Design.* London: Phaidon, pp. 156-166. On the fluid line between high and low culture, 1996

Lupton, E. and Miller, A .McPaper: USA Today and the Journalism of Hope. In: *Design Writing Research: Writing on Graphic Design.* London: Phaidon, pp. 142-155, 1996

Lupton, E. and Miller, A .Picture for Rent: From Stereoscope to Stereotype. In: *Design Writing Research: Writing on Graphic Design.* London: Phaidon, pp. 120-133. On stereotypes in stock photography, 1996

Lupton, E. and Miller, A .Subliminal Seduction. In: *Design Writing Research: Writing on Graphic Design.* London: Phaidon, pp. 134-141. On the myth of subliminal advertising, 1996

Lupton, E. and Miller, A .White on Black on Gray. In: *Design Writing Research: Writing on Graphic Design*. London: Phaidon, pp. 102-119. On representation and race in American advertising, 1996

M. Lynne Markus . Electronic Mail as the Medium of Managerial Choice. Organization Science, Vol. 5, No. 4. (1 November 1994), pp. 502-527, 1994

Marek, Kate. "Schoolbook Censorship USA." June 1987

Massachusetts: The MIT Press (also New York: McGraw-Hill, 1964; Critical edition, Gingko Press, 2003

McLuhan, Marshall . *Understanding Media: The Extensions of Man*. Cambridge, 1964

McQuail, D. and Windahl, S .*Communication Models for the Study of Mass Communications*. 2nd ed. London: Longman, 1993

Moon, J .Learning Journals: A Handbook for Academics, Students and Professional Development. London: RoutledgeFalmer,1999

National Coalition against Censorship (NCAC). "Books on Trial: A Survey of Recent Cases.", January 1985

Nava, M. et al. (eds) . *Buy this Book: Studies in Advertising and Consumption*. London: Routledge,1997

Neale, S .Questions of Genre. Screen, 31 (1). An influential but demanding essay in which Neale discusses cultural and generic verisimilitude. Extracts are also reproduced in Boyd-Barrett and Newbold (1995, pp. 460-72), 1990

Neale, S. (ed.) . *Genre and Contemporary Hollywood*. London: British Film Institute, 2002

Neale, S., *Genre and Hollywood*. London: Routledge, 2000

Newberry, Brian . "Media Richness, Social Presence and Technology Supported Communication Activities in Education", 2001

Newbold, C., Boyd-Barrett, O. and Van den Bulck, H. (eds) . *The Media Book*. London: Arnold, 2002

Ngwenyama, Ojelanki K., & Lee, Allen S.Communication richness in electronic mail: Critical social theory and the contextuality of meaning. MIS Quarterly, 21(2), 145-167, 1997

O'Reilly, Robert C. and Larry Parker. "Censorship or Curriculum Modification?" Paper presented at a School Boards Association, 1982

O'Shaughnessy, M .*Media and Society: An Introduction.* 2nd ed. Oxford: Oxford University Press, 2002

O'Sullivan, T. and Jewkes, Y .*The Media Studies Reader.* London: Arnold, 1997

O'Sullivan, T., Dutton, B. and Rayner, P .*Studying the Media: An Introduction.* 3rd ed. London: Arnold, 2003

Pinker, S .*The Language Instinct: The New Science of Language and Mind.* London: Allen Lane, 1994

Plato . *The Republic.* 3rd ed. Benjamin Jowett, trans. Oxford: Clarendon Press. Retrieved, 14 march 2005

Power, Catherine. "Overview of the Middle East and North Africa (MENA): Repression Revisited". *World Press Freedom Review.* International Press Institute region review, 2007

Ringmar, Erik A Blogger's Manifesto: Free Speech and Censorship in the Age of the Internet London: Anthem Press, 2007

Rose, B .TV Genres Re-Viewed. *Journal of Popular Film and Television.* 31(1) (Spring), pp. 2-4, 2003.

Saussure, F .*Course in General Linguistics.* Trans. Baskin, W. London: Peter Owen, 1964

Schor, J. B .*Born to Buy: The Commercialized Child and the New Consumer Culture.* New York: Scribner, 2005

Schwartz, T .*Media: The Second God.* Illustrated by Nurit Karlin. Garden City, NY: Anchor Books, 1983

Schwartz, T .*The Responsive Chord.* New York: Doubleday/ Anchor Press, 1974

Segal, R. A .*Joseph Campbell: An Introduction.* London: Taylor & Francis, 1987

Small, Robert C., Jr. "Preparing the New English Teacher to Deal with Censorship, or Will I Have to Face it Alone?" Annual Meeting of the National Council of Teachers of English, 1987

Starkey, D .Chasing Shadows. *The Sunday Times,* 2 July, p. 10. Retrieved 8 December 2006 from here, 1995

Starr, Paul . *The Creation of the Media: Political Origins of Modern Communications*. New York: Basic Books, 2004

Storey, J .*An Introduction to Cultural Theory and Popular Culture*. 2nd ed. Hemel Hempstead: Prentice Hall/Harvester Wheatsheaf, 1997

Storey, J .*An Introduction to Cultural Theory and Popular Culture*. 2nd ed. Athens, GA: niversity of Georgia Press, 1998

Strate, L .*Echoes and Reflections: On Media Ecology as a Field of Study*. Cresskill, NJ: Hampton Press, 2006

The Newspaper and Society: A Book of Reading, by George Lloyd Bird, Frederic Maton Mervin, Prentice-Hall, 1949

Thierer, Adam & Brian Anderson . *A Manifesto for Media Freedom*. New York: Encounter Books, 2008

Thwaites, T., Davis, L. and Mules, W .*Introducing Cultural and Media Studies: A Semiotic Approach*. Basingstoke: Palgrave, 2002

Trevino, L., Lengel, R., Bodensteiner, W., Gerloff, E. & Muir, N .The richness imperative and cognitive style: The role of individual differences in media choice behavior. Management Communication Quarterly, 4(2), 1990

Trevino, L.K., Lengel, R.K. & Daft, R.L .Media Symbolism, Media Richness and media Choice in Organizations. Communication Research, 14(5), 553-574, 1987

Tudor, A .Genre. In: Grant, B. K., ed. *Film Genre Reader III*. Austin, TX: University of Texas Press, pp. 3-11, 2003

Watson, J .*Media Communication: An Introduction to Theory and Process*. 2nd ed. Basingstoke : Palgrave Macmillan, 2003

Watson, J. and Hill, A. *Dictionary of Media and Communication Studies*. 7th ed. London: Hodder Arnold, 2006

Zamoyski, Adam. The *Polish Way*. New York: Hippocrene Books, 1987